Oxford International English

Teacher Resource Book

6

Moira Brown

OXFORD
UNIVERSITY PRESS

OXFORD
UNIVERSITY PRESS

Great Clarendon Street, Oxford OX2 6DP

Oxford University Press is a department of the University of Oxford.
It furthers the University's objective of excellence in research, scholarship,
and education by publishing worldwide in

Oxford New York

Auckland Cape Town Dar es Salaam Hong Kong Karachi
Kuala Lumpur Madrid Melbourne Mexico City Nairobi
New Delhi Shanghai Taipei Toronto

With offices in

Argentina Austria Brazil Chile Czech Republic France Greece
Guatemala Hungary Italy Japan Poland Portugal Singapore
South Korea Switzerland Thailand Turkey Ukraine Vietnam

© Oxford University Press 2013

British Library Cataloguing in Publication Data

Data available

ISBN 9780198388869

10

Printed in Great Britain by CPI Group (UK) Ltd, Croydon, CR0 4YY

Paper used in the production of this book is a natural, recyclable product made
from wood grown in sustainable forests. The manufacturing process conforms to
the environmental regulations of the country of origin.

Acknowledgements
Cover illustration: Patricia Castelao

The author and publisher are grateful for permission to include the following
copyright material in print, audio and digital formats in this package.

Isaac Asimov: 'The Fun They Had' in *Earth is Room Enough* (Granada, 1981), by
permission of The Trident Media Group, LLC.

Sara C Bisel: *The Secrets of Vesuvius* (Edward Arnold, 1990), by permission of Madison
Press Books.

Rhidian Brook: unpublished screenplay, *Africa United*, copyright © Rhidian Brook
2012, by permission of The Agency (London) Ltd on behalf of the author.

Jan Burchett and **Sara Vogler**: *Skeleton Island: Sam Silver: Undercover Pirate* (Orion
Children's Books, 2012), by permission of The Orion Publishing Group.

Dave Calder: 'Flood', copyright © Dave Calder 1989, from *Dolphins Leap Lampposts*,
poems by Dave Calder, Eric Finney and Ian Souter (Macmillan, 2002), by permission
of the author.

Suzanne Collins: *The Hunger Games* (Scholastic, 2009), © copyright Suzanne Collins
2009, by permission of the publishers.

Paul Cookson: 'Let No One Steal Your Dreams' from *The Very Best of Paul Cookson*
(Macmillan, 2001) copyright © Paul Cookson 2001, by permission of the author.

Terry Deary: *The Plot on the Pyramid* (A & C Black, 2004), copyright © Terry Deary
2004, by permission of the publishers, A & C Black, an imprint of Bloomsbury
Publishing Plc.

Philip Fisher: review of the 2011 RSC production of *Matilda, the Musical* from www.
britishtheatreguide, by permission of the British Theatre Guide and the author.

John Foster: 'The Price of Fame', copyright © John Foster 2007, from *The Poetry
Chest* (OUP, 2007), by permission of the author.

Clive Gifford: *Spies and Spying* (OUP, 2010), by permission of Oxford University
Press.

Nick Hale: *The Edge (Striker 3)* (Egmont, 2011), copyright © Nick Hale 2011, by
permission of the publisher.

Anthony Horowitz: *Stormbreaker* (Walker Books, 2012), copyright © Anthony
Horowitz 2000, and *Scorpia Rising* (Walker Books, 2011), copyright © Anthony
Horowitz 2011, by permission of Walker Books Ltd, London, SE11 5HJ,
www.walker.co.uk, and Philomel Books, an imprint of Penguin Group (USA).

Bobbi Katz: 'Heraklion: An Underwater City in the Bay of Abukir off the North
Coast of Egypt' from *Trailblazers: Poems of Exploration* by Bobbi Katz (Greenwillow
Books, 2007), copyright © Bobbi Katz 2007, by permission of the author.

Anabel Kindersley: *Celebration! Celebration! (Children Just Like Me)* (DK, 1997),
copyright © Dorling Kindersley Ltd 1997, by permission of Dorling Kindersley Ltd,
London.

John Kitching: 'Historian', copyright © John Kitching 2002, first published in
Brian Moses (ed): *The Works 2: Poems on Every Subject and For Every Occasion* (Macmillan
Children's Books, 2002), by permission of the author.

Elizabeth Laird: 'Pulling Together' from *Why Dogs Have Black Noses* (OUP, 2010),
copyright © Elizabeth Laird 2010, by permission of Oxford University Press.

Gill Lewis: *White Dolphin* (OUP, 2010), copyright © Gill Lewis 2010, by permission of
The Miles Stott Agency.

Loving Your Child: *History of Birthday parties* from www.lovingyourchild.com, by
permission of LYC.

Michael Morpurgo: *Kensuke's Kingdom* (Egmont, 1999), copyright © Michael
Morpurgo 1999, by permission of David Higham Associates.

Brian Moses: 'Salute', copyright © Brian Moses 2012, from *Olympic Poems* (by Brian
Moses and Roger Stevens (Macmillan, 2012), by permission of the author.

National Geographic: Instructions for making a kite from http://kids.
nationalgeographic.com, by permission of National Geographic Stock.

Kenn Nesbitt: 'My Dad's a Secret Agent', copyright © 2001 by Kenn Nesbitt from
The Aliens Have Landed at Our School (Meadowbrook, 2001, 2006) and 'When Sarah
Surfs the Internet', copyright © 2007 by Kenn Nesbitt from *Revenge of the Lunch
Ladies: the Hilarious Book of School Poetry* (Meadowbrook, 2007), both by permission of
Meadowbrook Press.

Scott O'Dell: 'The Iditarod Great Sled Race' from *Black Star, Bright Dawn* (Houghton
Mifflin Harcourt, 2008), copyright © Scott O'Dell 2008, by permission of McIntosh
and Otis, Inc for the author.

Lindsay Pickton and **Christine Chen**: *Myths and Legends: Treetops Teaching Notes,
Stages 15 & 16* (OUP, 2010), copyright © Oxford University Press 2010, by permission
of Oxford University Press.

James Putnam and **Scott Steedman**: *Egyptian News* (Walker Books, 2009), text
copyright © Scott Steedman 1997, by permission of Walker Books Ltd, London, SE11
5HJ, www.walker.co.uk.

Quark Expeditions: 'Antarctica cruises' at www.quarkexpeditions.co.uk, by
permission of Quark Expeditions UK, London, tel: + 44 203 514 2712.

Rick Riordan: *Heroes of Olympus: The Son of Neptune* (Puffin, 2011), copyright © Rick
Riordan 2011, by permission of Penguin Books Ltd, and United Agents
(www.unitedagents.co.uk) on behalf of the author.

Laura Amy Schlitz: *Fire Spell* (Bloomsbury Children's, 2012), by permission of the
publishers.

Owen Slot: *Cycling for Gold* (Puffin, 2012), copyright © Owen Slot 2012, by
permission of Penguin Books Ltd.

William Stafford: 'The Osage Orange Tree' in *Oregon Centennial Anthology: A
Collection of Prize-Winning Short Stories and Poems* (1959), copyright © William Stafford
1959, by permission of The Permissions Company Inc, on behalf of the Estate of
William Stafford.

Noel Streatfeild: *Circus Shoes* (Jane Nissen Books, 2006), copyright © Noel
Streatfeild 1938, by permission of A M Heath & Co Ltd for the Estate of Noel
Streatfeild.

Eleanor Watts: 'Who is this?', two kennings, copyright © Eleanor Watts 2012, by
permission of the author.

Kay Woodward: *Skate School: Stars on Ice* (Usborne Books, 2010), copyright ©
Chorion Rights Ltd 2010, by permission of Usborne Publishing, 83-85 Saffron Hill,
London, EC1N 8RT, UK. www.usborne.com.

WWF-New Zealand: bulletin about Hector's and Maui's dolphins from
www.wwf.org.nz with figures as at 13 March 2012, by permission of
WWF-New Zealand.

Laurence Yep: *The Star Maker* (HarperCollins, 2010), by permission of HarperCollins
Publishers, USA.

Although we have made every effort to trace and contact all copyright holders
before publication this has not been possible in all cases. If notified, the publisher
will rectify any errors or omissions at the earliest opportunity.

Any third party use of these extracts outside of this publication is prohibited, and
interested parties should apply directly to the copyright holders named in each case
for permission.

Contents

Introduction

How to use *Oxford International English* Level 6

This language and literacy course has been developed for and tested by teachers and students around the world in international schools and English medium schools. *Oxford International English* gives you the rich flavour of cultural diversity with all the quality ingredients of systematic literacy learning. It has been written and designed to complement both international curricula *and* national curricula.

Adding value

As a busy teacher, there are numerous demands on your time. *Oxford International English* supports your teaching goals by:

- Motivating and engaging your learners with dynamic themes and classroom activities.

- Delivering differentiated activities, allowing you to address the range of abilities in your class so each student works at his or her own level.

- Providing assessment: unit tests and termly check-up tests, clear mark schemes, as well as reading, writing and speaking and listening progress assessment criteria charts that help you level your students.

Student Book 6

 Every page of the Student Book has a clear **learning objective** for both teacher and student to use. The lesson notes in Teacher Resource Book 6 show you the **success criteria** for the learning objective and how to check that each student has achieved it. The CD-ROM has digital pages of all the learning objectives for you to display on the whiteboard.

Each **unit** of the Student Book is set out to allow a natural learning sequence of interest, inquiry, engagement, investigation and challenge. Using a rich range of literature — in various genres — and language, students interact with **cross-curricular topics** and themes whilst developing their English and literacy in a systematic and measurable way. The extra resources provided in Teacher

Resource Book 6 and Workbook 6 give students the chance to **consolidate and apply** what they have learnt in class time.

All units follow a clear logical pattern of **skills development**. Look out for the skills focus at the top of each Student Book page.

Speaking and listening	Vocabulary and spelling
Reading fiction	Spelling and grammar
Reading non-fiction	Reading poetry
Writing workshop	

Workbook 6

This Workbook provides a unit-by-unit match to the  Student Book topic with **further practice** and extension activities for independent work in class or as homework.

Students can do a **self-evaluation** of their learning at the end of each Workbook unit. This gives you and parents guidance on how to help them progress.

A **mini-dictionary** of vocabulary used in each unit is included at the end of the Workbook to help students work independently and develop their dictionary skills. There is space for them to write their own new vocabulary with definitions.

Digital classroom resources

E-books of all the fiction, non-fiction, poetry and corresponding Word Cloud lists are included on the CD-ROM. These can be used as interactive texts which can be manipulated on both a normal whiteboard and an interactive whiteboard. You can use these for whole class word and sentence focus. Each e-book also has audio recordings which allow students to practise listening and pronunciation. Please refer to the e-book user guide which can be found on the CD-ROM or the guided reading notes on page 194.

How is *Oxford International English* 'international'?

Culturally diverse classrooms

Oxford International English recognizes that your students are a diverse mixture of different nationalities using various different languages with different mother tongues. Even within a monolingual classroom, students are preparing to be global citizens aware of and engaged in cultural diversity in their communities. *Oxford International English* celebrates these aspects of your classes and facilitates both teacher and students to use this diversity as a learning tool so that students learn from each other as well with each other.

Maps

As a visual, colourful reference point, maps help students understand their place in the wider world and learn about other countries, languages and cultures. Maps are an integral part of the Student Book and can be used to locate where a person or story originates.

Stories, facts and poems from around the world

The reading extracts in each themed unit have been selected because they are either about a country or culture or have been written by a person from that country.

Global themes

From *Extreme Earth* to *Health and sport* each unit theme allows students to bring their own knowledge and experiences to the subject based upon their cultural heritage. The issues raised within the themes have a broad, universal appeal suitable for this age group.

How does it help students learning English as a second language?

Research has shown that learning a language and learning through that language are most successful when real contexts are used. *Oxford International English* uses authentic language and the type of real syntax that students would encounter in books, on the Internet, on television, and in magazines. With the right scaffolding, correct pace and structure that *Oxford International English* offers, students learning English as a second language can access, enjoy, and engage with English as both an academic subject and the means by which they will succeed across the curriculum.

Reading vocabulary in the Word Clouds and glossary definitions beforehand enables you to focus on low-frequency or difficult key words to aid understanding of the text extracts.

Audio recordings of Word Cloud vocabulary provide listening, phonics and spelling practice. Audio text extracts provide examples of different intonation, speech rhythms, and pronunciation patterns.

What about differentiation?

Your students, ranging from English as an additional or second language learners to English mother tongue learners, will have different cognitive abilities as well as different English language abilities. Some of your students will be brand new to your class *and* to learning English! To support you in this challenge *Oxford International English* uses differentiation in student activities.

A

This is for all ability students. In comprehension sections, these exercises are comprised of location and retrieval type questions for literal understanding.

B

This is slightly more challenging and for average ability students. In comprehension sections, these exercises consist of deduction and inference type questions.

C

This is the most challenging level and requires students to evaluate, interpret and create using what they have understood, their prior knowledge and their imagination. It is also the least structured type of activity.

····Challenge····

This is for high ability students to move onto after completing the other exercises or extension work.

How does *Oxford International English* help critical thinking skills?

Special features within Student Book 6 and Workbook 6 focus on developing students to be inquirers, questioning what they are discovering, prompting them to research further and encouraging them to consider how they learn.

Let's Talk! Allows students to practise guided speaking and listening skills. The theme of the unit and the visual stimuli also prompt students to consider what they want to know about the topic and how they will find out.

Discussion time
Is chocolate bad or good for us? Research and debate.

Structure and guidance for the teacher is given in the lesson notes of this Teacher Resource Book. Students are required to think critically, form an opinion, give reasons and evidence for their opinions and debate a topic with their classmates or present a viewpoint.

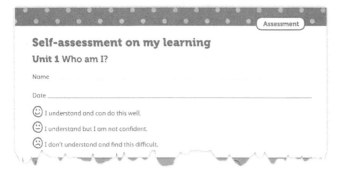

Assessment

Self-assessment on my learning

Unit 1 Who am I?

Name

Date

🙂 I understand and can do this well.

😐 I understand but I am not confident.

🙁 I don't understand and find this difficult.

Within Workbook 6, students have the chance to reflect on their own learning, decide what they can do well and where they need more help. This builds ownership of and responsibility for their learning and provokes them to plan how they learn.

Does it work alongside a reading scheme?

Oxford International English can be used as stand-alone classroom material delivering a core but comprehensive language and literacy programme for the whole year. However, it is strongly recommended that *Oxford International English* Level 6 is used alongside a broad reading scheme which allows students access to a wide range of fiction and non-fiction in the form of printed material and e-books. This is the best way for children to develop an enjoyment of and interest in reading. It helps them to be successful not only in their English literacy, but also produces excellent reading strategies and

comprehension skills across all areas of the curriculum. This is especially true for second language students whose overall academic success is dependent on their ability in English.

Oxford International English has been developed to link into and complement the **Oxford Reading Tree**, **TreeTops** and **Project X** reading schemes. There are extracts from books in these schemes in Student Book 6, as well as a complete short story from *TreeTops* with guided reading notes for your students to enjoy.

Look at the Oxford University Press International Schools website for reading books and e-books that connect with the unit themes of *Oxford International English* Level 6. Use *Oxford International English* together with a reading scheme for a robust and complete literacy strategy for your students. www.oup.com/oxed/international

How can I check students' progress and measure their English level?

End of unit tests appear after the teaching notes in Teacher Resource Book 6 as short review tests to check learning objectives have been achieved. There are also three **Revise and Check** tests which are longer and require some simple revision and preparation. Mark schemes, answers and model answers for all tests are provided on the CD-ROM.

On the CD-ROM there are separate **progress assessment charts** for speaking and listening, reading and writing. Mid-way through the year and at the end of the year, use the descriptions in the charts to measure an individual student's ability and allocate the numerical 'level' if needed.

What extra teacher's resources are there?

A literacy glossary appears at the end of this Teacher Resource Book giving explanations of teaching and literacy terms.

Photocopiable classroom activity sheets for writing and planning stories, are provided on the CD-ROM in the 'printable resources' tab.

Model answers for the Student Book 6 exercises are provided in the teaching notes in this Teacher Resource Book and the Workbook 6 answers are provided on the CD-ROM.

Guided reading notes on **page 194** of this Teacher Resource Book are to be used with the complete story after Unit 10 of the Student Book.

How do I use the CD-ROM and the e-books?

(1) Choose which resource you want and click on the tabs at the top of the screen.

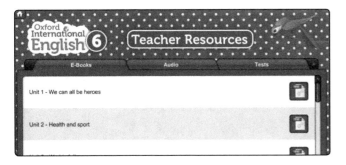

(2) Click on the file icon to select the e-book and unit you want to see.

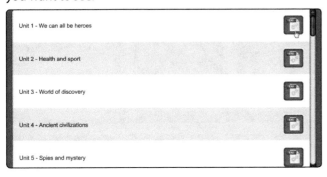

(3) Press the 'Play' button to hear the audio of the e-book you have chosen. The audio will stop at the end of the page and start again after you turn the page and press 'Play'.

CD-ROM minimum system requirements

PC

- Pentium® 4 1.5 GHz/ Intel® Core™2 Duo 1.2GHz processor or equivalent
- 16 x DVD-ROM drive speed
- 512 MB RAM
- 1024 x 768 screen resolution with 16-bit colour depth
- 16-bit sound card with speakers or headphones
- Mouse or equivalent pointing device
- Keyboard or equivalent input device
- Adobe® Reader® 7
- Microsoft® Office 2003
- Internet Explorer® 7

Supported operating systems:
- Windows® XP Service Pack 3
- Windows Vista®
- Windows® 7

Mac

- Intel® Core™ Duo 1.33 GHz processor or equivalent
- 16 x DVD-ROM drive speed
- 512 MB RAM
- 1024 x 768 screen resolution with 16-bit colour depth
- Sound card with speakers or headphones
- Mouse or equivalent pointing device
- Keyboard or equivalent input device
- Adobe® Reader® 7
- Microsoft® Office 2003
- Adobe® Flash® Player 9
- Safari 5

Supported operating systems:
- Mac OS 10.5.8 Leopard
- Mac OS 10.6.8 Snow Leopard
- Mac OS 10.7.2 Lion
- Mac OS 10.8.1 Mountain Lion

We can all be heroes

Speaking and listening

We can all be heroes

These children organized a real-life campaign against nuclear power stations. They protested using placards. Many people saw the newspaper picture and understood their message.

In the film *Africa United*, these children followed their dream and walked 4,800 km to the football World Cup in South Africa from Rwanda. They looked after each other through thick and thin. They were local heroes when they went home to Rwanda.

Fabrice: "Do you know how big Africa is? It's impossible."
Dudu: "Impossible is nothing. Anything is possible."
Africa United

Let's Talk

1 Who are your local and national heroes? What did they do?
2 Have you worked together in a team to help others?
3 List three advantages of working together as a team on a project.

8

① Warm up objective

Explore definitions and shades of meaning and use new words in context.

Discuss the definition of hero and evaluate the benefits of team work.

Remember to display the child-friendly learning objective to the class along with the child-friendly checklist that students can use to assess how well they achieve it.

We know that we have achieved this because:

▶ We are able to explain the definition of hero.

▶ We are now able to talk about heroic actions and their impact on people and society.

② Unit warm up

Books open. Read the text which accompanies the second photograph. Use a comparison to show how far 4,800 km is. *Example:* the distance between two cities within a country. Explain that 'thick and thin' means staying together in good times and bad, and idioms are everyday sayings.

Ask: *What heroic qualities are demonstrated by the children in the photograph?* (Perseverance, determination, solidarity, purpose, etc.) Write these on the board.

Focus students' attention on the first photograph, and read the text. Explain that 'campaign' means actions aimed at achieving a particular goal. Elicit students' understanding of placards. (To post or display a notice, inscription or opinion.)

Ask: *What local or national campaigns do students know of? What campaigns would they organize?*

Books open. Read the quote and ask each half of the class to read out the words of Fabrice and Dudu. Encourage the 'voice' of Dudu to be louder and more assertive.

③ Let's Talk

Tell students that they are going to talk about heroes and heroic actions. Read question 1. Split the class into small groups and ask them to identify a national hero and a local hero and their respective qualities. (A quality is a part of our character, of the way we are.) Ask for a volunteer from each group to share

these with rest of the class. Alternatively, names and qualities of heroes could be written on paper and displayed on a board for discussion.

Read question 2. Explain to students that such projects could be: community projects; team sports; charity involvement; campaigns, etc.

Read question 3. In pairs or small groups ask students to share and compare their feelings and emotions when working as part of a team. Elicit words like pride, happiness, fulfilled, pleased, etc. Ask each pair or group to say them aloud together, therefore sharing them with the whole class.

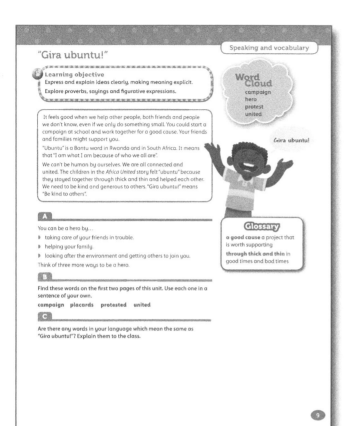

"Gira ubuntu!"

Learning objective
Express and explain ideas clearly, making meaning explicit.
Explore proverbs, sayings and figurative expressions.

Word Cloud
campaign
hero
protest
united

It feels good when we help other people, both friends and people we don't know, even if we only do something small. You could start a campaign at school and work together for a good cause. Your friends and families might support you.

"Ubuntu" is a Bantu word in Rwanda and in South Africa. It means that "I am what I am because of who we all are".

We can't be human by ourselves. We are all connected and united. The children in the *Africa United* story felt "ubuntu" because they stayed together through thick and thin and helped each other. We need to be kind and generous to others. "Gira ubuntu!" means "Be kind to others".

Gira ubuntu!

A
You can be a hero by...
▶ taking care of your friends in trouble.
▶ helping your family.
▶ looking after the environment and getting others to join you.
Think of three more ways to be a hero.

B
Find these words on the first two pages of this unit. Use each one in a sentence of your own.
campaign   placards   protested   united

C
Are there any words in your language which mean the same as "Gira ubuntu!"? Explain them to the class.

Glossary
a good cause a project that is worth supporting
through thick and thin in good times and bad times

9

Learning objective

(4)

Express and explain ideas carefully, making meaning explicit.
Explore proverbs, sayings and figurative expressions.

Students can explore and investigate proverbs, sayings and figurative expressions to understand their true meaning.

Remember to display the child-friendly learning objective to the class along with the child-friendly checklist that students can use to assess how well they achieve it.

We know that we have achieved this because:

▶ **We are able to investigate and explain vocabulary and proverbs associated with 'gira ubuntu'.**

▶ **We are now able to understand and talk about the qualities associated with 'gira ubuntu.'**

(5) Student Book teaching notes and speaking exercise answers

Read the text on 'Gira Ubuntu' with students. Write the words help, good cause, support, connected, united, helped, kind, and generous, on the board. Explain these ⇨

are to be emphasized in the reading. Other strategies could be used to help students read for meaning: a beat between each word; pronounced pause on full stops; enunciation of vowels and consonants.

A

Students can discuss their own experiences of taking care of friends in trouble, helping their families and looking after the environment. Ask students to write down other ways to be a hero. These could include: looking after someone or raising money for a good cause.

B

Students write the sentences in their notebooks. Ask volunteers to read their examples aloud to the class. To build on this exercise students can then write a short paragraph incorporating all four words.

C

Focus on the saying, 'gira ubuntu' (be kind to others) and revisit 'thick and thin'. Give some examples of comparable English proverbs. *Example:* 'a friend in need is a friend indeed' (a friend who helps out when we are in trouble is a true friend).

Ask students to provide a comparable saying from their own culture, or language. Students then read them aloud and explain them to the rest of the class.

(6) Word Cloud definitions

Write the Word Cloud words on the board and ask students to attempt their own definitions. Direct students to the Word Cloud definitions and ask them to compare these with their own. Do they match? Point out the different focus on hero. (Not the stereotype of the brave, handsome man of fiction.) Explain that 'protest' and 'campaign' can be used both as a verb and a noun. **Ask:** *Which of the following sentences uses the verb, and which uses the noun?* I am going to protest (verb) against this. I think this is a worthwhile protest (noun). In pairs ask students to add suffixes to: hero (heroine/heroic/heroically/heroism), campaign (campaigner/campaigning), and protest (protestor/protesting).

campaign work in an organized and active way towards a goal

hero person who is admired for their courage, or noble qualities

protest express an objection to what someone has said or done

united joined together politically, for a common purpose, or by common feelings

1 Learning objective

Begin to develop awareness that the context for which the writer is writing and the context in which the reader is reading can impact on how a text is understood.

Students consider how context is established and interpreted.

Remember to display the child-friendly learning objective to the class along with the child-friendly checklist that students can use to assess how well they achieve it.

We know that we have achieved this because:

▸ We can investigate the importance of context.

▸ We can understand that the time and place around which a book is set will mean that a particular 'world' and set of issues are created.

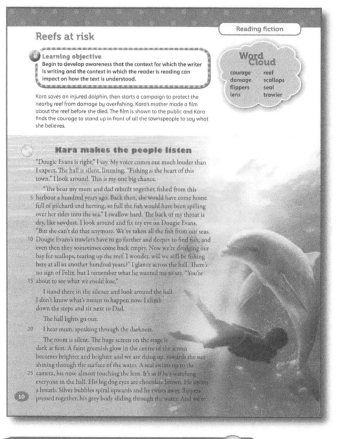

Reefs at risk

Reading fiction

Learning objective
Begin to develop awareness that the context for which the writer is writing and the context in which the reader is reading can impact on how the text is understood.

Kara saves an injured dolphin, then starts a campaign to protect the nearby reef from damage by overfishing. Kara's mother made a film about the reef before she died. The film is shown to the public and Kara finds the courage to stand up in front of all the townspeople to say what she believes.

Word Cloud

courage   reef
damage   scallops
flippers   seal
lens   trawler

Kara makes the people listen

"Dougie Evans is right," I say. My voice comes out much louder than I expect. The hall is silent, listening. "Fishing *is* the heart of this town." I look around. This is my one big chance.

"The boat my mum and dad rebuilt together, fished from this
5 harbour a hundred years ago. Back then, she would have come home full of pilchard and herring, so full the fish would have been spilling over her sides into the sea." I swallow hard. The back of my throat is dry, like sawdust. I look around and fix my eye on Dougie Evans. "But she can't do that anymore. We've taken all the fish from our seas.
10 Dougie Evans's trawlers have to go further and deeper to find fish, and even then they sometimes come back empty. Now we're dredging our bay for scallops, tearing up the reef. I wonder, will we still be fishing here at all in another hundred years?" I glance across the hall. There's no sign of Felix, but I remember what he wanted me to say. "You're
15 about to see what we could lose."

I stand there in the silence and look around the hall.
I don't know what's meant to happen now. I climb down the steps and sit next to Dad.

The hall lights go out.

20 I hear mum, speaking through the darkness.

The room is silent. The huge screen on the stage is dark at first. A faint greenish glow in the centre of the screen becomes brighter and brighter and we are rising up, towards the sun shining through the surface of the water. A seal swims up to the
25 camera, his nose almost touching the lens. It's as if he's watching everyone in the hall. His big dog eyes are chocolate brown. He snorts a breath. Silver bubbles spiral upwards and he twists away, flippers pressed together, his grey body sliding through the water. And we're

10

2 Reading fiction notes

Refer to the CD-ROM or read the text while students follow in their books.

Explain the setting of the story is a fishing village in Cornwall (south-west England). Ask students to find references to: fish and fishing/the sea/English names. This will enforce the idea of the different 'world' of the text. Direct them towards the title and what it suggests. (Kara takes action to make people notice and understand.)

Ask: *Whose comment, "Fishing is the heart of this town", is a platform for Kara's own argument?* (Dougie Evans.) Encourage class discussion on the meaning of the comment. (That too much fishing will mean a town without a heart – both physically and symbolically dead.)

Point out the transition from vocal to visual argument in the film made by Kara's mother.

Ask: *What imagery and tools has the writer used to emphasize a crucial moment?* (Darkness, and suspense of one line paragraphs.)

Ask: *How has the use of photographs in the story highlighted Kara's argument?* (They contrast the beauty of the sea with coral reef damaged by trawlers.)

Ask: *How do we know people have listened and understood Kara's argument?* (Applause, nodding, silence.)

3 Word Cloud definitions

Look at the Word Cloud words and refer to the CD-ROM. Ask students to find a type of shellfish (scallops). Explain what the verb trawl means (fish or catch with a net) and ask them to find the noun (trawler). Explain the meaning of flippers (flat limb), and why humans use these (swimming). **Ask:** *Why does the film focus on a seal?* (Beauty and nature — potentially spoiled by fishing.) *Which word means injury or harm to the world of the seal?* (Damage.) *Which word with the same suffix as 'damage' means being brave?* (Courage.) *Who shows courage?* (Kara.) *Which word in the sentence containing 'lens' gives us a clue to what it means?* (Camera.)

courage act on one's beliefs despite danger or disapproval

damage physical harm that spoils the value or function of something

flippers broad flat limbs without fingers, used for swimming by sea animals such as seals

lens the light-gathering part of a camera

reef a ridge of jagged rock, coral, or sand just above or below the surface of the sea

scallops small shellfish with ribbed fan-shaped shells

seal a fish-eating water based mammal with a streamlined body and flippers

trawler a type of fishing boat

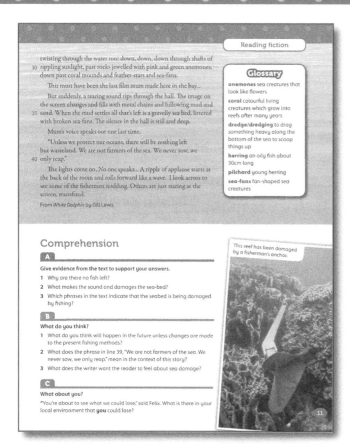

twisting through the water too: down, down, down through shafts of
30 rippling sunlight, past rocks jewelled with pink and green anemones,
down past coral mounds and feather-stars and sea-fans...

This must have been the last film mum made here in the bay...

But suddenly, a tearing sound rips through the hall. The image on
the screen changes and fills with metal chains and billowing mud and
35 sand. When the mud settles all that's left is a gravelly sea bed, littered
with broken sea-fans. The silence in the hall is still and deep.

Mum's voice speaks out one last time.

"Unless we protect our oceans, there will be nothing left
but wasteland. We are not farmers of the sea. We never sow, we
40 only reap."

The lights come on, No one speaks... A ripple of applause starts at
the back of the room and rolls forward like a wave. I look across to
see some of the fishermen nodding. Others are just staring at the
screen, transfixed.

From White Dolphin *by Gill Lewis*

Glossary

anemones sea creatures that look like flowers

coral colourful living creatures which grow into reefs after many years

dredge/dredging to drag something heavy along the bottom of the sea to scoop things up

herring an oily fish about 30cm long

pilchard young herring

sea-fans fan-shaped sea creatures

Comprehension

A

Give evidence from the text to support your answers.

1 Why are there no fish left?
2 What makes the sound and damages the sea-bed?
3 Which phrases in the text indicate that the seabed is being damaged by fishing?

B

What do you think?

1 What do you think will happen in the future unless changes are made to the present fishing methods?
2 What does the phrase in line 39, "We are not farmers of the sea. We never sow, we only reap." mean in the context of this story?
3 What does the writer want the reader to feel about sea damage?

C

What about you?

"You're about to see what we could lose," said Felix. What is there in your local environment that **you** could lose?

This reef has been damaged by a fisherman's anchor.

11

4 Student Book teaching notes and comprehension answers

Show students how to answer questions using evidence from the text. Use the second part of the question as the first part of the answer. Select the right quotation from the text, remembering to place inverted commas around it. **Example:** A hundred years ago, the boat would have brought back 'pilchard and herring', and been 'so full of fish'.

A

1 The fishermen have taken all the fish from the seas. They have overfished.
2 A trawler, or dredger is responsible for the damage to the sea bed.
3 Students read the text again and choose the phrases that describe the damage to the sea-bed.
Ask: *How many negative words can they find?* (tearing, billowing, littered, broken, few, no.)
Ask: *Which of these are focused on the actual sea bed?* (billowing, littered.)

➡

B

1 Ask students to suggest ideas and note them on the board.
2 Ask students which word — sowing and reaping — goes with which of the following meanings: scattering seeds on the earth so they can grow (sowing), and gathering/harvesting a crop (reaping). Discuss what this means in the context of this story. (We cannot keep on taking, if there is no growth.)
Ask: *If we carry on taking what do you think will happen?* **Example:** increased pollution and damage, the loss of livelihood for fishermen, the demise of fishing villages. Elicit answers and write on the board. Discuss with the class.
3 Ask the students how they feel about the sea damage. Do they feel sad and angry? Maybe they want to do something and feel that things have to change now before permanent damage is done.
Ask: *What do you think we could do?*

C

Elicit examples from the class. **Example:** fresh food, species of animals, balanced weather, fresh water, clean air, forests and fields, local industries, close communities. Write them on the board. Conduct a poll in the class to put the suggestions in order of importance and priority to students.

5 Extension

Students choose one of the suggestions from C that they have discussed. Ask them to create a poster using words and images to highlight the importance of their chosen issue. This can include a list of the causes and effects. Display them in the class and use as a discussion topic.

Learning objective

① Begin to show awareness of writers' choices of sentence length and structure.

Students show they can demonstrate the impact of short sentences, and understand how cutting down the use of 'and' could facilitate this.

Remember to display the child-friendly learning objective to the class along with the child-friendly checklist that students can use to assess how well they achieve it.

We know that we have achieved this because:

▶ **We know why writers use short sentences for effect.**

▶ **We know how to use short sentences in our own written work.**

② Student Book teaching notes and grammar exercise answers

A

1 Read the text with the class, clearly punctuating the full stops.

The lights come on *and* no one speaks *and* a ripple of applause starts at the back of the room *and* rolls forward like a wave *and* I look across to see some of the fishermen nodding *and* others are just staring at the screen.

2 Students read aloud the two different versions. (The original and the lengthier sentence.) The effect of losing the short sentences should then be self-evident. **Ask:** *What is the effect of losing the short sentences?* (There is a loss of impact in the long sentence, a change in pace between the two examples, and a loss of atmosphere.) Remind students that short sentences only have one verb.

To reinforce the point ask students to speak for one minute about what they have done so far that day, without using the word 'and'. This can only be managed if they speak in short sentences!

B

Read the initial text aloud, over-pronouncing the 'ands'. Explain that there will be 14 sentences in the rewritten text. Point out that 'and' will be needed to join clauses, but not clause after clause. Ask for volunteers to read their corrected text to the class. Correct common errors.

Ask: *Which short sentences did students think the most effective and why? What happens if you remove 'so'?* ('So' presents a consequence of an action. This means

⇨

Grammar

Sentence length in fiction texts

Learning objective
Begin to show awareness of writer's choices of sentence length and structure.

A

In the text extract from *White Dolphin* by Gill Lewis, the writer uses short sentences for dramatic effect. Look at the short sentences underlined below.

<u>The lights come on. No one speaks.</u> A ripple of applause starts at the back of the room and rolls forward like a wave. I look across to see some of the fishermen nodding. <u>Others are just staring at the screen.</u>

1 Join all the (short and long) sentences into one huge 'sentence', using 'and' to join each one.

2 What is the effect of 'losing' the short sentences?

Top Tips

▶ When you use 'and' consider whether you need to start a new sentence instead and get rid of the 'and'.

▶ Vary sentence length in your writing, so that there are both long and short sentences.

B

Look at the text below. The student has used too many 'ands' in their writing. Rewrite it so that these are taken out and a new sentence started instead. You will find that it is a much better piece of writing, with some very effective short sentences. (Note: A single 'and' should remain in the re-written text.)

It all started when I arrived home and I could see that the front door had been left open, so I felt a bit frightened and I wondered whether someone had broken in, so I opened the door very carefully and I tiptoed in and at first I couldn't see anything, so I breathed a huge sigh of relief and suddenly, I heard a noise and a scream and I wanted to run for my life, but I knew I had to investigate and slowly, I made my way to the living room and I opened the door very, very gently and I saw my mother with a broken television at her feet and she had bought a new television, brought it in herself and, as it was too heavy, had dropped it and she had been so busy struggling with all of this that she hadn't managed to close the door and there hadn't been a burglar after all!

C

Write a 10-sentence account of travelling home to your house late at night. Use at least five very short sentences for dramatic effect.

---

that we could remove 'so' and start a new sentence. This will break up the text and make it more interesting.)

C

Collect the 10-sentence accounts written by students and ask the class to tell a joint story using their examples. Highlight the impact of stretching out tension through using short sentences. 'I was walking home late at night. It was dark. I heard a noise. A sudden noise.' The story should not climax until the very last sentence.

③ Top Tip

Writers use short sentences to get an important point across to the reader. They may also use a short sentence to create tension, suspense or fear in the reader's mind. Good writing creates a balance between short and long sentences to break up the story and allow it to flow smoothly.

④ Extension

Ask students to look at, and review, a previous piece of writing, highlighting the number of times 'and' is used. They should tick those used correctly, cross out those that aren't, and place a question mark where they are undecided. Once completed ask students to swap their reviews with a partner to see if they agree with each other's assessment.

Main and subordinate clauses

Learning objective
Develop grammatical control of complex sentences, manipulating them for effect.

I like you when you are in a good mood.

A complex sentence consists of a **main clause** and one or more **subordinate** clauses. A subordinate clause cannot stand alone, and is usually introduced by a **subordinate connective** such as: who, what, that, why, when, which, where, if, although, since, until, as.

Examples: I like you **when you are in a good mood**.
The weather, **which was really sunny**, meant everyone went out.

Sometimes the subordinating connective is missed out. Here is a sentence from *White Dolphin* by Gill Lewis:
'I hear mum, speaking through the darkness.'
This could have been written as 'I hear mum, who is speaking through the darkness.'

Rewrite the following sentences, missing out the subordinating connective and making any necessary changes to the verb.
1 I saw my friend <u>who was</u> running up the stairs.
2 The boy <u>who was</u> waiting in the room expected a phone call.
3 The house <u>that</u> stands at the end of the street will soon be sold.

B

Sometimes a present participle verb (ending in '–ing') or past participle verb (ending in '–ed') can come at the beginning of a sentence.
Example: Tired and depressed, I slumped on the sofa
1 Start sentences with each of these participle verbs.
running   walking   laughing   exhausted   frightened

C

Subordinate clauses can be placed at different points in a sentence.
Example: Although Kara spoke clearly, they didn't listen. They didn't listen although Kara spoke clearly.
1 Complete this sentence and put the clauses in different positions.
When I have free time I...

13

Learning objective

(5)

Develop grammatical control of complex sentences, manipulating them for effect.

Students learn more ways of forming complex sentences.

Remember to display the child-friendly learning objective to the class along with the child-friendly checklist that students can use to assess how well they achieve it.

We know that we have achieved this because:
▶ **We can change 'who was/that shows' in sentences to a participle form.**
▶ **We can begin sentences with participle verbs.**
▶ **We can position a clause at the beginning and end of a sentence.**

(6) Student Book teaching notes and grammar exercise answers

A

1 Bring students' attention to how the comma has been used to separate the main clause from the subordinate clause.

If students need help, model the answer for the first sentence 'I saw my friend, running up the stairs', emphasizing how the comma has been used to separate off one clause from another. (The act of running up the stairs is emphasized.) After completing the next two examples, students could make up similar sentences, possibly transposing words of the original examples.

Answers:
1 I saw my friend, running up the stairs.
2 The boy, waiting in the room, expected a phone call.
3 The house, standing at the end of the street, will soon be sold.

B

Use the two examples to demonstrate that using a present or past participle verb at the beginning of a sentence can be an effective way to bring a feeling or an action to the attention of the reader.

Steer students into using suitably stretched phrases / clauses. ***Example:*** Running past my house . . . / Walking across the road ... / Laughing uncontrollably ... / Exhausted and tired . . . / Flabbergasted and amazed . . . / Frightened and alone . . .

C

Remind students that when you attach a subordinate clause in front of a main clause, you use a comma. When you attach a subordinate clause at the end of a main clause, you will generally use no punctuation.

Students write their sentences in their notebooks. Ask volunteers to share their answers with the class. Correct any common mistakes.

(7) Extension

Write the following three non-finite verbs on the board: startled, breathing, shouting. Ask students to write a sentence starting with each word. Ask volunteers to read out their sentences, and write the best ones on the board. Next, ask students to use these to write the first paragraph of a story which begins with an exciting piece of action.

Learning objective

1

Recognize key characteristics of non-fiction text types.

Students can demonstrate knowledge and understanding of the features of persuasive non-fiction texts.

Remember to display the child-friendly learning objective to the class along with the child-friendly checklist that students can use to assess how well they achieve it.

We know that we have achieved this because:

▶ **We are able to explain the conventions of persuasive texts.**

▶ **We are able to use persuasive techniques in our own non-fiction writing.**

② Reading non-fiction notes

Refer to the CD-ROM or read the text while students follow in their books.

Focus student's attention on the photograph. **Ask:** *How many students have seen a dolphin in real life?* Ask students what they know about them. Write their responses on the board, and then tick those that feature in the story.

Highlight how the article has been structured for persuasive effect. Explain that the problem has been put forward in some detail followed by the possibility of some hope, or solution, through WWF involvement. Show how emphasis is placed on how few Maui dolphins are left, heightening the urgency with words such as: only, rarest, extinct, etc. Stress the use of modal verbs, will/can, to emphasize what could happen in the future. Students should also understand words that suggest action. *Example:* regulate, produce, support, saved, etc.

The first three paragraphs give an overview of the story. Ask students to read the text. **Ask:** *Who is leading the campaign?* (World Wildlife Fund.) *What unanswered questions are researchers currently studying?* (Where do the dolphins live in winter months?) *How many of these tiny mammals are left?* (They estimate around 55.)

Ask students whether they think the WWF campaign will be successful and why. Explain that responses should be based on the information presented in the text. (Either a yes or no answer can be supported by research studies, school involvement and education, government regulation, global support from the WWF.)

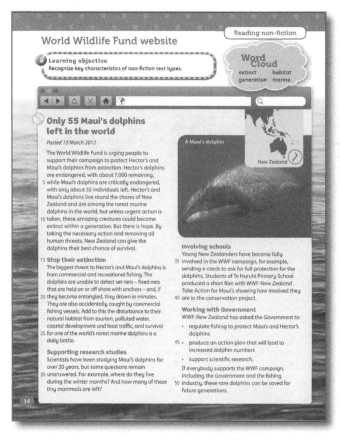

③ Word Cloud definitions

Refer to the CD-ROM. **Ask:** *If 'habitat' means home, what does 'inhabitant' mean?* (A person or animal that lives in or occupies a place.) Explain that the prefix 'mar' (mar/mer) means 'sea/pool'. Elicit related words from the class. *Example:* marina, maritime, mariner, mermaid, marsh. Explain that 'ex' is a prefix meaning 'out of', 'away from', 'lack of'. **Ask:** *How does that explain 'extinct' and words like 'expel', 'exhale'?* (force out, breathe out.) *The root 'gener' (genus) means birth and creation, so how does this relate to 'generation'?* (Relating to a specific time or era when a section of society was born.)

extinct no longer in existence; having no living members.

generation all of the people born and living at about the same time.

habitat the natural home or environment of an animal.

marine relating to, or found in, the sea.

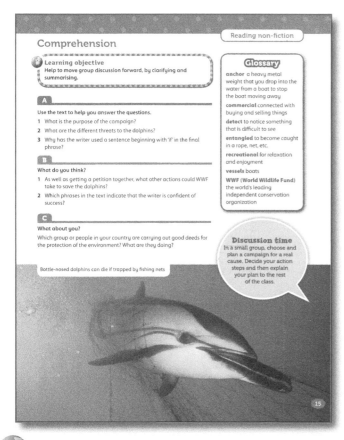

Comprehension

Learning objective
Help to move group discussion forward, by clarifying and summarising.

A

Use the text to help you answer the questions.
1 What is the purpose of the campaign?
2 What are the different threats to the dolphins?
3 Why has the writer used a sentence beginning with 'if' in the final phrase?

B

What do you think?
1 As well as getting a petition together, what other actions could WWF take to save the dolphins?
2 Which phrases in the text indicate that the writer is confident of success?

C

What about you?
Which group or people in your country are carrying out good deeds for the protection of the environment? What are they doing?

Bottle-nosed dolphins can die if trapped by fishing nets

Glossary
anchor a heavy metal weight that you drop into the water from a boat to stop the boat moving away
commercial connected with buying and selling things
detect to notice something that is difficult to see
entangled to become caught in a rope, net, etc.
recreational for relaxation and enjoyment
vessels boats
WWF (World Wildlife Fund) the world's leading independent conservation organization

Discussion time
In a small group, choose and plan a campaign for a real cause. Decide your action steps and then explain your plan to the rest of the class.

A

Answer:
1 To persuade readers to support the campaign and work of the WWF. (Lines 1–3)
2 Fixed nets, commercial fishing vessels, tourism, polluted water, coastal development, boat traffic, etc. (Lines 16–24)
3 The purpose of the final sentence is to give a conclusion some power, which means appealing to the reader emotionally. Explain that the use of the word 'if' emphasizes that there is still a lot of work to be done to ensure the future of these creatures.

B

1 The WWF could increase its educational programme and develop news stories for the media. It could seek endorsement for the cause from local firms or celebrities. All these tools will help support a wider, global petition.
2 Students should understand that these are positive statements. Elicit examples such as 'But there is hope.' 'If everybody supports…' etc.

C

Students may need reminding of what conservation groups are functioning in their country. Students can research a group on their own or in small groups.

4 Learning objective

Help to move group discussion forward, by clarifying and summarising.

Students use discussion as a tool to effectively summarize and clarify key points.

Remember to display the child-friendly learning objective to the class along with the child-friendly checklist that students can use to assess how well they achieve it.

We know that we have achieved this because:
▶ We can summarize the key points of a discussion.
▶ We understand how the writer uses persuasion and time references to underpin the key points of their discussion.

6 Discussion time

Students discuss local good causes, and choose one for the whole class to work on. In small groups students plan a campaign for the cause. Each group should then explain their plan to the rest of the class.

Once all plans have been presented and discussed, the groups can vote on the one they think will be most effective.

5 Student Book teaching notes and comprehension answers

Point to the glossary and read out the definitions. Ask students to locate these terms in the text. **Ask:** *Which other words do you think are important?*

Ask the students to work in pairs and list persuasive techniques of text, and share these with another pair.

1 Learning objective

Explore definitions, shades of meaning and use of new words in context.

Students learn new emotive words and understand how they are used to convince readers.

 Remember to display the child-friendly learning objective to the class along with the child-friendly checklist that students can use to assess how well they achieve it.

We know that we have achieved this because:

▶ We can identify emotive words in a text.

▶ We understand the function of emotive words in persuasive texts.

2 Student Book teaching notes and grammar exercise answers

A

Ask students to read 'Maui's Dolphins' again. Explain that the purpose of this task is to explore definitions.

Answers:

endangered in danger of becoming extinct

survival continuing to live in or after a difficult time

threat a person or thing that may damage or hurt somebody or something

protection safety or care for an animal in danger

B

Ask the class to read the first example aloud. Then write the same example on the board, omitting the emotive words so that it reads, '… among the (rarest) marine dolphins in the world, but unless (urgent) action is taken, these (amazing) creatures could become extinct (within a generation)'. **Ask:** *What has been lost by removing emotive words?* (Effect, strong dramatic message, etc.)

Answers:

'Hope' is the emotive word in example two. Reiterate that the short sentences stress the sense of drama.

Explain to students that the use of time is an emotive subject. In example three, 'minutes' is used to emphasize how quickly something can happen.

In the final example quantity (rarest) and time (daily battle) are used as emotive descriptions.

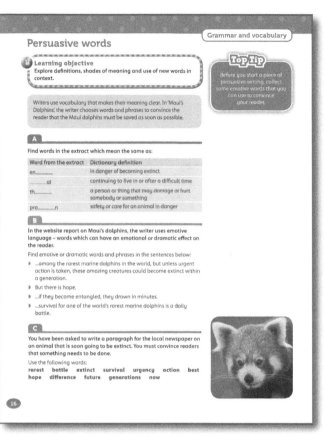

Persuasive words

Grammar and vocabulary

Top Tip
Before you start a piece of persuasive writing, collect some emotive words that you can use to convince your reader.

Learning objective
Explore definitions, shades of meaning and use of new words in context.

Writers use vocabulary that makes their meaning clear. In 'Maui's Dolphins', the writer chooses words and phrases to convince the reader that the Maui dolphins must be saved as soon as possible.

A

Find words in the extract which mean the same as:

Word from the extract	Dictionary definition
en_____	in danger of becoming extinct
_____al	continuing to live in or after a difficult time
th_____	a person or thing that may damage or hurt somebody or something
pro_____n	safety or care for an animal in danger

B

In the website report on Maui's dolphins, the writer uses emotive language – words which can have an emotional or dramatic effect on the reader.

Find emotive or dramatic words and phrases in the sentences below:

▶ …among the rarest marine dolphins in the world, but unless urgent action is taken, these amazing creatures could become extinct within a generation.

▶ But there is hope.

▶ …if they become entangled, they drown in minutes.

▶ …survival for one of the world's rarest marine dolphins is a daily battle.

C

You have been asked to write a paragraph for the local newspaper on an animal that is soon going to be extinct. You must convince readers that something needs to be done.

Use the following words:
rarest battle extinct survival urgency action best hope difference future generations now

16

C

Direct students to write a paragraph of up to 100 words. Encourage the use of two or three of the words in a headline. ***Example:*** Is there any hope for the future? The battle for survival.

Reiterate the importance of planning, ordering and structure in persuasive writing, and ask students to arrange vocabulary in the order they might use it. Students can also use words more than once for impact and effect. Ask for volunteers to read out their paragraphs, and ask the class to decide which one is the most persuasive. **Ask:** *Which of the words do students find most emotive?* (Sense of time, quantity, loss, etc.)

3 Top Tip

When writing persuasively, always refer to your list of emotive vocabulary for a suitable choice. Don't just use the first word that you think of. The precise choice of words matter!

4 Extension

Students review a selection of non-fiction texts such as leaflets and advertisements, and copy down some effective emotive vocabulary which they can then use in their own writing. Then they create their own poster or advertisement for their own campaign.

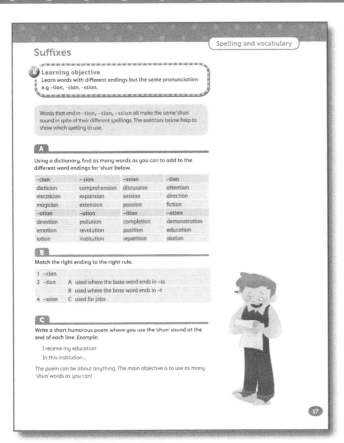

Spelling and vocabulary

Suffixes

Learning objective
Learn words with different endings but the same pronunciation
e.g –tion, –cian, –ssion.

Words that end in –tion, –cian, –ssion all make the same 'shun' sound in spite of their different spellings. The exercises below help to show which spelling to use.

A
Using a dictionary, find as many words as you can to add to the different word endings for 'shun' below.

–cian	– sion	–ssion	–tion
dietician	comprehension	discussion	attention
electrician	expansion	session	direction
magician	extension	passion	fiction
–otion	–ution	–ition	–ation
devotion	pollution	completion	demonstration
emotion	revolution	position	education
lotion	institution	repetition	station

B
Match the right ending to the right rule.

1 –cian	
2 –tion	A used where the base word ends in –ss
	B used where the base word ends in –t
4 –ssion	C used for jobs

C
Write a short humorous poem where you use the 'shun' sound at the end of each line. *Example:*

I receive my education
In this institution...

The poem can be about anything. The main objective is to use as many 'shun' words as you can!

17

A

Explain that in this lesson, students are going to work out the different ways of spelling the 'shun' ending, matching rules to endings. Ask students to add words to the list, checking the spelling in a dictionary first.

B

Advise students to use the lists in A to help them with this exercise.

Answers:

1 C, **2** B, **3** A

Ask students to copy these rules, with examples, in their notebooks.

C

Direct students towards the words in their 'shun' list, and ask them to read these aloud, really enunciating the 'shun' ending. This will draw their attention to all the 'shun' words which they could use to write the poem.

Students should use a 'shun' word in the title of their poem. Advise that lines be kept roughly the same length. If students want to use longer lines, they could extend the two lines given in the student book, so they have a platform to start their poem. *Example:* 'I receive my daily education/ In this excellent institution . . .'

Write suggestions for the last line 'shun' word on the board. Ask volunteers to read out their poems to the class.

---

(7) Extension

1   Ask students to continue collecting words with different 'shun' endings. Who can make the longest list? Students can create 'shun' posters to display in class on which they can add new 'shun' words as they find them.
2   Using the list provided in the student book hold a class spelling competition to reinforce students understanding of the spelling rules.

---

(5) Learning objective

Learn words with different endings but the same pronunciation. *Example:* **–tion, –cian, –ssion.**

The purpose of the lesson is for students to find out the different spellings of the 'shun' ending, and which spelling to use.

Remember to display the child-friendly learning objective to the class along with the child-friendly checklist that students can use to assess how well they achieve it.

We know that we have achieved this because:

▶ **We can use the correct –shun ending in our writing.**
▶ **We know how to use –shun endings to spell words correctly.**

---

(6) Student Book teaching notes and spelling exercise answers

Tell students they are going to work on a word ending which sounds the same but has different spellings. Ask different students how they spell: magician, explosion, session, direction, lotion. Write the correct spellings on the board, underlining the endings.

① Learning objective

Develop awareness of context for both the writer and reader of a text.

Students develop their understanding of context, and understand the particular life circumstances and experiences which make characters behave the way they do.

Remember to display the child-friendly learning objective to the class along with the child-friendly checklist that students can use to assess how well they achieve it.

We know that we have achieved this because:

▸ We can gauge the context of a text through its portrayal of the characters.

▸ We understand, and can use in context, the words associated with play scripts.

② Teaching notes on the play

Focus attention on the small map of Africa. Point out the distance between Rwanda and South Africa, where the World Cup was held. Emphasize the effort and determination required to complete such a journey. Explain that the script is going to show how the dream began. Read through the contextual overview which gives the reasons why the characters decide to do what they do.

Use the glossary on page 19 to explain 'directions' and 'play script'.

Ask if students are familiar with scripts and know the difference between a script and prose?

Script	Prose
Written for actors	Written for readers
Performed	Read
Focus is on the words spoken by the actors.	Focus is on a diverse use of language to give information, ideas, instructions, explanations, etc. If there is direct speech, it is placed in quotation marks.
Focus is on performance, so there are directions for actors on how they should speak and move.	Does not need stage directions.
No narrator. A director will rehearse the play with actors so that it seems real on the stage, and makes sense.	The writer will often act as a narrator.

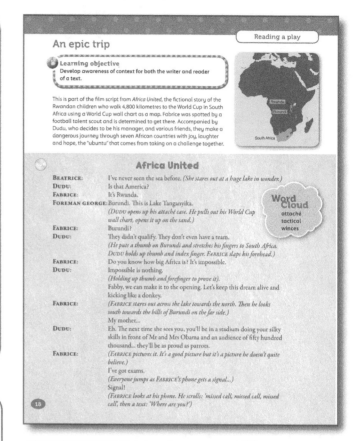

An epic trip

Learning objective
Develop awareness of context for both the writer and reader of a text.

This is part of the film script from *Africa United*, the fictional story of the Rwandan children who walk 4,800 kilometres to the World Cup in South Africa using a World Cup wall chart as a map. Fabrice was spotted by a football talent scout and is determined to get there. Accompanied by Dudu, who decides to be his manager, and various friends, they make a dangerous journey through seven African countries with joy, laughter and hope, the "ubuntu" that comes from taking on a challenge together.

Africa United

BEATRICE: I've never seen the sea before. *(She stares out at a huge lake in wonder.)*
DUDU: Is that America?
FABRICE: It's Rwanda.
FOREMAN GEORGE: Burundi. This is Lake Tanganyika.
(DUDU opens up his attaché case. He pulls out his World Cup wall chart, opens it up on the sand.)
FABRICE: Burundi?
DUDU: They didn't qualify. They don't even have a team.
(He puts a thumb on Burundi and stretches his fingers to South Africa. DUDU holds up thumb and index finger. FABRICE slaps his forehead.)
FABRICE: Do you know how big Africa is? It's impossible.
DUDU: Impossible is nothing.
(Holding up thumb and forefinger to prove it).
Fabby, we can make it to the opening. Let's keep this dream alive and kicking like a donkey.
FABRICE: *(FABRICE stares out across the lake towards the north. Then he looks south towards the hills of Burundi on the far side.)*
My mother...
DUDU: Eh. The next time she sees you, you'll be in a stadium doing your silky skills in front of Mr and Mrs Obama and an audience of fifty hundred thousand... they'll be as proud as parrots.
FABRICE: *(FABRICE pictures it. It's a good picture but it's a picture he doesn't quite believe.)*
I've got exams.
(Everyone jumps as FABRICE's phone gets a signal...)
Signal!
(FABRICE looks at his phone. He scrolls: 'missed call, missed call, missed call', then a text: 'Where are you?')

18

Word Cloud
attaché
tactical
winces

③ Word Cloud definitions

Read out the words in the Word Cloud and refer to the CD-ROM. Can students work out their meanings from the context?

attaché case a small case in which documents etc. may be carried

tactical The noun 'tactics' is the method you use to achieve something or gain an advantage

winces make a slight movement because of pain or embarrassment

④ Extension

Randomly write the differences between scripts and prose on the board, mixing up the answers. Working in pairs, ask students to complete the table below. It is important students understand the 'features' of the particular form they will be exploring.

Script	Prose

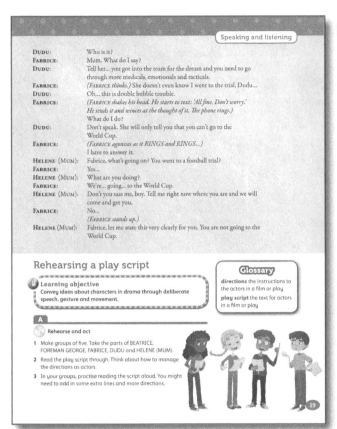

DUDU:	Who is it?
FABRICE:	Mum. What do I say?
DUDU:	Tell her… you got into the team for the dream and you need to go through more medicals, emotionals and tacticals.
FABRICE:	*(FABRICE thinks.)* She doesn't even know I went to the trial, Dudu…
DUDU:	Oh… this is double bubble trouble.
FABRICE:	*(FABRICE shakes his head. He starts to text: 'All fine. Don't worry.' He sends it and winces at the thought of it. The phone rings.)* What do I do?
DUDU:	Don't speak. She will only tell you that you can't go to the World Cup.
FABRICE:	*(FABRICE agonises as it RINGS and RINGS…)* I have to answer it.
HELENE (MUM):	Fabrice, what's going on? You went to a football trial?
FABRICE:	Yes…
HELENE (MUM):	What are you doing?
FABRICE:	We're… going… to the World Cup.
HELENE (MUM):	Don't you sass me, boy. Tell me right now where you are and we will come and get you.
FABRICE:	No…
	(FABRICE stands up.)
HELENE (MUM):	Fabrice, let me state this very clearly for you. You are not going to the World Cup.

Rehearsing a play script

Learning objective
Convey ideas about characters in drama through deliberate speech, gesture and movement.

Glossary
directions the instructions to the actors in a film or play
play script the text for actors in a film or play

A
Rehearse and act

1 Make groups of five. Take the parts of BEATRICE, FOREMAN GEORGE, FABRICE, DUDU and HELENE (MUM).
2 Read the play script through. Think about how to manage the directions as actors.
3 In your groups, practise reading the script aloud. You might need to add in some extra lines and more directions.

19

Learning objective

Convey ideas about characters in drama through deliberate speech, gesture and movement.

Students develop their knowledge of scripts, and can use speech and movement to express character.

Remember to display the child-friendly learning objective to the class along with the child-friendly checklist that students can use to assess how well they achieve it.

We know that we have achieved this because:
▶ We understand the need for the directions used in play scripts.
▶ We can follow the directions in play scripts to portray characters and emotions.

⑥ Student Book teaching notes and speaking exercise answers

Books closed. Before students start their reading, ask the following questions to generate a class discussion.

Ask: *What advice would students give the actors on how to play the different characters? How would they explain and direct changes in voice, mannerisms, and gestures to create different dramatic effects? How could directions be used to build up tension? How would some of the film script directions be managed, such as the close-up of a text message on a phone?*
Refer to the e-book on the CD-ROM and listen to the play script as many times as necessary.

A

1 On the board write the traits of the characteristics of the characters:

FABRICE – concerned about his mother and school (hesitant, anxious, more pauses in speech, fidgeting, constantly looking around, slower walk)

DUDU – unworried, cool, and often uses rhyming slang (confident, swaggers and bounces as he walks, uses lots of gestures, speech emphatic and clear)

HELENE (MUM) – poised, hands folded, voice clear and firm, authoritative, voice of reason, sensible

BEATRICE – curious

FOREMAN GEORGE – informative

Split the class into groups of five. Each group should choose a character to play (extra lines will need to be created for Beatrice and Foreman George).

Students practise facial expressions and body posture, walking, and tone of speech.

2 Books open. Ask students to read the script to themselves. Ensure students understand they are not just reading the content of the script but also the directions. Ask students to stop reading at random points and ask them to explain what their character is feeling at this point in the script.
3 Students rehearse their script. Set aside an area where the audience will sit. Encourage them to look at this area and to move around keeping in clear sight of the audience. Reiterate the importance of clarity and enunciation in their dialogue. Encourage students to add additional lines or stage directions.

⑦ Extension

Ask students to assess their own performances based on the following criteria:

▶ How convincing was their character?
▶ Did they speak loudly and clearly?
▶ Did they gesture and move as directed in the script?
▶ What directions would they add for their character?

① Learning objective

Adapt the conventions of the text type for a particular purpose.

Students learn the conventions of writing a script.

Remember to display the child-friendly learning objective to the class along with the child-friendly checklist that students can use to assess how well they achieve it.

We know that we have achieved this because:
- ▶ We can write dialogue and directions.
- ▶ We can adapt stories and plots around specific images.

② Writing workshop teaching notes

Take students through the three script 'accident' writing scenarios, using the images to clarify the characters, setting and incident.

In pairs or small groups ask students to list three things they think could happen next.

Examples:

Storyline 1:

- – The two boys stop to help and talk to the elderly woman. They reassure her and get help.
- – A passing driver phones for an ambulance.
- – The elderly woman is taken to the hospital and thanks the boys.

Storyline 2:

- – The girl drinks the water and is slightly dazed. The woman and man watching in the background rush over to help.
- – The girl stands up and picks up her bike up and thanks everyone for helping. She isn't hurt or injured.
- – The three girls then walk away together laughing and talking about what happened.

Storyline 3:

- – The boys are running away and looking at the girl who is shouting but don't realize that another boy is standing in front of them.
- – The boys are stopped by the other school boy.
- – They return the school bag to the crying boy, the owner of the bag, and say sorry.

  Write the suggestions for each writing scenario on the board. With the class, decide on which endings are more plausible than others. Ask students to consider these in context of a class performed drama. Students should consider area, props, stage directions, etc.

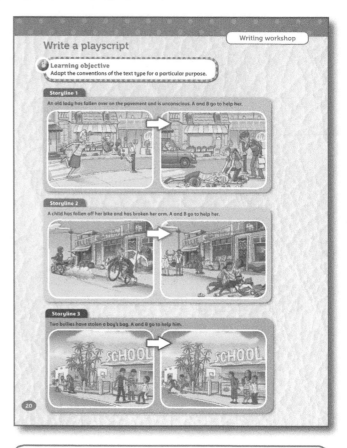

- ▶ The speaker's name is written in the left-hand margin.

- ▶ In a printed play script directions are in italics.

- ▶ In a handwritten play script, directions are written inside brackets.

- ▶ Directions are written in the present tense.

- ▶ In directions, character names are written in capital letters.

- ▶ Directions that are sentences/phrases are written with a capital letter at the beginning and a full stop at the end.

③ Extension

Books closed. Working in pairs, allow students five minutes to list the conventions of writing a play script. Then get students to check their list against the list in the teaching notes. Highlight and discuss any differences.

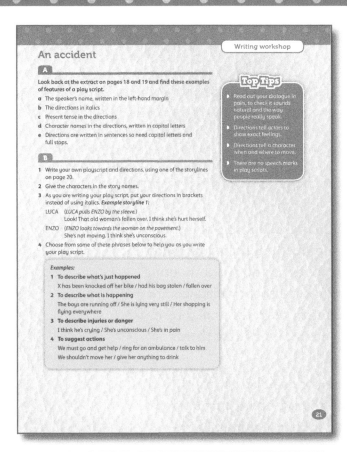

④ Writing workshop teaching notes and exercise answers

Refer students back to the 'Africa United' script. Elicit example answers from the class.

Possible answers:

a BEATRICE
b *DUDU opens up his attaché case...*
c *He puts a thumb on Burundi...*
d *FABRICE pictures it.*
e *FABRICE stands up.*

Explain that in the preceding pages of the Student Book students have learned quite a lot about the conventions of how a play script is written, and they are now going to use this information to write their own play script!

1 Students choose a storyline from page 20, using scenarios that you have discussed as a class.

2 When choosing names, ask students to consider how a name might help shape a character, rather than choosing a name they like. ***Example:*** Mr Blunt is a very direct-speaking teacher.

3 As students write their directions, remind them to look at the characters in each frame of the story-line. They will need to give direction for all people in the scene, even if they are not 'speaking' roles.

4 Students can choose phrases from examples provided in the Student Book.

Example play script for storyline 1

(*LOLA, an elderly woman, is crossing a zebra crossing. LOLA is carrying her shopping in a little basket and it has lots of vegetables and some eggs in it. LOLA trips just as she reaches the pavement.*)

LOLA: Ohhhh! My shopping!

(*JUAN and BEN are walking along the street and see LOLA fall. They are concerned and stop. BEN kneels down to talk to LOLA.*)

BEN: Are you hurt? (*In a concerned voice.*)

LOLA: My head hurts. (*LOLA is dazed and confused.*)

(*A man drives past in his car and stops.*)

DRIVER: Do you need any help? (*In a concerned voice.*)

BEN: Could you take her to the hospital please? She has hurt her head. (*In a very sad, concerned voice.*)

DRIVER: I will call for help. (*DRIVER takes a mobile phone out of his pocket and calls for an ambulance. He is standing to one side talking to the operator on the phone.*)

Possible ending

(*A few minutes pass and then the ambulance arrives.*)

LOLA: Thank you boys. I am fine. You are very kind. (*LOLA is very grateful.*)

AMBULANCE CREW: Lola is going to be fine. She has a few cuts which we will clean up at the hospital and she can then go home. Thank you boys. You were very brave. (*The ambulance crew is very grateful to BEN, JUAN and the DRIVER for looking after her. LOLA is taken in the ambulance but she is smiling and waving goodbye to the boys. The AMBULANCE CREW are carrying her shopping which is now back in the basket.*)

⑤ Extension

Students can write scripts for the two storylines they didn't use in the previous task. As this will not be performed in class, encourage them to be creative and elaborate with plot development and stage directions.

End of Unit Test

Question Paper

Reading: fiction

Read the extract and answer the questions.

On the run

The world has transformed into one of flame and smoke. Burning branches crack from trees and fall in showers of sparks at my feet. All I can do is follow the others, the rabbits and the deer, and I even spot a wild-dog pack shooting through the woods. I trust their sense of direction because their instincts are
5 sharper than mine. But they are much faster, flying through the underbrush so gracefully as my boots catch on roots and fallen tree limbs, that there's no way I can keep pace with them.

The heat is horrible, but worse than the heat is the smoke, which threatens to suffocate me at any moment. I pull the top of my shirt up over
10 my nose, grateful to find it soaked in sweat, and it offers a thin veil of protection. And I run, choking, my bag banging against my back, my face cut with branches that materialize from the grey haze without warning, because I know I am supposed to run.

From *The Hunger Games* by Suzanne Collins

Glossary
instincts fixed patterns of behaviour in animals in response to certain stimuli

Comprehension

A

Give evidence from the extract to support your answers.

1 What parts of the trees are burning?

_____ [1]

2 List three animals that are on the run.

_____ [1]

3 Explain why the writer wants to follow the animals.

_____ [1]

4 What poses the greatest danger to the writer? Tick the correct box.

  a Heat   ☐

  b Smoke   ☐

  c Wild animals   ☐

  d Falling over   ☐   [1]

B

Give evidence from the extract to support your answers.

1 Does the writer keep up with the animals? Explain your answer.

_____ [2]

2 Why is the writer grateful to find his shirt _'soaked in sweat'_?

_____ [2]

3 _'And I run, choking...'_ What is making the writer choke?

_____ [1]

4 What is the writer most afraid of?

_____ [1]

C

Give evidence from the extract to support your answers.

1 What does the _'grey haze'_ refer to? Tick the correct box.

a Fog ☐

b Smoke ☐

c Sky ☐

d Forest ☐ [1]

2 Which adverb shows the contrast between how the animals run and how the writer runs?

_____ [1]

3 _'... a thin veil of protection.'_ What figure of speech is this? Tick the correct box.

a Alliteration ☐

b Metaphor ☐

c Simile ☐

d Onomatopoeia ☐

e Personification ☐

_____ [1]

4 Find two examples of alliteration in the extract.

_____

_____ [2]

Reading: non-fiction

Read the extract and answer the questions.

In recognition

The National Bravery Award for Indian Children is a series of five awards, given each year by the Government of India to Indian children for 'meritorious acts of bravery against all odds.' The awards are given to about 24 children below the age of 16. The two most popular awards are the Sanjay Chopra Award
5   and Geeta Chopra Award — given in memory of the Chopra children who demonstrated great bravery while confronting kidnappers. The Bharat Award was instituted in 1987, and the Bapu Gayadhani Award in 1988. The highest award is the Bharat Award.

An award will include a medal, a certificate, and money. Financial
10   assistance is also provided for schooling.

The origin of the award dates back to 2 October 1957, when India's first Prime Minister, Jawaharlal Nehru, was watching a performance at Delhi's Ramlila grounds, at the Red Fort, when a fire broke out in a shamiana (decorated tent) due to an electrical fault. Harish Chandra, a 14-year-old
15   scout, promptly took out his knife, and ripped open the burning shamiana — saving the lives of hundreds of trapped people. Inspired, Nehru asked the authorities to constitute an award to honour brave children from all over the country. It was called the National Bravery award and Harish Chandra was the first recipient. Among the 21 bravery awards for 2009 was Thoi Thoi
20   Khumanthem, a class II student of Manipur, who jumped into a five-foot-deep pond and rescued four-year-old Maison Singh from drowning.

The awards for each year are presented in January, in the week prior to the Republic Day. The awardees are then able to take part in the Delhi Republic Day parade.

Adapted from www.wikipedia.org/wiki/National_Bravery_Award

Glossary
meritorious praiseworthy or worthy

Comprehension

A

Give evidence from the extract to support your answers.

1 Which award was started in 1957 and in 1988?

_____ [2]

2 Give the names of the five awards.

_____

_____ [3]

3 What acts of bravery were performed by the Chopra children, Harish Chandra, and Thoi Thoi Khumanthem?

_____

_____ [3]

Give evidence from the extract to support your answers.

1 Explain how an award could help the winner.

_____ [3]

2 Why are the awards presented in January?

_____ [2]

Give evidence from the extract to support your answer.

1 Give another word or phrase that can be used instead of 'confronting'.

_____ [1]

Writing: fiction

Write the beginning of a story where someone is trying to run away from someone – or something. Please use a separate sheet of paper.

The action could take place in a forest, by a river, or even in a busy town.

The piece of writing should be three paragraphs long, stopping just at the point when someone — or something — is getting much nearer.

[30]

Writing: non-fiction

Often heroes are quite ordinary, everyday people. Write a profile of someone you know for a website entitled 'Everyday Heroes.' Please use a separate sheet of paper.

The first paragraph should provide personal details/background of your hero.

The second paragraph should describe their heroic actions. This could be helping someone in the community, organizing a protest, standing up to bullies, etc.

The third paragraph should give your views on why you think they are heroic.

[20]

2 Health and sport

1 Warm up objective

Paraphrase explicit meanings based on information at more than one point in the text.

Students learn that to paraphrase information is to retell it in their own words. They understand that to copy directly is plagiarism and they know that they need to understand a text before they can paraphrase or summarize in their own words.

Remember to display the child-friendly learning objective to the class along with the child-friendly checklist that students can use to assess how well they achieve it.

We know that we have achieved this because:

▷ We are able to paraphrase specific textual information.

▷ We understand the difference between paraphrasing and copying (plagiarism).

Speaking and listening

2 Health and sport

Sachin Tendulkar batting for India

Saudi women's team

New Zealand player Lydia Ko, aged 15

Fiji playing against Samoa

Let's Talk

1 Name the sports in each picture.
2 Is it more important to win a sporting event, or to just take part?
3 What are the most popular sports in your country?

"Obstacles don't have to stop you... don't give up."
Michael Jordan

22

2 Unit warm up

Books closed. Write the unit title on the board and ask students to explain how the two words, health and sport, go together. Confirm that participation in sport means you are much more likely to be healthy. Ask the class which sports they participate in. **Ask:** *Why do you play sport?* This should elicit suggestions linking sport and health. Write the responses on the board.
Example: improve strength, endurance, stamina, keeps your mind active. Point out that people who do regular activity have a lower risk of contracting a disease than those who don't.

Books open. Read the quote and ask students to emphasize 'don't give up.' Write the word 'obstacles' on the board and then list possible obstacles, such as:

▷ eating too much/eating the wrong food
▷ prefer watching television/playing video games
▷ don't have time/too much homework
▷ no sports facilities nearby
▷ not very good at sport

Explain that Michael Johnson is a runner who has won four Olympic gold medals and eight World Championships gold medals. He began running competitively at the age of ten. Explain that the quote from Johnson is about not letting obstacles such as these take over.

3 Let's Talk

Focus students' attention on the photos. Explain that each shows a particular sport.

1 Timed activity: Ask students to identify the four sports correctly. Go through the answers with the class. Students who play these sports could be selected to explain the sport to the rest of the class.

Answers:

Cricket, Basketball, Golf, Rugby

2 Ask students to vote either yes or no; write the respective numbers on the board. Select students from each side of the argument to explain their views to the rest of the class. Points could be written on separate sides of the board:

Taking part: participation, good use of leisure time, enjoyment, individual fitness, good health, etc.
Winning: individual excellence, high levels of fitness and health, sense of achievement, etc.

Ask students if they have changed their minds.

3 In turn, each student says which sport they think is the most popular sport in their country. Keep a tally to find out which is considered to be the most popular.

⑤ Student Book teaching notes and speaking exercise answers

Read through each of the multiple choice 'Health Quiz' questions, and explain to students how the answer key works, and how to work out the final score/profile.

Students complete the quiz on their own, then share their answers with a partner. Give students a speaking frame to follow or model ways of managing their explanations. ***Example:*** *'The first question asked how often you have a sports lesson or physical activity at school. I didn't do very well, as I only got one point. That's because I do very little exercise, and I know I really should do more . . .'*

⑥ Word Cloud definitions

Focus students' attention on the Word Cloud and ask them to identify the class of words on the list. (Nouns.)

Explain that deep-fried food is unhealthy because it means cooking food in enough fat or oil to cover it completely.

exercise activity requiring physical effort, carried out to sustain or improve health and fitness

free time your own time outside of school or work

fried food cooked in hot fat or oil, typically in a shallow pan

physical relating to the body as opposed to the mind

sports day a day in schools and colleges where the students compete in various sports

④ Learning objective

Express and explain ideas clearly, making meaning clear.

Students complete a 'Health Quiz' and explain the results to a partner. Students also explain their participation in a recent sporting activity.

Remember to display the child-friendly learning objective to the class along with the child-friendly checklist that students can use to assess how well they achieve it.

We know that we have achieved this because:

▶ We are able to explain the results of a 'Health Quiz' and the ways we have participated in sport.

▶ We can listen to the explanations of others, and ask questions to help make explanations clearer.

⑦ Challenge

Explain that an activity can be anything physical — not necessarily a sport. Model how to avoid saying 'and' — that is, by starting a new sentence instead, very deliberately stopping and beginning each one, so there is less chance of filling the gap with 'and'.

Learning objective

Analyse the success of writing in evoking particular moods.

Students consider how specific features of language are used to evoke a mood of extreme conditions, tension and excitement.

Remember to display the child-friendly learning objective to the class along with the child-friendly checklist that students can use to assess how well they achieve it.

We know that we have achieved this because:

▶ We can identify specific language features such as short sentences, movement verbs and literary features.

② Reading fiction notes

Use the illustrations to explain that a dogsled race is a winter dog sport popular in the Arctic regions of the USA, Canada, Russia, and some European countries. It involves the timed competition of teams of dogs that pull a sled with the dog driver standing on the runners. Confirm that this race will be especially difficult because of the extreme weather conditions in Alaska.

Explain to students that the extract they are about to read highlights significant dangers, so conveying the determination of Bright Dawn and her team of dogs (especially the leader, Black Star) in overcoming them. Books open: Students scan the text. **Ask:** *Which words or phrases highlight the extreme conditions?* (Wild, forsaken, temperature well below zero, eyelashes gathered frost, thin ice.)

Refer to the CD-ROM once students are ready to read the text in full. Otherwise, read out the extract aloud to the class.

③ Word Cloud definitions

Refer to the CD-ROM. Explain that 'scooped' means to pick up something in quick movements. **Ask:** *Why are the dogs scooping up snow with their jaws?* (It would be their only way to get a drink of water.) Explain 'billowing' by fluttering a piece of cloth to show it rising and swelling out. Explain that the ice would be so dense that it would be billowing like this. Explain that 'dazed' means a state of confusion and bewilderment.

Inform students that the dog race can be described as 'gruelling' because it is extremely demanding and tiring. Explain that 'lagoon' is a geographical term, meaning a stretch of salt water separated from the sea.

Alaskan adventure

Learning objective
Analyze the success of writing in evoking particular moods.

A young Alaska native girl, Bright Dawn, takes her father's place in a gruelling dogsled race that covers 1600 kilometres. Running with ears laid back and nose in the air Black Star, leader of her dog team, guides them through dangers on the race trail.

Word Cloud

billowing   ragged
dazed   runners
gruelling   scooped
handlebar   seized
lagoon

The Iditarod Great Sled Race

The country beyond looked wild and forsaken. Scattered trees were ragged and bent over by fierce winds. It was very cold. My feet stuck to the [sled] runners. They felt as if they belonged to somebody else.

I drove the team faster than I ever had before. At times we were
5 running at fifteen miles an hour. The dogs opened their jaws and scooped up snow as they ran...

The trail wound through steep hills and the temperature was now much below zero. My eyelashes gathered frost and began to feel like splinters. I had a hard time seeing and had to depend on Black Star.
10 I was travelling on a lagoon formed by the Innoko River, when the trail began to tremble. At once I realized that we were on ice, thin ice, no more than a couple of inches thick. Ahead of us it was billowing like waves on the sea.

Black Star saw the billows too and stopped the dogs. If we went
15 on, the whole team, all of us, would go crashing down into the rushing river. We were trapped. Panic seized me. Black Star stood with his ears curled back tight against his head. He was trying to decide where to go, to the right or to the left. I was of no help. It was Black Star's decision.
20 At last he turned toward a line of trees that marked the shore. He went slowly and the team followed him.

The ice grew thinner. It creaked beneath the weight of the sled. Through the ice I could see fish swimming and blue water racing over the rocks. Black Star's head was up and his ears alert, his bushy tail
25 curved high over his back. The rest of the team were dragging their tails. Suddenly Black Star pulled up. Then, slowly gathering speed, with the bank only a few yards away, he made a dash and scrambled safely to shore. The next five dogs followed him. Then the ice broke and the rest of the team fell through
30 into the swirling water. The sled went with them and I went with the sled.

24

Ask: *What does 'ragged' mean in the context of its use in paragraph one?* (Bare, irregular and without leaves, or suffering from exhaustion because of the fierce winds and cold, hostile landscape.) Explain this is called personification — where something not human is given human qualities. Point out that the word 'seized' in the sentence, 'panic seized me' heightens the suddenness of what happens. The two remaining terms are 'handlebars' (steering bar) and 'runners' (underside of sledge that forms the contact with the ground.)

billowing rising, swelling

dazed reaction to an emotional or physical shock, unable to think or react properly

gruelling extremely tiring and demanding

handlebar the steering bar of a bicycle, motorbike, or other vehicle

lagoon stretch of salt water separated from the sea by a low sandbank

ragged suffering from exhaustion or stress

runners the long pieces on the underside of a sledge that forms the contact in sliding

scooped picked up (someone or something) in a swift, fluid movement

seized taken hold of suddenly and forcibly

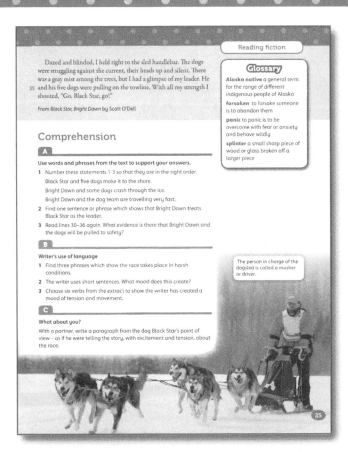

Dazed and blinded, I held tight to the sled handlebar. The dogs were struggling against the current, their heads up and silent. There was a gray mist among the trees, but I had a glimpse of my leader. He
35 and his five dogs were pulling on the towline. With all my strength I shouted, "Go, Black Star, go!"

From Black Star, Bright Dawn by Scott O'Dell

Comprehension

A

Use words and phrases from the text to support your answers.

1 Number these statements 1-3 so that they are in the right order.
   Black Star and five dogs make it to the shore.
   Bright Dawn and some dogs crash through the ice.
   Bright Dawn and the dog team are travelling very fast.
2 Find one sentence or phrase which shows that Bright Dawn treats Black Star as the leader.
3 Read lines 30–36 again. What evidence is there that Bright Dawn and the dogs will be pulled to safety?

B

Writer's use of language

1 Find three phrases which show the race takes place in harsh conditions.
2 The writer uses short sentences. What mood does this create?
3 Choose six verbs from the extract to show the writer has created a mood of tension and movement.

C

What about you?

With a partner, write a paragraph from the dog Black Star's point of view – as if he were telling the story, with excitement and tension, about the race.

> The person in charge of the dogsled is called a musher or driver.

25

④ Student Book teaching notes and comprehension answers

Tell students that in this lesson, they will analyse and discuss how the author uses language to evoke (create) a particular mood in a story, such as excitement and tension. They will focus on how short sentences, movement verbs, and similes are used by the writer.

A

1 Ask students to work in pairs and, using a 6–8 box narrative frame, to write one sentence in each box summing up each stage of the story.

   Answers:

   1 Bright Dawn and the dog team are travelling very fast.
   2 Bright Dawn and some dogs crash through the ice.
   3 Black Star and five dogs make it to the shore.

2 Explain that the lead dog, Black Star, would be a crucial part of the team. Although Bright Dawn is navigating and managing the team, it is Black Star who will be leading. Direct students to find evidence in the text where he does this.

Answer:

'It was Black Star's decision.' (Lines 18–19)

3 Direct students to re-read the final paragraph, and select words and phrases that evidence Bright Dawn and the dogs will be saved.

Answer:

'He and his five dogs were pulling on the towline. With all my strength I shouted, 'Go, Black Star, go!' (Lines 34–36)

This shows the human and animals working together – in tandem – for a common purpose.

B

1 The first paragraph sets the scene of the story. Point out that the writer uses short sentences to add impact to the dramatic scenery and harsh conditions.

Answers:

'The country beyond looked wild and forsaken.' (Line 1)

'It was very cold.' (Line 2)

'We were on ice, thin ice, no more than a couple of inches thick…' (Lines 11–12)

2 Remind students that a short sentence will only have one verb. Direct students to finding the short sentences in paragraphs 5, 6 and 7. The short sentences could be joined up with 'and'. *Example:* It was very cold./We were trapped./Panic seized me.

3 **Ask:** *What is a verb?* (Word used to describe action.) Encourage students to read out their choices. Less effective verbs or wrong word classes chosen can then be countered by the teacher.

Answers:

drove, running, scooped, tremble, billowing, etc.

C

In pairs students write a paragraph of the story from the perspective of Black Star. If students struggle, suggest they use the action in the extract as the basis for their work. The ice crossing will be particularly effective from the viewpoint of the animal.

Remind students that excitement and tension can be enhanced with the correct punctuation, sentence structure and vocabulary.

Learning objective

1

Identify uses of the colon and semicolon.

Students learn what a colon is and what a semicolon is, and how they are used and what their function is in a sentence.

 Remember to display the child-friendly learning objective to the class along with the child-friendly checklist that students can use to assess how well they achieve it.

We know that we have achieved this because:

▶ We are able to recognize a colon and understand its function in a sentence.
▶ We are able to recognize a semicolon and understand that it can separate items in a list within a sentence.
▶ We are also able to use a colon and semicolon correctly in a sentence.

2 Student Book teaching notes and punctuation exercise answers

Read the definitions of colons and semicolons with the class. Point out the examples and elicit any queries as to the function and use of colons and semicolons.

A

Students exercise their understanding of the function of a colon.

Answers:

1 I have lived in many cities: San Francisco, Rome, Sydney, Dubai, New Delhi, and London.
2 The plan you have suggested has three advantages: it is cheap, it is sensible, and it will be popular.
3 Roald Dahl is the author of: *Charlie and the Chocolate Factory*, *James and the Giant Peach*, *The BFG*, and *The Twits*.

B

Students exercise their understanding of the function of a semicolon.

Answer:

The dogs pulled the sled holding: a pair of old walking boots; a mobile phone; a large red apple; a bottle of water; a fur hat; half a chocolate bar; a notebook; a first aid kit; a sleeping bag.

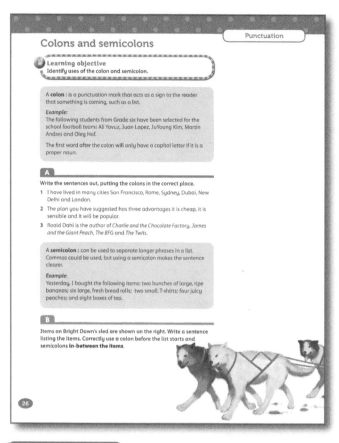

Colons and semicolons

Learning objective
Identify uses of the colon and semicolon.

A **colon :** is a punctuation mark that acts as a sign to the reader that something is coming, such as a list.

Example:
The following students from Grade six have been selected for the school football team: Ali Yavuz, Juan Lopez, JuYoung Kim, Martin Andres and Oleg Hof.

The first word after the colon will only have a capital letter if it is a proper noun.

A

Write the sentences out, putting the colons in the correct place.
1 I have lived in many cities San Francisco, Rome, Sydney, Dubai, New Delhi and London.
2 The plan you have suggested has three advantages it is cheap, it is sensible and it will be popular.
3 Roald Dahl is the author of *Charlie and the Chocolate Factory*, *James and the Giant Peach*, *The BFG* and *The Twits*.

A **semicolon ;** con be used to separate longer phrases in a list. Commas could be used, but using a semicolon makes the sentence clearer.

Example:
Yesterday, I bought the following items: two bunches of large, ripe bananas; six large, fresh bread rolls; two small, T-shirts; four juicy peaches; and eight boxes of tea.

B

Items on Bright Dawn's sled are shown on the right. Write a sentence listing the items. Correctly use a colon before the list starts and semicolons **in-between the items.**

26

3 Extension

Give students a selection of texts. ***Example:*** a leaflet, a photocopied page from a fiction book, a set of instructions, etc. and ask them to highlight examples of the use of colon and semicolon.

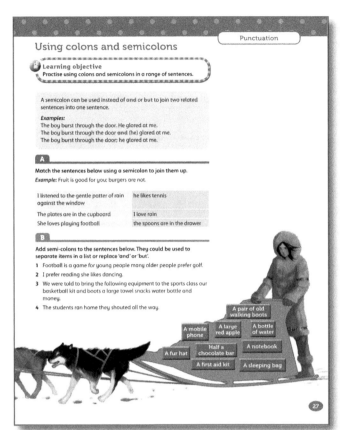

Using colons and semicolons

Punctuation

Learning objective
Practise using colons and semicolons in a range of sentences.

A semicolon can be used instead of and or but to join two related sentences into one sentence.

Examples:
The boy burst through the door. He glared at me.
The boy burst through the door and (he) glared at me.
The boy burst through the door; he glared at me.

A

Match the sentences below using a semicolon to join them up.
Example: Fruit is good for you; burgers are not.

I listened to the gentle patter of rain against the window	he likes tennis
The plates are in the cupboard	I love rain
She loves playing football	the spoons are in the drawer

B

Add semi-colons to the sentences below. They could be used to separate items in a list or replace 'and' or 'but'.
1 Football is a game for young people many older people prefer golf.
2 I prefer reading she likes dancing.
3 We were told to bring the following equipment to the sports class our basketball kit and boots a large towel snacks water bottle and money.
4 The students ran home they shouted all the way.

27

Learning objective

④ **Practise using colons and semicolons in a range of sentences.**

Students learn how use a semicolon as a conjunction and to recognize how the colon and semicolon can be included in a range of punctuation.

Remember to display the child-friendly learning objective to the class along with the child-friendly checklist that students can use to assess how well they achieve it.

We know that we have achieved this because:
▶ We are able to recognize that a semicolon can be used to separate items in a list and as a conjunction.
▶ We are also able to use correctly them in a sentence which includes a range of punctuation.

---

⑤ **Student Book teaching notes and punctuation exercise answers**

A

Students implement their understanding of semicolons in this practise exercise.

Answers:
1 I listened to the gentle patter of rain against the window; I love rain.
2 The plates are in the cupboard; the spoons are in the drawer.
3 She loves playing football; he likes tennis.

B

Point out to students that semicolons can be used to separate items instead of 'and' or 'but'.

Answers:
1 Football is a game for young people; many older people prefer golf.
2 I prefer reading; she likes dancing.
3 We were told to bring the following equipment to the sports class: our basketball kit and boots; a large towel; snacks; water bottle; and money.
4 The students ran home; they shouted all the way.

⑥ **Extension**

Ask students to describe a room in their house, listing all the items and furniture that it has in it, using the colon and semicolon correctly.

Learning objective

①

Recognize key text features of journalistic interviews.

Students explore the question types used and how these elicit factual and personal information which will be of interest to the reader.

Remember to display the child-friendly learning objective to the class along with the child-friendly checklist that students can use to assess how well they achieve it.

We know that we have achieved this because:

▶ We are able to identify different question styles and types.

▶ We are able to create our own interview questions.

② **Reading non-fiction notes**

Read the summary for 'We Salute You'. Emphasize the skill, determination and expertise that would be required to perform stunts in a wheelchair and perform these all over the world.

Ask students to find one word in the summary which sums up what is important about what Aaron is doing (pioneer). Explain that spina bifida is a defect of the spine, which some people are born with. Explain that a healthy spine is closed to protect the spinal cord (a bundle of nerves that sends messages back and forth between your brain and the rest of your body). The messages tell your muscles to move so you can kick a ball or pick up a pencil. The spine of someone with spina bifida is open, so is not protected. This means that the spine cannot get messages to and from the brain. People with spina bifida cannot move their muscles the way other people do. This is called paralysis. The person cannot move some muscles or feel things on some parts of the body.

Refer to the CD-ROM or read the text while students follow in their books. Point to the glossary and read out the definitions. Explain that the title, 'We Salute You', means that the writer wants us to honour Aaron because of his sporting skills and qualities of determination and perseverance, so effectively overcoming his disability.

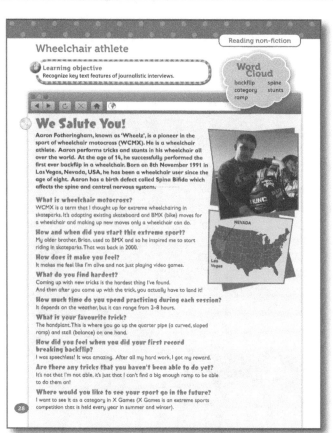

We Salute You!

Aaron Fotheringham, known as 'Wheelz', is a pioneer in the sport of wheelchair motocross (WCMX). He is a wheelchair athlete. Aaron performs tricks and stunts in his wheelchair all over the world. At the age of 14, he successfully performed the first ever backflip in a wheelchair. Born on 8th November 1991 in Las Vegas, Nevada, USA, he has been a wheelchair user since the age of eight. Aaron has a birth defect called Spina Bifida which affects the spine and central nervous system.

What is wheelchair motocross?
WCMX is a term that I thought up for extreme wheelchairing in skateparks. It's adapting existing skateboard and BMX (bike) moves for a wheelchair and making up new moves only a wheelchair can do.

How and when did you start this extreme sport?
My older brother, Brian, used to BMX and so he inspired me to start riding in skateparks. That was back in 2000.

How does it make you feel?
It makes me feel like I'm alive and not just playing video games.

What do you find hardest?
Coming up with new tricks is the hardest thing I've found. And then after you come up with the trick, you actually have to land it!

How much time do you spend practising during each session?
It depends on the weather, but it can range from 2–8 hours.

What is your favourite trick?
The handplant. This is where you go up the quarter pipe (a curved, sloped ramp) and stall (balance) on one hand.

How did you feel when you did your first record breaking backflip?
I was speechless! It was amazing. After all my hard work, I got my reward.

Are there any tricks that you haven't been able to do yet?
It's not that I'm not able, it's just that I can't find a big enough ramp to be able to do them on!

Where would you like to see your sport go in the future?
I want to see it as a category in X Games (X Games is an extreme sports competition that is held every year in summer and winter).

28

③ **Word Cloud definitions**

Focus students' attention on the Word Cloud and refer to the CD-ROM. Ask students to think about the meaning of 'backflip' (to turn over with a sudden quick movement). Ask students to consider how exceptional it must be to do a backflip in a wheelchair. Explain that the verb 'flip' is used to represent a quick movement. Explain that in sporting competitions, which include disabled athletes, getting a new sport (category) accepted will be very important.

backflip a backward somersault done in the air

category a class or division of people or things, with shared characteristics

ramp sloping surface joining two different levels

spine series of vertebrae extending from the skull to the small of the back

stunt an action displaying spectacular skill and daring

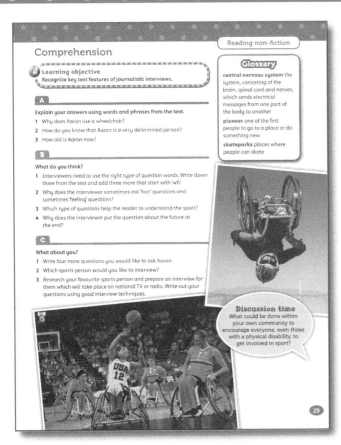

Comprehension

Reading non-fiction

Learning objective
Recognize key text features of journalistic interviews.

A

Explain your answers using words and phrases from the text.
1 Why does Aaron use a wheelchair?
2 How do you know that Aaron is a very determined person?
3 How old is Aaron now?

B

What do you think?
1 Interviewers need to use the right type of question words. Write down three from the text and add three more that start with 'wh'.
2 Why does the interviewer sometimes ask 'fact' questions and sometimes 'feeling' questions?
3 Which type of questions help the reader to understand the sport?
4 Why does the interviewer put the question about the future at the end?

C

What about you?
1 Write four more questions you would like to ask Aaron.
2 Which sports person would you like to interview?
3 Research your favourite sports person and prepare an interview for them which will take place on national TV or radio. Write out your questions using good interview techniques.

Glossary
central nervous system the system, consisting of the brain, spinal cord and nerves, which sends electrical messages from one part of the body to another
pioneer one of the first people to go to a place or do something new
skateparks places where people can skate

Discussion time
What could be done within your own community to encourage everyone, even those with a physical disability, to get involved in sport?

29

 Student Book teaching notes and comprehension answers

A

Students should provide evidence for their answers.

Answers:
1 Aaron has spina bifida which effects his central nervous system. (Lines 7–8)
2 Aaron has been involved in wheelchair sport since he was eight. He cites coming up with new tricks as "…*the hardest thing I've found.*" (Line 19). Aaron practises for between 2–8 hours each session. (Line 22).
3 Aaron is 21, his birth date is 8 November 1991. (Line 5)

B

Explain that all the questions help the reader understand the sport from both a factual and personal angle. The facts are tied up with feelings because a person is being interviewed. Factually based questions have been used to illicit underlying qualities such as endurance and determination.

Ask students to identify which questions are focused on 'fact' or 'feeling'.

What is wheelchair motocross? Fact. *How does it make you feel?* Feeling.

Answers:
1 What? How? Where? When? Why? Which? Who?
2 So that he can give information and also convey the essential qualities of a Paralympics athlete to the reader.
3 What and how questions encourage the interviewee to convey both facts and opinion.
4 Interviews usually begin when the interviewee is young, and starting out on their career or sport. An interview will usually conclude with what the interviewee hopes to achieve in the future.

C

1 Ask students to read out their questions so that overlong and inappropriate questions rectified.
2 Steer students towards a suitable sports personality, and encourage some variation if students' choices are the same!
3 For this question ensure that:
▶ A range of question stems are used.
▶ A range of fact and feeling questions are used.
▶ The interview starts logically at the outset of the sportsperson's career, culminating in what they hope to achieve in the future.
▶ Research is duly carried out, so that the questions asked can be answered.

 Discussion time

Ask students for their ideas to encourage locally inclusive sporting activities and events. Collate the ideas, and help students draft a class letter to the town council (or equivalent), suggesting these opportunities.

Learning objective

Investigate meanings and spellings of connectives.

Students learn about the categories of connective words and phrases to help them explain and persuade their audience.

 Remember to display the child-friendly learning objective to the class along with the child-friendly checklist that students can use to assess how well they achieve it.

We know that we have achieved this because:

▶ We know that the right type of connective must be used to join sentences.
▶ We can use the right type of connective to join sentences in our own writing.

② Student Book teaching notes and grammar exercise answers

A

Read through the explanation of connectives. Explain that they are words or phrases that link one sentence to the next for the reader, so helping them follow ideas and make sense of things.

Students complete the task on their own. They should read through their sentences to check they make sense and then swap with a partner for correction. Elicit feedback on incorrect answers to clarify for the whole class.

Example answers:

2 Some people think that young people do not do enough sport. Moreover, they spend too much time playing computer games.

3 Swimming increases fitness. In addition it really helps build strength.

4 Sports require skill and team work. For example, successful teams cannot be formed if every individual on the team is trying to act on their own.

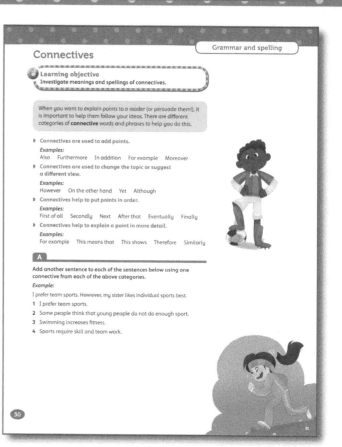

Connectives

Learning objective
Investigate meanings and spellings of connectives.

When you want to explain points to a reader (or persuade them!), it is important to help them follow your ideas. There are different categories of **connective** words and phrases to help you do this.

▶ Connectives are used to add points.
Examples:
Also Furthermore In addition For example Moreover
▶ Connectives are used to change the topic or suggest a different view.
Examples:
However On the other hand Yet Although
▶ Connectives help to put points in order.
Examples:
First of all Secondly Next After that Eventually Finally
▶ Connectives help to explain a point in more detail.
Examples:
For example This means that This shows Therefore Similarly

A

Add another sentence to each of the sentences below using one connective from each of the above categories.
Example:
I prefer team sports. However, my sister likes individual sports best.
1 I prefer team sports.
2 Some people think that young people do not do enough sport.
3 Swimming increases fitness.
4 Sports require skill and team work.

30

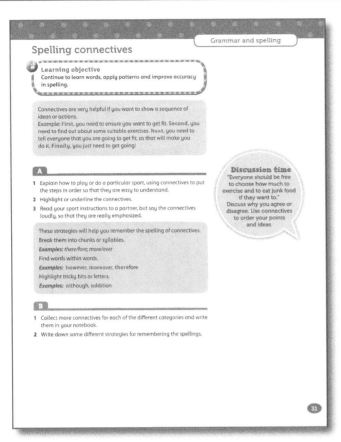

Page 31 student book reproduction:

Spelling connectives

Learning objective
Continue to learn words, apply patterns and improve accuracy in spelling.

Connectives are very helpful if you want to show a sequence of ideas or actions.
Example: First, you need to ensure you want to get fit. Second, you need to find out about some suitable exercises. Next, you need to tell everyone that you are going to get fit, as that will make you do it. Finally, you just need to get going!

A
1 Explain how to play or do a particular sport, using connectives to put the steps in order so that they are easy to understand.
2 Highlight or underline the connectives.
3 Read your sport instructions to a partner, but say the connectives loudly, so that they are really emphasized.

These strategies will help you remember the spelling of connectives. Break them into chunks or syllables.
Examples: there/fore; more/over
Find words within words.
Examples: however, moreover, therefore
Highlight tricky bits or letters.
Examples: although, addition

B
1 Collect more connectives for each of the different categories and write them in your notebook.
2 Write down some different strategies for remembering the spellings.

Discussion time
"Everyone should be free to choose how much to exercise and to eat junk food if they want to." Discuss why you agree or disagree. Use connectives to order your points and ideas.

Example:

How to play football

<u>First</u>, you need to create a team. Football usually is played between two teams with 11 players playing for each team at a time.

<u>Secondly</u>, you need to create your football field.

<u>Next</u>, you need to create goal posts at either end of the field. This is where your team will score goals.

<u>After that</u>, choose the player positions. Everyone needs to have a role so they know what to do when the game starts.

<u>Finally</u>, you can start the game!

As students read their instructions to a partner check for any incorrect terms and correct.

 B

1 Students find more connectives for each of the categories. When they have written them in their notebooks elicit responses from the class and write these on the board. Ask students to write down any connectives they have not already written in their notebooks.

Additional connectives:

Add points: and, as well as
Change topic: unless, except, apart from
Ordering: meanwhile, then
Explaining: such as, for instance, in the case of

2 Ask students if they use particular strategies to remember spellings and share these with the class. Explain some simple techniques to them. ***Example:***

LOOK carefully at the new word. How can you break it into smaller bits?

THINK about the parts of the words which might cause problems — double letters for instance, or a vowel that isn't pronounced as you would expect.

COVER the word and close your eyes. Try to see it in your mind.

WRITE the word down without looking back.

CHECK to see if you're right. If not, look carefully at where you went wrong and try again.

③ Learning objective

Continue to learn words, apply patterns and improve accuracy in spelling.

Students understand and use new vocabulary and implement techniques to remember spellings.

Remember to display the child-friendly learning objective to the class along with the child-friendly checklist that students can use to assess how well they achieve it.

We know that we have achieved this because:

▶ **We understand a range of connectives and how they are used.**
▶ **We can spell new words correctly.**
▶ **We can use techniques to help us remember how to spell words correctly.**

④ Student book teaching notes and grammar exercise answers

Read the information in the box with the class. Explain that they are going to write explanations guiding readers through the rules and techniques of a particular sport. To do this they will need to use connectives to sequence events and provide additional information.

A

Students choose a sport to explain and write the steps, underlining connectives.

⑤ Discussion time

As a class discuss the issues surrounding too much junk food and too little exercise. Elicit the effects of these from the class (poor health, low level of fitness, obesity, etc.). Once students have decided if they agree or disagree with the statement they write a list of points using connectives to sequence them for clarity and importance. Ask for volunteers to read their arguments to the class. Check for any common errors and clarify.

Learning objective

Explore how poets manipulate and play with words and their sounds.

Students identify and then explain how the poet uses words and sound to achieve the message of the poem.

  Remember to display the child-friendly learning objective to the class along with the child-friendly checklist that students can use to assess how well they achieve it.

We know that we have achieved this because:

▶ We can identify the features used by the poet.

▶ We can explain the effects of these.

▶ We can understand how they enhance the meaning of the poem.

② Teaching notes on the poem

Ask students if they watched the London Paralympics on television. Explain that the name 'Paralympics' comes from the Greek prefix 'para', meaning 'alongside' the main Olympics. Its motto is 'Spirit in Motion'.

Explain that the competition is targeted at people who have some disability but also the highest athletic ability. Sports include archery, cycling, football, horse riding, judo, power lifting, rowing, sailing, shooting, swimming, table tennis, volleyball, wheelchair basketball, wheelchair fencing, wheelchair rugby, and wheelchair tennis.

The poem, 'Salute' describes the obstacles, challenges and in turn, the almost superhuman qualities and skills required to become a Paralympic athlete.

Tell students that Brian Moses is a very experienced children's poet, having performed in over 2000 schools. Explain that Brian said he began writing poetry when he realized he would never be a rock star: "*I put the guitar to one side, but the songs carried on and became poems.*" That original musical influence can still be heard in his work, with its regular beat and steady rhyme.

Books open. Refer to the CD-ROM or read out the poem aloud to the class. Focus attention on the photographs of Paralympics athletes. **Ask:** *What do the photographs make you think of as you read the poem?*

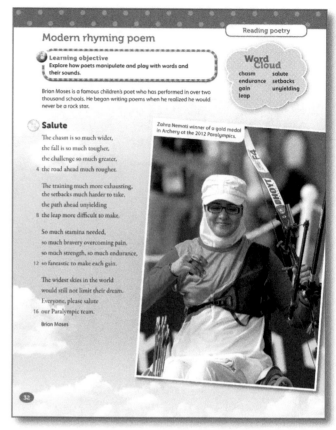

Modern rhyming poem

Reading poetry

Learning objective
Explore how poets manipulate and play with words and their sounds.

Brian Moses is a famous children's poet who has performed in over two thousand schools. He began writing poems when he realized he would never be a rock star.

Word Cloud

chasm · salute
endurance · setbacks
gain · unyielding
leap

Salute

The chasm is so much wider,
the fall is so much tougher,
the challenge so much greater,
4 the road ahead much rougher.

The training much more exhausting,
the setbacks much harder to take,
the path ahead unyielding
8 the leap more difficult to make.

So much stamina needed,
so much bravery overcoming pain,
so much strength, so much endurance,
12 so fantastic to make each gain.

The widest skies in the world
would still not limit their dream.
Everyone, please salute
16 our Paralympic team.

Brian Moses

Zahra Nemati winner of a gold medal in Archery at the 2012 Paralympics.

32

③ Word Cloud definitions

Refer to the CD-ROM. Explain that many of the words in the poem are to do with the obstacles Paralympians need to overcome.

Ask students to find a word in the Word Cloud that means going back to the beginning again (setbacks). **Ask:** *Which word means not ever giving up, never changing their course of action?* (Unyielding.)

Direct students to the first line, '*The chasm is so much wider*', and explain that 'chasm' means a huge space between progress and achievement. **Ask:** *Which word means to put up with something, and not give up?* (Endurance.) Ask students to find two words in the Word Cloud which indicate moving forward; both are nouns (leap, gain). Tell students that these can be used as verbs. ***Example:*** to leap (jump) over the wall, and to gain (add) a friend. Refer back to the non-fiction extract 'We Salute You!' to tease out the meaning of the title of the poem, to give the Paralympics athletes a gesture of respect.

chasm a profound difference between people, viewpoints, feelings, etc

endurance the ability to endure an unpleasant process or situation without giving way

gain increase the amount or rate of

leap jump or spring a long way, to move forward

salute gesture of respect, homage, or polite recognition or acknowledgment

setbacks reversals or checks in progress

unyielding unlikely to be swayed

Comprehension

A

Give evidence from the poem to support answers to A and B.

1 The poet has called the poem 'Salute'. Which statement below explains the reason for the poem's title?
  a To express admiration for the courage and determination of the paralympic team.
  b To show that the paralympic team normally salute at the end of a sporting event.
  c To ask the readers to salute at the end of the poem.
2 Name three qualities a paralympic athlete needs.
3 The paralympic athlete has to put in great effort. Which two words emphasize this throughout the poem?
4 Which sentence explains that the athlete will not stop competing?

B

Poet's use of language

1 Look again at the first three verses. What do you notice about how each line starts?
2 The poet uses rhyme at the end of some lines to emphasize his feelings and create a rhythm. Write down the rhyming word pairs.
3 The poet refers to 'our Paralympic team'. Which word class is 'our'?
  a pronoun
  b adjective
  c preposition
4 Why has the poet used the word 'our' and not 'the'?

C

What about you?

Tell a partner about the most challenging situation you have been in. It could be:
▶ moving to a new school or country.
▶ taking part in a competition or an exam.
▶ helping to care for a sick family member.
Listen to each other, and then ask and answer these questions:
a How did you overcome the difficulties?
b What advice would you give to someone facing the same challenge?

Tanni Grey Thompson, paralympic athlete

'88 SEOUL PARALYMPICS

The logo of the first ever paralympic games

33

emphasize the difficulties athletes have to face. Verse three is focused on the special qualities needed by athletes: stamina (the ability to sustain prolonged physical or mental effort) bravery, strength, endurance. The final verse focuses on the extent of their hopes — widest skies, dream. In cumulatively listing the obstacles faced and qualities required, the poem builds up to the request to the reader to salute these unsung heroes.

Answers:

1 The first two verses begin with 'The'. The additional features are the repeat of the phrase 'so much', which emphasizes the effort required by the athletes, and the use of comparatives: wider, tougher, greater, rougher.
2 Alternate lines (Note difference in 3rd and 4th verses): Wider/greater; rougher/tougher; exhausting/unyielding; take/make; pain/gain; dream/team).
3 a – pronoun
4 They are part of the community/country; they belong to us.

C

Students may write about their own experiences or use the suggestions provided.

Students could be given only one to two minutes to describe their challenging situation — speed telling. More time should be given for each student to ask questions. Remind students of appropriate question stems. ***Example:*** interrogative words: What? When? Who? Where? Which?

④ Student Book teaching notes and comprehension answers

Read the poem, emphasizing the words repeated, steady rhythm and end rhymes. Ask students to join in, adding a steady beat by tapping desks. The poem should build up in volume and emphasis. The class could be divided into four groups, and allocated one stanza each to perform to the rest of the class. The class could all salute on the last two lines, 'Everyone, please salute/our Paralympic team.'

A

Students can complete this activity in pairs. Check the answers with the whole class.

Answers:

1 a
2 determination, stamina, bravery, strength, endurance
3 so/much
4 'The widest skies in the world would still not limit their dream.'

B

Explain how the first verse focuses on the general nature of the challenge facing the athletes — wider, tougher, and greater. Having these words at the end further emphasizes them for the reader. In verse two, words like exhausting and unyielding again seem to

⑤ Extension

Ask students to write a short letter to Brian Moses saying what they liked about his poem, 'Salute'.

⇨

Learning objective

Argue a case in writing, developing points logically and convincingly.

Students will explore how to structure an argument and what persuasive techniques to use. They will then write their own arguments using these techniques.

Remember to display the child-friendly learning objective to the class along with the child-friendly checklist that students can use to assess how well they achieve it.

We know that we have achieved this because:

- **We are able to identify topic sentences.**
- **We know how to structure a persuasive argument.**
- **We are able to identify persuasive techniques such as: examples, facts and statistics, anecdotes, sets of three, emotive vocabulary, short sentences, rhetorical questions.**
- **We know how to write a persuasive argument using these techniques.**

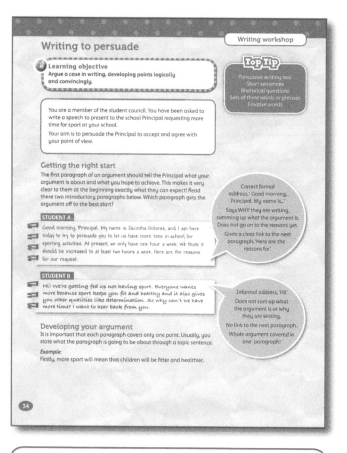

② Writing workshop teaching notes

Tell students that they are going to write their own speech to the Principal, asking for more time for sports. Confirm that there will be much that they can use from the samples provided.

First ask students to write a four paragraph plan. The first and final paragraphs will be the introduction and conclusion. The second and third paragraphs should be a topic sentence for each. Students should therefore write the plan as follows:

Paragraph 1 Introduction
Paragraph 2 More hours for sports will make students healthier
Paragraph 3 Students who are fit and healthy will work better at their school work
Conclusion

Read through the writing task, putting emphasis on the persuasive aspect of the task, and that it's a written speech, not a letter.

Ask: *What are the formal features of the writing by Student A?* Formal address, gives name, states intentions, and suggests they will provide reasons for their argument.

Ask: *What are the informal features of the writing by Student B?* Inappropriate greeting – Hi, expresses irrelevant feelings, lacks clarity of argument, bluntness 'I want to hear back from you.'

Getting the right start

Students should now write their introduction. Encourage students to use the format and number of sentences used in Student A's example.

Developing your argument

Explain how the topic sentences (the sentences which essentially tell the reader what the paragraph is about) need to be proved. This can be done through using real life examples; facts and statistics; story of someone you know; finishing with a sentence which points out the difference between the change being put forward and the conditions at present. **Ask:** *Which examples can you find in the texts from Student A and Student B?* Student A: 'I am here today to try and persuade you to let us have more time in school for sporting activities.' Student B: 'We're getting fed up not having sport.'

③ Top Tip

Students write two short sentences, two rhetorical questions, and choose three emotive words that they will use in their own writing.

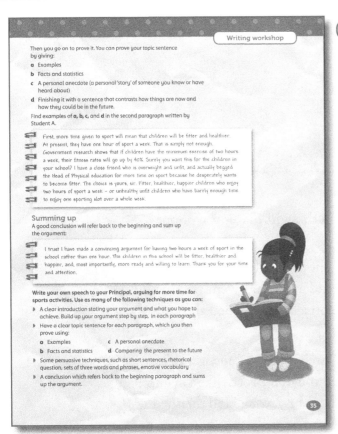

Writing workshop

Then you go on to prove it. You can prove your topic sentence by giving:

a Examples

b Facts and statistics

c A personal anecdote (a personal 'story' of someone you know or have heard about)

d Finishing it with a sentence that contrasts how things are now and how they could be in the future.

Find examples of **a**, **b**, **c**, and **d** in the second paragraph written by Student A.

> First, more time given to sport will mean that children will be fitter and healthier. At present, they have one hour of sport a week. That is simply not enough. Government research shows that if children have the minimum exercise of two hours a week, their fitness rates will go up by 40%. Surely you want this for the children in your school? I have a close friend who is overweight and unfit, and actually begged the Head of Physical education for more time on sport because he desperately wants to become fitter. The choice is yours, sir. Fitter, healthier, happier children who enjoy two hours of sport a week – or unhealthy unfit children who have barely enough time to enjoy one sporting slot over a whole week.

Summing up

A good conclusion will refer back to the beginning and sum up the argument:

> I trust I have made a convincing argument for having two hours a week of sport in the school rather than one hour. The children in this school will be fitter, healthier and happier, and, most importantly, more ready and willing to learn. Thank you for your time and attention.

Write your own speech to your Principal, arguing for more time for sports activities. Use as many of the following techniques as you can:

▸ A clear introduction stating your argument and what you hope to achieve. Build up your argument step by step, in each paragraph

▸ Have a clear topic sentence for each paragraph, which you then prove using:

a Examples　　c A personal anecdote

b Facts and statistics　　d Comparing the present to the future

▸ Some persuasive techniques, such as short sentences, rhetorical question, sets of three words and phrases, emotive vocabulary

▸ A conclusion which refers back to the beginning paragraph and sums up the argument.

35

⑤ Extension

Split the class into groups of four, and ask them to read their speeches to each other. Choose one to read to the rest of the class. If real issues have been used, and it is appropriate to do so, arrange for students to present their arguments to the Principal.

The techniques used in the writing of the persuasive speech could be subsequently used as assessment criteria.

④ Writing workshop teaching notes

As students write their second and third paragraphs, they should be encouraged to:

▸ Improve their respective topic sentences using examples.

Example: At present we only have one hour of sport a week. This is not enough time to … .

▸ Implement statistics and research.

Example: Recent research shows that … .

▸ Highlight personal anecdotes.

Example: I have a friend who … .

Confirm with students that they can create impact with a final, contrasting sentence. ***Example:*** What would you like, Sir? Healthy or unhealthy children?

Encourage students to use sets of three (health, fitness, stamina); emotive words (dramatically improve children's futures); rhetorical questions, (Surely this is not what you want for your school?)

Summing up

Students write the conclusion, referring to the content and sentence structure of the example conclusion.

Explain that a good conclusion will refer back to the beginning, and sum up the argument, with the first sentence of the last paragraph summing up the argument. The rest of the paragraph will then expand on this, finishing by thanking the Principal for their attention and time.

End of Unit Test

Question Paper

Reading: fiction

Read the extract and answer the questions.

> **Morning Cycle Race**
>
> Every morning started with a bike race and Sam thought that it was about time he won one.
>
> Every morning at Mr Parrott's newsagents' shop — early. They started at 6.30 am, Sam versus Nate, ready, steady go — and away they went for thirty
> 5 eight minutes of frantic pedalling, thirty nine on a bad day when the weather wasn't friendly.
>
> The race record was thirty-seven minutes and twelve seconds, and it was Sam who held it. The day he set it, he flew on his bike through the roads like a maniac; the wind and every single traffic light seemed to be in his favour. He'd thrashed
> 10 Nate easily. But that was a month ago. Now it seemed he was losing more than he won — and that meant that he was not only losing the race, but money too...
>
> Mr Parrott would always have his customers' papers laid out in two piles, all in perfect order. On the left was the pile for what he called the 'west circuit' and on the right was the pile for the 'east circuit.'
>
> 15 'Which do you fancy today, Nate?' Sam asked. 'West or east?'
>
> Whoever won the previous day could decide whether he did the east or west the following morning. The west was slightly longer, with more countryside, longer roads and fewer newspapers to deliver. The east circuit was shorter, with more newspapers for more houses that were closer
> 20 together. Whichever you picked, though, your time on the road was almost exactly the same. It was the perfect race.
>
> From *Cycling for Gold* by Owen Slot
>
> ---
>
> **Glossary**
> **frantic** conducted in a hurried, excited, and disorganized way

Comprehension

A

Give evidence from the extract to support your answers.

1 How often did the two boys race?

_____ [1]

2 What has been the fastest race time?

_____ [1]

3 Explain what the east and west circuit is, and how they are different.

_____ [2]

B

Give evidence from the extract to support your answers.

1 Give two reasons why Sam is unhappy.

_____

_____ [2]

2 Who had won the previous day? Nate or Sam? Explain the reason for your choice.

_____ [2]

3 Find evidence which shows that Mr Parrott is an organized person.

_____ [1]

4 Why does the writer refer to the _'perfect race'_?

_____ [2]

C

Give evidence from the extract to support your answers.

1 _'...when the weather wasn't <u>friendly</u>.'_ Replace the underlined word with a word or phrase that means the same.

_____ [1]

2 _'...he flew on his bike through the roads <u>like a maniac</u>.'_ Identify the figure of speech. Tick the correct box.

  a Metaphor ☐

  b Alliteration ☐

  c Personification ☐

  d Simile ☐

  e Onomatopoeia ☐ [1]

3 What do you think will happen next in the story? Give reasons for your answer.

_____ [2]

Reading: non-fiction

Read the extract and answer the questions.

Get on your bike!

Cycling is one of the easiest ways to exercise. You can ride a bicycle anywhere, and at any time of the year — and all without spending a fortune. Sometimes people are put off doing sports because of the high level of skill that seems to be required, or perhaps they cannot commit to a team sport due to time pressures.
5　But with cycling, all you need is a bike, a half an hour here or there where it suits, and a bit of confidence.

　　You might go along with the common perception that cycling only exercises the legs, but you would be wrong. It actually builds strength in a holistic manner, since every single part of the body is involved. Cycling also improves
10　general muscle function and cardiovascular fitness. In addition, cycling burns 300 calories per hour, so if you cycle 30 minutes every day it means an 11 lb loss over the year. As it also helps to build muscle, cycling will continue to boost your metabolic rate long after you've finished your ride.

　　Cycling also makes you smarter. Teachers often comment that children
15　who walk or cycle to school arrive brighter and more ready to learn than those who arrive by car.

　　You don't need to spend a fortune when purchasing a bike, but it is imperative that it is the right size! A bike that is too big or too small can be dangerous. The balls of the feet should just touch the ground – and you should
20　be able to turn the handlebars, brake, and change gear without over stretching.

Glossary
holistic the treatment of the whole person
metabolic processes that occur in a living organism to maintain life

Comprehension

A

Give evidence from the text to support your answers.

1 Find three statements in the text which suggest cycling is a good sport to be involved in.

_____

_____ [3]

2 Why does a bike need to be the right size for the rider?

_____ [1]

3 What word class is the word 'you'?

_____ [1]

B

Give evidence from the extract to support your answers.

1 Give one fact from the extract about cycling, and one opinion.

_____

_____ [2]

2 Why would a _'bike that is too big or too small'_ be dangerous? Explain in your own words.

_____

_____ [3]

C

Give evidence from the extract to support your answers.

1 _'You don't need to spend a fortune when purchasing a bike, but it is <u>imperative</u> that it is the right size!'_ Why has the writer used an exclamation mark?

_____ [2]

2 Give another word or phrase that could be used instead of the word _'imperative.'_

_____ [1]

3 Explain why the writer has used _'you'_ so often throughout the text.

_____ [2]

Writing: fiction

Write three paragraphs about someone in a race. Please use a separate sheet of paper.

Remember!

The race should present difficulties for the competitor. Perhaps a competitor is ahead of them, or just catching up.

You will need to make the decision as to whether they win or lose the race, and what effect it has on them.

Write in the first person.

[30]

Writing: non-fiction

Choose a sport you know well and write three paragraphs for a website on why children should take it up as a keep-fit activity. Please use a separate sheet of paper.

Remember!

Use some of the same techniques that have been used in the cycling text.

[20]

3 World of discovery

Speaking and listening

3 World of discovery

① Warm up objective

Discuss and express preferences in terms of language, style and themes.

Students develop their understanding and skills to discuss their preferences.

Remember to display the child-friendly learning objective to the class along with the child-friendly checklist that students can use to assess how well they achieve it.

We know that we have achieved this because:
▶ We are able to identify our preferences.
▶ We can explain our preferences.

"Judge a man by his questions rather than by his answers."
Voltaire, 1694–1778

Let's Talk
1 Why do you think it is important to find out about our world and the past?
2 What would you like to find out about the world?

36

② Unit warm up

Books closed. Write the words 'world' and 'discovery' on the board and ask students to suggest what the words make them think of. Then write the unit title, 'World of discovery'. Confirm that it means finding out and learning about the earth we live on. These discoveries can be about people, animals, and places.

Explain there are people whose jobs are focused on discovery, such as historians, astronauts, scientists, and explorers. This unit will focus on some important discoveries about the past.

Books open. Read the quote and ask students to repeat it chorally.

Ask students to write down in large letters on a piece of paper what they think Voltaire means in this quote.

Write students' responses on the board, and use these to tease out the meaning. (It is more important to find out and discover the answers than just have the answers.) Reinforce this meaning by writing the following on the board, 'If we don't ask and enquire, we will not discover or learn'.

Ask students how they could explain Voltaire's quote to younger students. Create a quote cloud filled with students' answers that could be displayed in the classroom.

③ Let's Talk

1 Generate a class discussion with the 'Let's Talk' question. Elicit ideas such as: our past and our history help us to understand our present; we learn from our mistakes, etc.
2 Develop the discussion by asking students what they would like to find out about the world – and the universe. **Ask:** *What do you think there is still left to discover?* (Technology, new planets, energy sources, etc.)

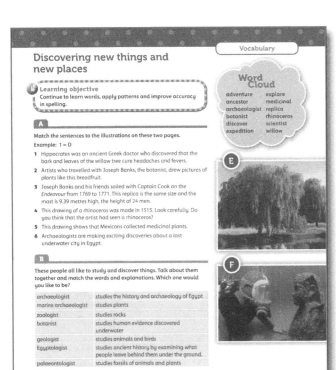

Learning objective

④ **Continue to learn words, apply patterns and improve accuracy in spelling.**

Students are introduced to new words linked to discovery and associated occupations. They are then given the opportunity to discuss these terms and to write about them.

Remember to display the child-friendly learning objective to the class along with the child-friendly checklist that students can use to assess how well they achieve it.

We know that we have achieved this because:

▶ We are able to talk and write about these new terms.

▶ We are able to understand them and use them in context.

⑤ **Word Cloud definitions**

Focus students' attention on the Word Cloud. **Ask:** *Which words are to do with discovery?* (Adventure, discover, expedition, explore.)

adventure an unusual and exciting, experience
ancestor a person from whom one is descended
archaeologist someone who studies ancient history by examining what people leave behind them
botanist someone who studies plants
discover to notice or learn
expedition journey undertaken by a group of people with the purpose of exploration or research
explore to travel through (an unfamiliar area) in order to learn about it
medicinal relating to medicine or drugs
replica an exact copy or model of something
rhinoceros a large mammal with one or two horns on the nose and thick folded skin
scientist an expert in science
willow a type of tree

⑥ **Student Book teaching notes and vocabulary exercise answers**

A

Ask students to look at the pictures. **Ask:** *Which of the Word Cloud words can they place under each picture?* Read these through with students, eliciting responses to see who is correct.

Answers:

1 E, **2** B, **3** A, **4** C, **5** D, **6** F,

B

Explain that the suffix '–ist' at the end of a word indicates a person involved in a particular activity or area.
Example: scientist, cyclist. Working in pairs, students match the terms.

Answers:

archeologist studies ancient history by examining what people leave behind them underground
marine archeologist studies human evidence discovered underwater
zoologist studies animals and birds
botanist studies plants
geologist studies rocks
Egyptologist studies the history and archaeology of Egypt
paleontologist studies bones and dinosaurs

① Learning objective

Understand aspects of narrative structure, e.g. the handling of time.

Students consider how narrative time and sequence is managed through respective journal entries.

Remember to display the child-friendly learning objective to the class along with the child-friendly checklist that students can use to assess how well they achieve it.

We know that we have achieved this because:

▶ We can infer how time has progressed.

▶ We understand that there are different ways of suggesting time within a narrative structure.

▶ We can identify features of narrative structure.

② Reading fiction notes

Ask students to imagine how exciting it must be to be involved in a major discovery. Books open. Read the text summary. Tell them that the *Endeavour* was sent on a voyage of discovery to New Zealand and Australia, led by Captain Cook. Explain that a journal is a personal diary of the news and events on the ship and will therefore give the reader quite a lot of information, albeit from one viewpoint.

Ask for volunteers to read the glossary explanations, steering them towards correct pronunciation. Repeat this exercise so that a definition is read out more than once.

Refer to the CD-ROM or read the text while students follow in their books.

③ Word Cloud definitions

Refer to the CD-ROM. Explain the differences between a 'diary' (personal feelings about experiences, events), 'journal' (personal diary about a journey) and 'log' (record of facts/events of a journey). **Ask:** *Is 'itch' used in the text as a noun or a verb?* (Verb.) **Ask:** *What is causing Nicholas to itch?* (Salt water and fleas.) Elicit responses from the class as to what three other words are to do with ships? (Deck, stowaway, voyage.) **Ask:** *Which plural is another word for animals?* (Creatures.) *Which word refers to something which could orbit around the sun?* (Planet.) Point out that 'presence' can also suggest a particular sort of personal quality — both negative and positive.

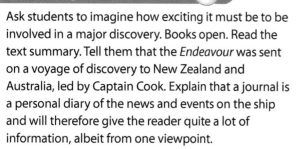

The diary of a stowaway

Learning objective
Understand aspects of narrative structure, for example the handling of time.

This is from the imaginary journal of a real boy, Nicholas Young, who was a stowaway on the ship *Endeavour*. He helped Joseph Banks on the ship and was given a job by him when they returned home. The 'Gentlemen' are Mr Banks, the scientists and artists. The author used Captain Cook's real journal to help her write this fictional journal.

Word Cloud

creatures   log
deck   planet
diary   presence
itch   stowaway
journal   voyage

The Start of a Great Adventure

Sunday 7th to Friday 19th August 1768 (Plymouth). I have managed to keep my presence aboard *Endeavour* secret. The three seamen I paid to get me on bring biscuits and water. It's a good hiding place I've got, in the aft of the Pinnace, a
5 small boat *Endeavour* carries aboard her. I can look over the edge and see the deck without being noticed. I've chickens for neighbours, and a goat. They cluck and bleat all day and night, in pens on deck. I'm glad of their company and wish I might go near them more often. I've had milk out of the goat. John
10 Ramsay says she's aboard for the Gentlemen and officers, so they might have fresh cream when they please...

Tuesday 23rd August (Plymouth). Last night the servant boy came right to my hiding place.
"Lad," he whispered, "are you still alive in there?" I held
15 silent. After a moment he poked his head into the Pinnace and stared straight at me. When he made out I was well, he smiled. He dropped some hardtack into my hand...

Tuesday 6th September (Off the coast of Spain). Mr Parkinson and Mr Buchan, the artists aboard, must be very busy men to draw all the
20 creatures Mr Banks discovers. Now his discoveries are all recorded in Mr Parkinson's and Mr Buchan's pictures...

Thursday 8th September (Off the coast of Spain). John Ramsay says, "We're pulling away from Cape Saint Vincent, lad, the last of Europe. And soon you shall come out."
25 It's difficult deciding what to do first. A wash — what with the fleas and a coat of saltwater on my skin, I itch like mad — or dinner. I think it shall be dinner...

38

Glossary

aboard on a ship
hardtack hard bread, like a biscuit
journal a diary kept on a journey
pinnace a small boat, kept on a ship

creatures animals

deck the planks of wood across the floor of a boat

diary a book in which someone's writes a daily record of events and experiences

itch to have, or feel, a tingling of the skin that causes a desire to scratch

journal a personal diary about a journey

log facts and information recorded by a captain on a ship's voyage

planet a body that orbits the sun, and is big enough for its own gravity to make it round

presence person, or thing, that exists or is present in a place but is not seen

stowaway a person who secretly hides on a vehicle such as an aeroplane, ship or train

voyage a long journey involving travel by sea or space

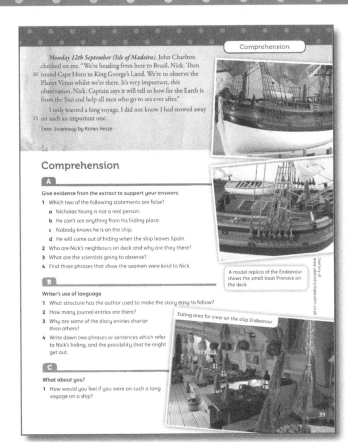

Monday 12th September (Isle of Madeira). John Charlton checked on me. "We're heading from here to Brasil, Nick. Then round Cape Horn to King George's Land. We're to observe the Planet Venus whilst we're there. It's very important, this observation, Nick. Captain says it will tell us how far the Earth is from the Sun and help all men who go to sea ever after."

I only wanted a long voyage. I did not know I had stowed away on such an important one.

From Stowaway by Karen Hesse

Comprehension

A

Give evidence from the extract to support your answers.

1 Which two of the following statements are false?
   a Nicholas Young is not a real person.
   b He can't see anything from his hiding place.
   c Nobody knows he is on the ship.
   d He will come out of hiding when the ship leaves Spain.
2 Who are Nick's neighbours on deck and why are they there?
3 What are the scientists going to observe?
4 Find three phrases that show the seamen were kind to Nick.

B

Writer's use of language

1 What structure has the author used to make the story easy to follow?
2 How many journal entries are there?
3 Why are some of the diary entries shorter than others?
4 Write down two phrases or sentences which refer to Nick's hiding, and the possibility that he might get out.

C

What about you?

1 How would you feel if you were on such a long voyage on a ship?

A model replica of the *Endeavour* shows the small boat Pinnace on the deck

Eating area for crew on the ship *Endeavour*

39

(4) Student Book teaching notes and comprehension answers

Students will learn how a journal can be used to sequence narrative structure, and indicate the passage of time and build up of plot. Highlighting the use of narrative, point out how the extract begins, '*I have managed to keep my presence on the Endeavour secret*', creates an immediate narrative hook.

A

1 Remind students that they have to consider the multiple choice questions and answers before selecting what they think is the correct answer. Students should provide quotes from the text or supporting information to qualify their answers.

Answers:

b He can't see anything from his hiding place.
c Nobody knows he is on the ship.

2 Explain 'neighbours' in this context means other people on the boat who are living next to Nicholas. On a long voyage a ship would function like a small town, with many different types of people, jobs and activities.

Ask students to create a list of people and animals on the ship. They must directly reference the text extract.

➡

Answers:

Three Seamen, officers, gentlemen, servant boy, John Ramsay, Mr Parkinson and Mr Buchan (artists), John Charlton, Mr Banks, Captain, chickens, goat.

Elicit reasons from the class as to why they are there.

3 Ask students to find the word 'observe' in the text. The scientists were there to observe the planet Venus in order to find out the distance of Earth from the Sun. This information will help with the development of navigational tools.

4 'The three seamen I paid to get me on bring biscuits and water.'
   'John Ramsay says, "We are pulling away from Cape Saint Vincent, lad, the last of Europe. And soon you shall come out".'
   'John Charlton checked on me.'

B

1 Students should refer to the dated entries. They should also identify the locations refered to in the journal. **Ask:** *Which three locations does Nick refer to in his diary entries?* (Plymouth, off the coast of Spain, the Isle of Madeira.)

Answer:

1 The author has used dated journal entries, so that the reader can follow the passage of time and location, and subsequent build up of plot and tension.

2 There are five diary entries.

3 The first entry is the longest. It summarizes Nicholas's experience on the journey so far, and explains how he is on board. The following entries are shorter. There isn't much to report on as he is in hiding. His days are defined by his interaction with others and his thoughts.

4 'John Ramsay says, "We are pulling away from Cape Saint Vincent, lad, the last of Europe. And soon you shall come out."'

C

Explain that in 1768, boats were often the only form of transport. There were no cars, trains, or airplanes. Long distances could take months by boat. The *Endeavour* sailed 17,004.47 kilometres on its journey to Australia, and was away for two years.

Ask students to write a short journal entry for their first day at sea. Ask them to consider how they would feel (excited, nervous, fearful, etc.), as well as the practicalities of being on board a ship at this time in history.

Learning objective

1 **Begin to show awareness of the impact of writers' choices of sentence length and structure.**

Students learn why and when different sentence lengths and structures are needed. They also learn about finite verbs, simple, compound and complex sentences.

Remember to display the child-friendly learning objective to the class along with the child-friendly checklist that students can use to assess how well they achieve it.

We know that we have achieved this because:

▶ We are able to recognize simple, compound and complex sentences in a text and use them in our own writing.

2 **Student Book teaching notes and grammar exercise answers**

Read the grammar explanation box. Ask students to write in large letters on three separate pieces of paper an example of a simple sentence with one finite verb; a compound sentence with clauses joined by 'and', 'but' or 'or'; and a complex sentence with a main and subordinate clause.

Refer students to the grammar box for help in this task.

Answers:

held, cluck, bleat, wanted, came

1 Ask students to read the summary box for definitions of compound and complex sentences.

Answer:

'I can look over the deck and see the deck without being noticed.' 'After a moment, he poked his head into the Pinnace and stared straight at me.'

Explain that 'I've got chickens and a goat' is not a compound sentence, as there is only one finite verb.

2 Direct students to read through the text again on their own, referring them to the rules in the grammar box to help them identify the answers.

Answers:

John Ramsay says (that) she's aboard for the gentlemen and the Officers, <u>so they might</u> have fresh cream when they please.

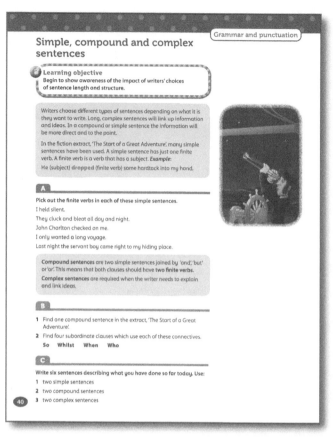

We're to observe the planet Venus <u>whilst we're there.</u>

<u>When he made</u> (that) out I was well, he smiled.

Nick says it will tell us far the Earth is from the Sun and help all the men <u>who go to the sea ever after.</u>

Before starting this task, remind students that each clause in a compound sentence must have a verb. Students share their sentences with the class and they agree or disagree with the intended structure.

3 **Extension**

Ask students to keep a tally of the number of simple, compound, and complex sentences used in their own writing over a period of time. Alternatively they can refer to an extract from a book by their favourite author.

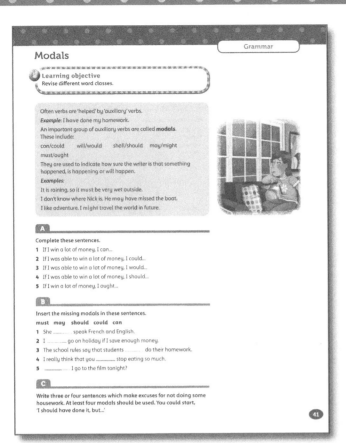

Grammar

Modals

Learning objective
Revise different word classes.

Often verbs are 'helped' by 'auxiliary' verbs.
Example: I have done my homework.
An important group of auxiliary verbs are called **modals**.
These include:
can/could   will/would   shall/should   may/might
must/ought
They are used to indicate how sure the writer is that something happened, is happening or will happen.
Examples:
It is raining, so it must be very wet outside.
I don't know where Nick is. He may have missed the boat.
I like adventure. I might travel the world in future.

A
Complete these sentences.
1 If I win a lot of money, I can...
2 If I was able to win a lot of money, I could...
3 If I was able to win a lot of money, I would...
4 If I was able to win a lot of money, I should...
5 If I win a lot of money, I ought...

B
Insert the missing modals in these sentences.
must may should could can
1 She _____ speak French and English.
2 I _____ go on holiday if I save enough money.
3 The school rules say that students _____ do their homework.
4 I really think that you _____ stop eating so much.
5 _____ I go to the film tonight?

C
Write three or four sentences which make excuses for not doing some housework. At least four modals should be used. You could start, 'I should have done it, but...'

41

Learning objective

(4)

Revise different word classes.

Students learn the range of modal verbs. They also learn how to use these for a specific meaning in different sentences.

Remember to display the child-friendly learning objective to the class along with the child-friendly checklist that students can use to assess how well they achieve it.

We know that we have achieved this because:

▶ **We know the full range of modal verbs and how they can make a subtle but crucial difference to a verb's meaning.**

▶ **We can use the full range of modal verbs in our own construction of sentences.**

(5) **Student Book teaching notes and grammar exercise answers**

A

Emphasize that can/could/should/may/might/ought are about intention while will/would/shall are focused on definite action. Ask students to complete the sentences in their notebooks and then compare with a partner.

Students could be asked to find more examples of modals from the text. ***Example:***

I can look over the edge . . ., I might go there more often, I think it shall be dinner, etc.

B

Explain to the class that there are different possibilities. Ask students to work in pairs to identify what these possibilities are.

Answers:

1 She *can* speak French and English. (could, should)
2 I *could* go on holiday if I save enough money. (can)
3 The school rules say that students *must* do their homework. (should)
4 I really think that you *should* stop eating so much. (must)
5 *May* I go to the film tonight? (can)

C

Tell students that the choice of modal will depend on the context of the sentence – that is, its intended meaning.

They will do it: can

Willing to do something: will, shall, could

Prediction: might

Possibility: may

Essential that they do it: must

They should do it: ought

Guess: might

Ask students to read out their sentences using modals to a partner. Do they make sense? If not, what suggestions would their partner make to correct them?

(6) **Extension**

Divide the class into two groups. Hand out paper to all the students. Instruct those in the first group to write simple sentences with 'must'. Choose a student in turn to read out their sentence. ***Example:*** 'My brother *must* pick up his clothes from the floor.' Tell the second group to change the modal so that the meaning is different. ***Example:*** 'My brother *should* pick his clothes up from the floor'.

Learning objective

Analyse how paragraphs and chapters are structured and linked.

Students create subheadings for a text, using evidence from the content.

 Remember to display the child-friendly learning objective to the class along with the child-friendly checklist that students can use to assess how well they achieve it.

We know that we have achieved this because:

▶ We are able to create suitable headings within a text that will help the reader.

2 Reading non-fiction notes

Explain that 2500 years ago there was once an ancient harbour of Alexandria as well as two other nearby holiday resorts, Herakleion and Canopus, but the remains of these cities are now underwater. These underwater cities are now major archaeological sites. Explain that these are places that archaeologists are studying so that they can find out how people used to live all those years ago.

Refer to the CD-ROM or read the text while students follow in their books. Ask students to list words they are unsure of. Then list these on the board to explain to the whole class.

Read out the glossary definition, and ask students to locate the term in the text. Ask students which three other words they think should go in the glossary that are not in the Word Cloud. This will give teachers more information on vocabulary not yet fully grasped.

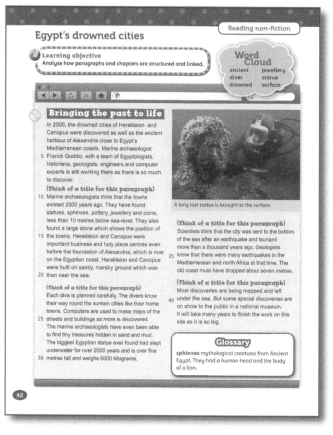

3 Word Cloud definitions

Refer to the CD-ROM. As each word is explained to students, ask individual students to find the sentence with the word, and to transpose it accordingly.
Example: 'The ancient (STOP) – *that means it has been in existence for a long time* – (CONTINUE) harbour of Alexandria.'

ancient having existed for a very long time

diver person who wears a diving suit to work underwater

drowned died through submersion and inhalation of water

jewellery personal ornaments, such as necklaces

statue a carved or cast figure of a person or an animal

surface the outside part or uppermost layer of something

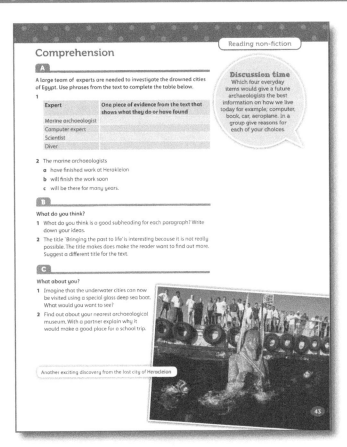

B

1 Before students embark on this task, explain that paragraph titles should give the reader a clue to what the paragraph is about, and so helps with their reading; they know what to expect. Sometimes a title can be a rhetorical question. ***Example:*** the first paragraph could be 'Exciting Finds!' or 'What has been found?'

If students have problems coming up with suitable headings, ask them to select the most important piece of information in each paragraph and either condense it into two or three words, or re-use it. ***Example:*** the heading for the first paragraph could be 'Drowned Cities'.

2 Ask students to come up with titles and rhetorical questions in pairs, and then compare them. Which ones are the most effective? Emphasize that the headings should catch the reader's eye and make them WANT to read. Sometimes alliteration is used. ***Example:*** 'Divers go down deep'.

C

1 As a class discuss what students would like to see. Ask them to back up their answers with reasons. ***Example:*** I would like to see the size of the streets to compare them to our roads now.

2 If students do not know of any local museum discoveries direct them to research online. The students will need to be given some guidance. ***Example:*** search terms and key words. Students share their research with the class. With students working in pairs elicit reasons as to why this would make a good trip. ***Example:*** educational, historically important, to understand how people used to live, etc.

④ Student Book teaching notes and comprehension answers

Working in groups, and structured as a timed activity, ask students the following: *What is the text about?* Elicit responses which incorporate the following detail. An earthquake and tsunami caused the underwater cities of Herakleion, Canopus and harbour of Alexandria to be flooded, ending up under the sea. A team of experts are examining what has been left so that they can discover information about the past 2500 years ago.

A

1 Students re-read the text in order to find evidence for their answers.

Answers:

Marine archaeologists '... have found statues, sphinxes, pottery...' (Lines 11–13)

Computer expert 'Computers are used to make maps of the streets and buildings...' (Lines 24–25)

Scientist '... think that the city was set to the bottom of the sea after an earthquake and tsunami...' (Lines 32–34)

Diver 'The divers know their way round the sunken cities like their home towns.' (Lines 22–24)

2 C - The marine archaeologists will be there for many years.

⑤ Discussion time

Students generate ideas for items that best inform on our current lives. Explain that students need to reinforce their suggestions with reasons. ***Example:*** Smartphone: So in the future people can understand how we communicated with others.

① Learning objective

Continue to learn words, apply patterns and improve accuracy in spelling.

Students learn about homophones, and how to distinguish one spelling from another.

 Remember to display the child-friendly learning objective to the class along with the child-friendly checklist that students can use to assess how well they achieve it.

We know that we have achieved this because:

▶ We know that certain words sound the same but are spelled differently. These words will have a different meaning and often be a different part of speech.

▶ We know that strategies have to be used to remember homophones.

▶ We are able to spell the words correctly.

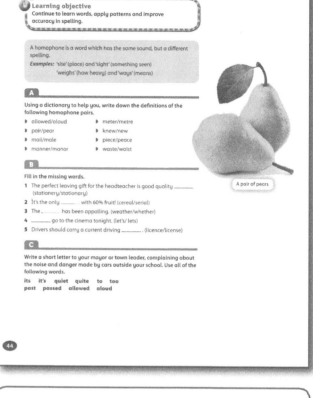

Grammar and spelling

Homophones

Learning objective
Continue to learn words, apply patterns and improve accuracy in spelling.

A homophone is a word which has the same sound, but a different spelling.
Examples: 'site' (place) and 'sight' (something seen)
'weighs' (how heavy) and 'ways' (means)

A

Using a dictionary to help you, write down the definitions of the following homophone pairs.
▶ allowed/aloud ▶ meter/metre
▶ pair/pear ▶ knew/new
▶ mail/male ▶ piece/peace
▶ manner/manor ▶ waste/waist

B

Fill in the missing words.
1 The perfect leaving gift for the headteacher is good quality _____ (stationery/stationary)
2 It's the only _____ with 60% fruit! (cereal/serial)
3 The _____ has been appalling. (weather/whether)
4 _____ go to the cinema tonight. (let's/ lets)
5 Drivers should carry a current driving _____ . (licence/license)

C

Write a short letter to your mayor or town leader, complaining about the noise and danger made by cars outside your school. Use all of the following words.
its it's quiet quite to too
past passed allowed aloud

A pair of pears

44

② Student Book teaching notes and grammar exercise answers

Read the explanation on what a homophone is. Ask students to provide examples of homophones, using drawings on the board to elicit these. **Example:** write the number 2 to elicit 'to/two/too'; draw sun and rain to elicit 'weather/whether'; draw a flower to elicit 'flower/flour'. In each case, the homophones should be written on the board and their different spellings highlighted so that the differences are clear to the student.

Ask students to read the two words aloud, so they can hear that they sound the same. Point out that strategies are required to help them remember the different spellings. **Example:** 'too', uses the 'oo' sound; 'two' has the double stroke of the 'w', reminding us it has two 'o's; 'to' is either used as a preposition or part of an infinitive, so it is not a lexical word – 'to' only has two letters.

A

Students to say the words out loud first, then write their meanings using a dictionary. Ask students to work in pairs. On completion, pick pair words from a hat, and ask students to explain the difference between the two. Give them the opportunity to ask or confer with another student.

Answers:

Aloud means out loud. Allowed means permitted.

Pair means a couple. Pear refers to the fruit.

Mail means letters and parcels sent by post. Male refers to a male person, animal, or plant.

Manner means a way in which something is done. Manor means a large country house.

Meter is a device that records something. Metre is a unit of measurement.

Knew, the past tense of know, means to understand. New means not previously used.

Piece refers to a portion of something. Peace means freedom of disturbance.

Waste means to use something carelessly. Waist is the part of the body above the hips.

B

Students can complete this exercise individually. Go through the answers with them in class.

1 The perfect leaving gift for the Headmaster is good quality *stationery*.
2 It's the only *cereal* with 60% fruit.
3 The *weather* has been appalling.
4 *Let's* go to the cinema tonight.
5 Drivers should carry a current driving *licence*.

To extend this task ask students to use the other homophone correctly in a sentence.

C

Check that students understand the difference between the homophones before they start writing.

Grammar

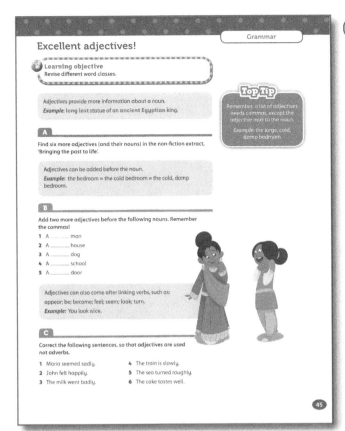

Excellent adjectives!

Learning objective
Revise different word classes.

Adjectives provide more information about a noun.
Example: long lost statue of an ancient Egyptian king.

Top Tip
Remember, a list of adjectives needs commas, except the adjective next to the noun.
Example: the large, cold, damp bedroom

A
Find six more adjectives (and their nouns) in the non-fiction extract, 'Bringing the past to life'.

Adjectives can be added before the noun.
Example: the bedroom = the cold bedroom = the cold, damp bedroom.

B
Add two more adjectives before the following nouns. Remember the commas!
1 A _____ man
2 A _____ house
3 A _____ dog
4 A _____ school
5 A _____ door

Adjectives can also come after linking verbs, such as:
appear; be; become; feel; seem; look; turn.
Example: You look nice.

C
Correct the following sentences, so that adjectives are used not adverbs.
1 Maria seemed sadly.
2 John felt happily.
3 The milk went badly.
4 The train is slowly.
5 The sea turned roughly.
6 The cake tastes well.

45

Learning objective

3

Revise different word classes.

Students will learn that an adjective gives more information about the noun.

Remember to display the child-friendly learning objective to the class along with the child-friendly checklist that students can use to assess how well they achieve it.

We know that we have achieved this because:
▶ We know that adjectives make detail precise.

4 ## Student Book teaching notes and grammar exercise answers

 A

Students can do this exercise in pairs. The text could be read without the adjectives, and students asked what difference does it make?

Answers:

drowned cities, ancient harbour, marine archaeologist, computer experts, large stone, etc.

B

Students should appreciate that adjectives make detail precise, and that adding adjectives before the noun will create a very definite picture in the reader's head. Adding two adjectives can increase the emphasis. ***Example:*** 'cold, damp house'.

Ask each student to read out what they consider to be their most effective example. Agree the best ones with the class and write them on the board.

C

To build on this task ask students to write additional sentences, using the linking verbs listed.

Answers:

Maria seemed *sad*.

John felt *happy*.

The milk went *bad*.

The train is *slow*.

The sea turned *rough*.

The cake tastes *good*.

5 **Top Tip**

Remind students that commas indicate a pause between parts of a sentence or they separate items in a list.

6 **Extension**

Ask students to describe their bedroom, or another room in their house, using adjectives to give a precise image to the reader. The description could be written as if the writer is a television commentator, 'Well first, of all, let's go up the back stairs, then through the old, oak door into my untidy bedroom. . . .' All adjectives used should be underlined.

53

① Learning objective

Explore how poets manipulate and play with words and their sounds.

Students identify the dialogue form used to express opposing points of view.

 Remember to display the child-friendly learning objective to the class along with the child-friendly checklist that students can use to assess how well they achieve it.

We know that we have achieved this because:

▶ We understand that the poem provides a form that enables two points of view to be clearly expressed.

▶ We can identify key words and phrases.

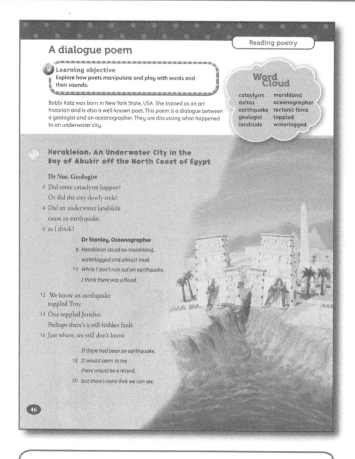

A dialogue poem

Learning objective
Explore how poets manipulate and play with words and their sounds.

Bobbi Katz was born in New York State, USA. She trained as an art historian and is also a well-known poet. This poem is a dialogue between a geologist and an oceanographer. They are discussing what happened to an underwater city.

Word Cloud

cataclysm marshland
deltas oceanographer
earthquake tectonic force
geologist toppled
landslide waterlogged

Herakleion: An Underwater City in the Bay of Abukir off the North Coast of Egypt

Dr Nur, Geologist
2 Did some cataclysm happen?
  Or did the city slowly sink?
4 Did an underwater landslide
  cause an earthquake,
6 as I think?

        Dr Stanley, Oceanographer
      8 Herakleion stood on marshland,
        waterlogged and almost mud.
     10 While I don't rule out an earthquake,
        I think there was a flood.

12 We know an earthquake
   toppled Troy.
14 One toppled Jericho.
   Perhaps there's a still-hidden fault
16 Just where, we still don't know.

        If there had been an earthquake,
     18 It would seem to me
        there would be a record,
     20 but there's none that we can see.

46

② Teaching notes on the poem

Explain that the word 'dialogue' means a conversation between two people. If a person is speaking on their own, it is a monologue.

Read the summary and remind students that the non-fiction text suggested that an earthquake and tsunami may have caused Herakleion to be sent to the bottom of the sea, but this poem presents another point of view. Read through the poem, asking students to repeat more difficult, unfamiliar words. They can use the glossary to help them. Refer to the CD-ROM to hear how words are pronounced. **Example:** cataclysm, waterlogged, tectonic force, Jericho, delta.

Ask one half of the class to read the first, third and fifth verses, taking on the voice of Dr Nur who thinks the cause is an earthquake, and the other half to read the second, fourth and sixth verses, taking on the voice of Dr Stanley who thinks the cause was a flood. Ask the whole class to read the final verse aloud.

③ Word Cloud definitions

Refer to the CD-ROM or read the line 'Did some cataclysm happen?'. Ask students if can they work out from this what 'cataclysm' means? **Ask:** *What is another word which starts with 'cata' and means everything is going wrong?* (Catastrophe.) Explain that words like 'landslide, marshland, waterlogged' would originally have been two words, but have been merged together to give a precise geographical description. The word 'tectonics' refers to how the Earth is built of different parts. **Ask:** *Which word means to 'fall over'?* (Toppled.)

cataclysm a large-scale and violent event in the natural world

deltas landforms that are formed at the mouth of a river, where the river flows into a large body of water

earthquake a sudden violent shaking of the ground

geologist a scientist who deals with the physical structure and substance of the Earth

landslide collapse of a mass of earth or rock

marshland an area of low-lying land which is generally waterlogged

oceanographer a scientist who deals with the physical and biological properties of the sea

tectonic force relating to the structure of the Earth's crust and its movements

toppled overbalanced and fell

waterlogged saturated with or full of water

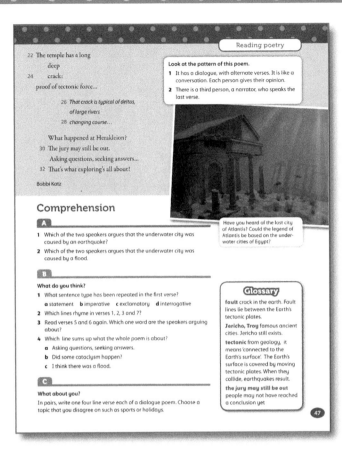

4 Student Book teaching notes and comprehension answers

A

Refer students to the summary to remind them that the poem is a dialogue between two experts with opposing points of view.

Dr Nur, Geologist, offers his opinion in verses 1, 3 and 5. Dr Stanley, Oceanographer, offers his opinion in verses 2, 4 and 6

1 Dr Nur's opinion is the first to be addressed in the poem. He argues that the underwater city was caused by an earthquake. Ensure that students understand what a geologist does.

Answer:

Dr Nur's opinion is addressed in the final two lines of the first verse, 'Did an underwater landslide cause an earthquake, as I think?' (Lines 4–5)

2 Dr Stanley's opinion is the second to be addressed in the poem. Ensure that students understand what an oceanologist does.

Answer:

Dr Stanley's opinion is addressed in the final two lines of the second verse, 'While I don't rule out an earthquake, I think there was a flood.' (Lines 9–10)

B

1 Confirm with students that three questions are asked in the first verse.

Answer:

d interrogative

2 Ask students to re-read the poem, making notes of the words and lines that rhyme.

Answers:

Verse 1: Lines 3 and 6
Verse 2: Lines 9 and 11
Verse 3: Lines 14 and 16
Verse 7: Lines 30 and 32

3 Ask students to find the word that is repeated (crack). Explain that the existence of this crack is the basis for both experts' argument as to the cause of the flood.

Answer:

crack (Line 24 and Line 26)

4 Confirm with students that they understand that the poem is a dialogue and discussion between two experts. As scientists they will continually ask questions and seek answers, looking for evidence to prove their theories.

Answer:

a Asking questions, seeking answers

C

In order to help students write out their dialogue poems, suggest the following structure:

Introduce your characters in the first two verses.
Example: 'Mary Smith, football fan . . . John Rogers, non-football fan . . .'

Start each successive verse with words such as, 'I think that', and ending with, terms such as 'Don't you agree?'

The final verse can be the same as the one used in the poem but changing the topic to reflect the students' own work.

① Learning objective

Develop skills of writing biography and autobiography in role.

Students consider how to construct a journal, and the various narrative 'ingredients'. They decide on the number of entries they will write and the information they will include in each one.

Remember to display the child-friendly learning objective to the class along with the child-friendly checklist that students can use to assess how well they achieve it.

We know that we have achieved this because:

▶ We are able to consult appropriate sources to find the information we need.

▶ We know how to divide our journal text into different entries.

② Writing workshop teaching notes

Ask students asked to revisit the 'The Start of a Great Adventure' so they remember how a journal is written. Revisit the elements included in a travel journal such as date, place, distances travelled, fellow passengers, conditions, weather, etc.

Confirm that journals are generally written after actions have happened. *Example:* 'Today we travelled to the Australian coast. It was a long and hard journey.' Some features can be in present tense, such as direct speech, rather than reported speech, 'He says, "We have arrived!"'. Emotions, too, may be conveyed in the present tense, 'Now, at the end of the day, I feel so excited at what has taken place.'

An imaginary journey

Tell students that they are going to write a journal of a voyage. Ask them first to choose what kind of ship they are on, and where they are going. Students may need some detail on types of ship such as a cargo ship holds cargo, a cruise ship is a large passenger ship used for pleasure.

Before students start work on the template point out that if they choose to travel to a country they are not familiar with, or are writing an historical account, they will need to research it so that they are able to write about what they see and experience. They will also need to look at the map to see which seas they are travelling across, and the countries and places they will pass en route.

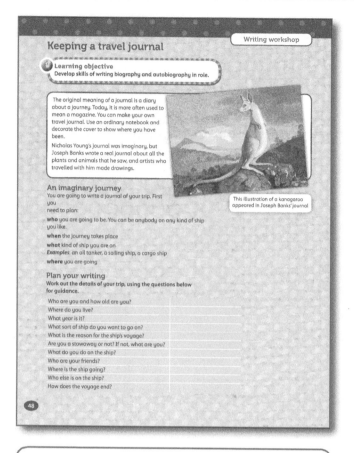

Keeping a travel journal

Writing workshop

Learning objective
Develop skills of writing biography and autobiography in role.

The original meaning of a journal is a diary about a journey. Today, it is more often used to mean a magazine. You can make your own travel journal. Use an ordinary notebook and decorate the cover to show where you have been.

Nicholas Young's journal was imaginary, but Joseph Banks wrote a real journal about all the plants and animals that he saw, and artists who travelled with him made drawings.

This illustration of a kanagaroo appeared in Joseph Banks' journal

An imaginary journey
You are going to write a journal of your trip. First you
need to plan:
who you are going to be. You can be anybody on any kind of ship you like.
when the journey takes place
what kind of ship you are on
Examples: an oil tanker, a sailing ship, a cargo ship
where you are going

Plan your writing
Work out the details of your trip, using the questions below for guidance.
Who are you and how old are you?
Where do you live?
What year is it?
What sort of ship do you want to go on?
What is the reason for the ship's voyage?
Are you a stowaway or not? If not, what are you?
What do you do on the ship?
Who are your friends?
Where is the ship going?
Who else is on the ship?
How does the voyage end?

48

Working in pairs or small groups students share their initial ideas and ask and answer questions about each other's journals. Write question stems for students to consider on the board. *Example:* Why? How? What if . . . ? Suppose that . . . I don't think that would make sense because . . . etc.

Ask students to copy out the template questions onto paper, and complete the task. Pin the profiles on the classroom wall, so they can be seen by the whole class. Encourage a discussion focusing on the feasibility of some of these profiles. Elicit suggestions on how they can be improved.

Make the point that unless something happens — or is suggested might happen — there will be little narrative tension. This tension could be to do with the weather, running out of supplies, an accident, pirates, running low on fuel or power, etc.

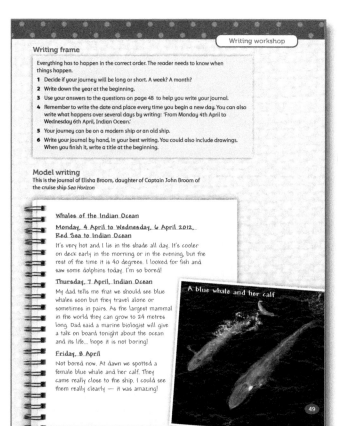

Writing frame

Everything has to happen in the correct order. The reader needs to know when things happen.

1 Decide if your journey will be long or short. A week? A month?

2 Write down the year at the beginning.

3 Use your answers to the questions on page 48 to help you write your journal.

4 Remember to write the date and place every time you begin a new day. You can also write what happens over several days by writing: 'From Monday 4th April to Wednesday 6th April, Indian Ocean.'

5 Your journey can be on a modern ship or an old ship.

6 Write your journal by hand, in your best writing. You could also include drawings. When you finish it, write a title at the beginning.

Model writing

This is the journal of Elisha Broom, daughter of Captain John Broom of the cruise ship *Sea Horizon*

Whales of the Indian Ocean

Monday, 4 April to Wednesday, 6 April 2012, Red Sea to Indian Ocean

It's very hot and I lie in the shade all day. It's cooler on deck early in the morning or in the evening, but the rest of the time it is 40 degrees. I looked for fish and saw some dolphins today. I'm so bored!

Thursday, 7 April, Indian Ocean

My dad tells me that we should see blue whales soon but they travel alone or sometimes in pairs. As the largest mammal in the world they can grow to 24 metres long. Dad said a marine biologist will give a talk on board tonight about the ocean and its life... hope it is not boring!

Friday, 8 April

Not bored now. At dawn we spotted a female blue whale and her calf. They came really close to the ship. I could see them really clearly — it was amazing!

A blue whale and her calf

49

When students have completed their journals they exchange their draft with a classmate for suggested corrections. Once they are satisfied that they have followed all the guidelines, they copy out their final version and hand it in for review and assessment.

④ Extension

1 To extend the activity students can include labelled drawings to describe key points in their journal, such as the boat they are travelling on, people they meet, and objects they have found. Ask students to draw maps detailing their routes, these can be annotated through the journal to show what progress has been made on their journey.

2 Students can be asked to keep a journal of their own lives for a week or longer. They should employ the techniques used in the previous activities. Alternatively they can research famous journals and write a short summary of who wrote them and what they were about.

③ Writing workshop teaching notes

Your journal

Take students through the guidance given regarding the length of the journey and the number of journal entries. Read through the example journal, and point out the introductory sentence, 'This is the journal of Elisha Broom, daughter of Captain John Broom of the cruise ship *Sea Horizon*.' Confirm that this sort of introduction would have been commonplace in case there was an accident or a death, as the journal would be the only record of events left behind. Students should copy this introduction when starting their own journal.

Ask students to find references in the journal entry example relating to dates, places, weather, people, and atmosphere (danger or tension). Remind students that information like this should be used in their own journals.

Explain to students that for the purpose of an engaging narrative they should write in the first person, using the present and past tense, and include a variety of sentence structures to create drama, and enhance their descriptions of objects or events.

Ask students to write the first two or three entries, and to read these out in class, or within a group. This would enable some constructive feedback to be given before any more is written. Remind them to consult the dictionary if they have doubts about the spelling or meaning of a word.

End of Unit Test

Question Paper

Reading: fiction

Read the extract and answer the questions.

The adventurer

Sam stumbled out onto a wooden deck, blinking in the bright sunlight.
He could see barrels and rigging and rows of cannon and the deep blue sea
beyond. He was on a ship! And one thing was certain. He wasn't in Backwater
Bay. The weather was far too hot and there was no land in sight. Men, dressed
5   like the boy behind him, were busy on the long, narrow deck, mending sails,
sawing wood and painting things with tar. Three towering masts, their sails
billowing, rose above him. A flag fluttered in the wind from the highest mast.
It was black, with a picture of what looked like a snarling dog's head over a pair
of crossed bones. Sam knew a pirate flag when he saw one!

10   A tall man strode up to them. He wasn't dressed like the others. His long
coat had deep cuffs and shiny brass buttons. His hair and beard were braided
with threads, and on his finger a ring with a blood red stone glinted fiercely.

'By the stars, a stowaway?' he declared, his hand on the hilt of a vicious-
looking cutlass. His voice was deep and commanding. 'How did you slip on
15   board, boy?'

'I have no idea,' said Sam, bewildered.

From *Skeleton Island* by Jan Burchett and Sara Vogler

Glossary
cutlass a short sword with a slightly curved blade

Comprehension

A

Give evidence from the extract to support your answers.

1 How do we know it is daytime on the ship?

_____ [1]

2 Where had Sam originally come from?

_____ [1]

3 *'He was on a ship!'* Give three examples which support this statement.

_____

_____

_____ [2]

4 What do you think Sam is thinking and feeling? Write a quote from Sam.

_____

_____ [2]

B

Give evidence from the extract to support your answers.

1 How do we know Sam is experiencing changing weather conditions?

_____ [1]

2 Why would Sam be worried when he saw the pirate flag?

_____ [1]

3 Which sentence explains that the tall man might be the captain of the ship?

_____ [1]

4 What do you think might happen next? Explain your answer.

_____

_____ [1]

C

Give evidence from the extract to support your answers.

1 Give two words or phrases which make the tall man appear frightening.

_____

_____ [2]

2 Provide one example of alliteration from the text.

_____ [1]

3 *'He was on a ship!'* Explain why an exclamation mark has been used.

_____ [2]

Reading: non-fiction

Read the extract and answer the questions.

Who was Tutankhamen?

Tutankhamen was probably born in Akhetaten, then the capital city of Egypt. He became pharaoh at the tender age of nine, reigning from 1337 BCE to 1328 BCE — the year of his death.

ADD YOUR SUBHEADING HERE _____

5   The reason that Tutankhamen is so well known today is that his tomb, containing fabulous treasures, was discovered in 1922 by the British archaeologist, Howard Carter — nearly 3000 years after he died.

How did Howard Carter know where he was buried?

Several finds made in the Valley of the Kings led Howard Carter to believe that the king was buried there. For example, an archaeologist called Theodore Davis found a cup and other fragments bearing the name of

10   Tutankhamen and his queen!

ADD YOUR SUBHEADING HERE _____

During an X-ray of the mummy in 1968, scientists found bone fragments in Tutankhamen's skull, prompting a sensational theory that the boy king had been murdered. Another recent theory is that King Tutankhamen was not murdered after all, but died from a broken leg. According to *National*

15   *Geographic* (December 2006) a new scan of King Tutankhamen's mummy showed a thin coating of embalming resin around the leg break, suggesting that Tutankhamen broke his leg just before he died and that his death may have resulted from an infection or other complications.

Adapted from www.woodlands-junior.Kent.sch.uk

Glossary
embalming preserving a corpse from decay

Comprehension

A

Give evidence from the extract to support your answers.

1 When did Tutankhamen die?

_____ [2]

2 How did Howard Carter know to look for Tutankhamen's tomb in the Valley of the Kings?

_____

_____ [3]

B

Give evidence from the extract to support your answers.

1 Tutankhamen was born in Akhetaten. Is this a fact or an opinion?

_____

_____ [3]

2 Which reason for Tutankhamen's death is more likely? Explain your answer.

_____

_____ [3]

C

Give evidence from the extract to support your answers.

1 Provide the two missing subheadings. Write them as questions.

_____

_____ [2]

Writing: fiction

Imagine you have been transported to a different time and place. Write two paragraphs describing this transformation. Please use a separate sheet of paper.

Remember!

The first paragraph could be about what the new place (and time) is like.

The second paragraph could describe an important character approaching you, then asking about who you are, and why you are there.

[30]

Writing: non-fiction

Imagine an archaeologist has discovered a village thousands of years old buried underneath fields near where you live. Give this lost village — and the archaeologist — a name, and describe the moment leading up to the discovery (one paragraph) and the actual discovery itself (second paragraph). What will the archaeologist find? Please use a separate sheet of paper.

Remember!

This could be written up as a report for the local television news.

[20]

Ancient civilizations

(1)

Warm up objective

Express and explain ideas clearly, making meaning explicit.

Students apply strategies to express themselves more fluently. They explain ideas effectively.

Remember to display the child-friendly learning objective to the class along with the child-friendly checklist that students can use to assess how well they achieve it.

We know that we have achieved this because:
▸ We are able to express our ideas effectively.
▸ We are able to explain our ideas clearly.

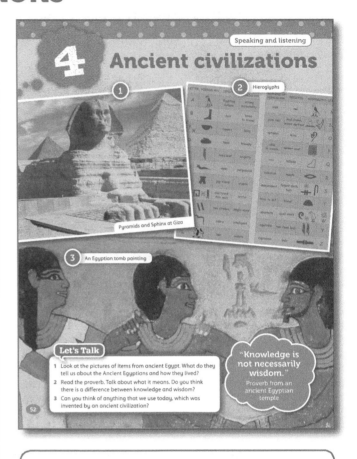

(2) Unit warm up

Books closed. Write the unit title on the board and ask students to explain what 'ancient' means. Explain that although it is a word commonly used to describe a person or an idea that seems old and out of date, a key meaning is as an adjective to describe a time in history which is very old, and no longer in existence. *Example:* the cultures of Rome, Greece and Egypt. 'Civilization' means a particular society at a particular time and place, but also means that this society is advanced in its social development — government, housing, art, leisure, education, etc. **Ask:** *What does the phrase 'ancient civilizations' mean?* Confirm that it refers to societies that were around in a certain part of the world up to about 1600 years ago, but died out for various reasons. All we have are records of what they were like.

Books open. Read the quote. In pairs, ask students to confer and agree on what the quote means. Confirm that wisdom means to be wise — that is, to have experience, and demonstrate good judgment. Knowledge is knowing key information and facts. **Ask:** *Which attribute sounds a better one to have?* Confirm that it is the application of knowledge for good that is important.

(3) Let's Talk

1 Focus students' attention on the pictures of items from ancient Egypt. Explain that the pyramids and Sphinx at Giza were built over 4500 years ago. The pyramids are the stone tombs of Egypt's kings — the pharaohs. The Sphinx stands in front of the pyramids in Giza. It has the body of a lion and the head of a pharaoh.

Explain that hieroglyphs were a formal writing system used by the Ancient Egyptians. Each hieroglyph represents a common object in Ancient Egypt. It could represent the sound of the object or an idea associated with the object.

Ask: *What does the scene in the tomb mural represent?* Elicit responses such as the life of the pharaoh, what animals they kept, what animals they hunted, and what sort of clothes they wore, etc.

2 Explain that proverbs were a very important part of the ancient religion of Egypt, creating a code of behaviour as to how people should live. **Ask:** *What values are important in society today?* Elicit responses such as friendship, communication, tolerance, human worth, help, perseverance, etc. Point out that you can have knowledge without wisdom.

3 Take suggestions from students on what the Egyptians invented that we use widely today. Direct them towards 'paper.' Explain that the Egyptians used the papyrus plant as paper. The plant was sliced open, soaked in water and pressed under a heavy rock for 21 days — the juice of the plant acting like glue and bonding the strips together into a sheet. This was hammered flat and dried in the sun. Before papyrus, writing had been done through carving on clay tablets.

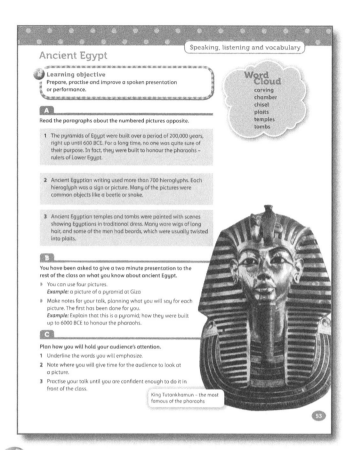

King Tutankhamun – the most famous of the pharaohs

death, the pharaoh would live forever. Explain that the tomb contained thousands of objects, many were richly decorated and covered in gold. It was thought they would be needed by the king in his afterlife. Explain that 'traditional dress' means dressing in accordance with tradition.

 B

Students could be given a short quiz on ancient Egypt, so as to refresh their knowledge. These questions could encompass: papyrus and writing, hieroglyphics, pharaohs, pyramids, features of traditional dress, etc.

Point out that students need to be careful on which pictures they choose, as these will be what they talk about.

Explain that the notes students make for the talk should:

▶ Be in order.
▶ Be largely words/phrases – and not always full sentences.
▶ Be 4–6 points for each picture, as they only have two minutes to present.
▶ Incorporate pictures that are as big and clear as possible.

Students could practise their talk in front of their partner.

 C

Demonstrate what an unsatisfactory presentation could sound like. ***Example:*** a rushed monotone. Re-read, building in emphasis on key words, slowing the pace, so that each word is enunciated clearly; deliberate pauses which give the audience time to look at the pictures.

Students practise a similar delivery (marking up presentation notes appropriately), and then make a presentation to the class or to a group.

Learning objective
④ **Prepare, practise, and improve a spoken presentation or performance.**

Students give a prepared talk on features of Ancient Egypt, varying tone and vocabulary so as to engage the listener.

Remember to display the child-friendly learning objective to the class along with the child-friendly checklist that students can use to assess how well they achieve it.

We know that we have achieved this because:
▶ **We are able to give a talk with pictures to an audience.**
▶ **We are able to understand what vocabulary should be emphasized for the benefit of the audience.**

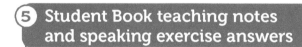
⑤ **Student Book teaching notes and speaking exercise answers**

A

Direct students' attention to the photograph of the pyramids and Sphinx at Giza. It was believed that if the pharaoh's body was mummified (preserved) after

⑥ **Word Cloud definitions**

Focus students' attention on the Word Cloud and ask them to identify the class of words on the list. (They are all nouns.)

carving cutting into a hard material to make an image, decoration or word
chamber a closed-off space underground
chisel a long-bladed hand tool which is struck with a hammer or mallet, to cut or shape wood, stone, or metal
plaits lengths of hair made up of three or more interlaced strands
temples buildings devoted to the worship of gods.
tombs large burial rooms

Learning objective

(1)

Consider how characters and settings are presented.

Students explore how the writer has presented character and setting and why.

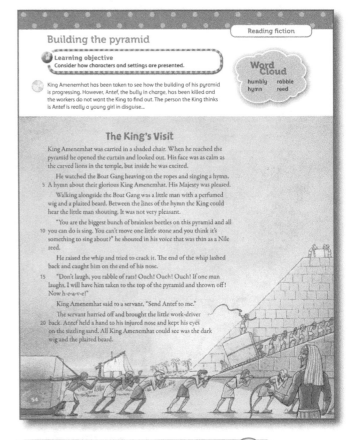

Remember to display the child-friendly learning objective to the class along with the child-friendly checklist that students can use to assess how well they achieve it.

We know that we have achieved this because:

▶ We are able to identify the use of adjectives to create atmosphere in fiction.

(2) Reading fiction notes

Remind students of the time and work involved in building a pyramid. *Example:* the Great Pyramid of Giza was built by tens of thousands of skilled workers, and took over 20 years. Explain that the extract students are now going to read, or listen to, shows the power that pharaohs had, and what happens when something goes wrong.

Read the summary. Working in pairs, ask students to find the words from the glossary in the text, and to re-read the sentence with the respective explanation. *Example:* 'heaving on the ropes' will then be read as, 'lifting and moving something heavy on the ropes.'

Read the extract. Explain that the king (a pharaoh) has come along to see how his pyramid is progressing. This is a symbol of his power and money. The king will be thinking about how all of this work is just for him. Confirm that King Amenemhat was actually a real king. Point out that there are suggestions throughout the extract that things are not quite right, but the king does not pick up on this. This creates suspense. Will he find out?

Refer to the CD-ROM or read the text while students follow in their books. **Ask:** *How do we find out that the king has a high position and is powerful?* (He is 'carried in a shaded chair' – to keep him out of the direct glare of the sun.)

Tell students that the summary has let them know that Antef, the leader of the Boat Gang, is not really Antef, but someone else. They know something the King doesn't. **Ask:** *What clues should the King have picked up on that Antef is not really Antef?* (Thin voice; little; cannot control the whip; does not look at the King directly; refers to accidents; sniffles over a crushed beetle.)

Reading fiction

Building the pyramid

Learning objective
Consider how characters and settings are presented.

King Amenemhat has been taken to see how the building of his pyramid is progressing. However, Antef, the bully in charge, has been killed and the workers do not want the King to find out. The person the King thinks is Antef is really a young girl in disguise...

Word Cloud

humbly   rabble
hymn   reed

The King's Visit

King Amenemhat was carried in a shaded chair. When he reached the pyramid he opened the curtain and looked out. His face was as calm as the carved lions in the temple, but inside he was excited.

He watched the Boat Gang heaving on the ropes and singing a hymn.
5 A hymn about their glorious King Amenemhat. His Majesty was pleased.

Walking alongside the Boat Gang was a little man with a perfumed wig and a plaited beard. Between the lines of the hymn the King could hear the little man shouting. It was not very pleasant.

"You are the biggest bunch of brainless beetles on this pyramid and all
10 you can do is sing. You can't move one little stone and you think it's something to sing about?" he shouted in his voice that was thin as a Nile reed.

He raised the whip and tried to crack it. The end of the whip lashed back and caught him on the end of his nose.

15 "Don't laugh, you rabble of rats! Ouch! Ouch! Ouch! If one man laughs, I will have him taken to the top of the pyramid and thrown off! Now h-e-a-v-e!"

King Amenemhat said to a servant, "Send Antef to me."

The servant hurried off and brought the little work-driver
20 back. Antef held a hand to his injured nose and kept his eyes on the sizzling sand. All King Amenemhat could see was the dark wig and the plaited beard.

54

(3) Word Cloud definitions

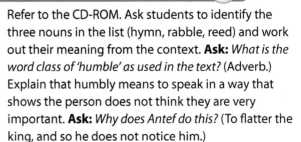

Refer to the CD-ROM. Ask students to identify the three nouns in the list (hymn, rabble, reed) and work out their meaning from the context. **Ask:** *What is the word class of 'humble' as used in the text?* (Adverb.) Explain that humbly means to speak in a way that shows the person does not think they are very important. **Ask:** *Why does Antef do this?* (To flatter the king, and so he does not notice him.)

humble showing a modest or low estimate of one's importance

hymn religious song or poem

rabble a disorderly crowd

reed tall, slender-leaved plant of the grass family

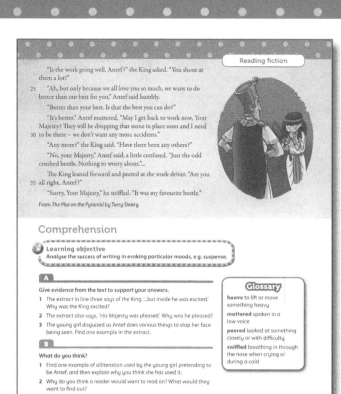

"Is the work going well, Antef?" the King asked. "You shout at them a lot!"

25   "Ah, but only because we all love you so much, we want to do better than our best for you," Antef said humbly.

"Better than your best. Is that the best you can do?"

"It's better," Antef muttered, "May I get back to work now, Your Majesty? They will be dropping that stone in place soon and I need

30   to be there – we don't want any more accidents."

"Any more?" the King said. "Have there been any others?"

"No, your Majesty," Antef said, a little confused. "Just the odd crushed beetle. Nothing to worry about."...

The King leaned forward and peered at the work-driver. "Are you

35   all right, Antef?"

"Sorry, Your Majesty," he sniffled. "It was my favourite beetle."

From The Plot on the Pyramid by Terry Deary

Comprehension

 Learning objective
Analyse the success of writing in evoking particular moods, e.g. suspense.

A

Give evidence from the text to support your answers.

1   The extract in line three says of the King, '...but inside he was excited.' Why was the King excited?

2   The extract also says, 'His Majesty was pleased.' Why was he pleased?

3   The young girl disguised as Antef does various things to stop her face being seen. Find one example in the extract.

B

What do you think?

1   Find one example of alliteration used by the young girl pretending to be Antef, and then explain why you think she has used it.

2   Why do you think a reader would want to read on? What would they want to find out?

C

What about you?

What do you think Antef should do next?

Glossary

heave to lift or move something heavy

muttered spoken in a low voice

peered looked at something closely or with difficulty

sniffled breathing in through the nose when crying or during a cold

55

---

2   The King was pleased as the workers were singing 'a hymn about their glorious King Amenemhat.'

3   'Antef held a hand to his injured nose and kept his eyes on the sizzling sand.' (Lines 20–21) Confirm that students understand that Antef's impersonator was doing this to hide their face.

B

Students locate the necessary information in the text. Then they compare their answers in pairs.

1   Confirm that the use of alliteration makes 'Antef' sound more insulting and forceful.

Answers:

'… biggest bunch of brainless beetles …' (Line 9)

'… rabble of rats!' (Line 15)

2   Explain that it is important that readers want to read on. Creating on-going narrative suspense is what writers do.

Answers:

To find out if the King discovers the truth.

To see how long the young girl pretending to be Antef can keep up her change of identity.

C

Ask students what they would do if they were Antef. **Ask:** *Would they carry on pretending to be Antef? Would they try to run away? Would they own up to the deceit?*

Encourage students to work through the possible outcomes of their answers and what effect their chosen actions would have on the rest of the characters featured in the story.

Learning objective

④ **Analyse the success of writing in evoking particular moods, e.g. suspense.**

Students analyse and discuss how successful the writer is in creating a mood of suspense.

 Remember to display the child-friendly learning objective to the class along with the child-friendly checklist that students can use to assess how well they achieve it.

We know that we have achieved this because:

▶ **We are able to track and list evidence of the developing plot.**

▶ **We are able to identify tools used to create suspense.**

⑤ **Student Book teaching notes and comprehension answers**

A

Direct students to read the extract again. Confirm that they understand they need to directly reference the text to provide evidence for their answers.

1   The King was excited in anticipation as to how his pyramid was progressing/how much bigger it was.

Learning objective

1 **Punctuate speech and use apostrophes accurately.**

Students learn that when there is a new speaker in a dialogue, a new line is taken. They also learn that there should be variations on the verb, 'said.'

 Remember to display the child-friendly learning objective to the class along with the child-friendly checklist that students can use to assess how well they achieve it.

We know that we have achieved this because:

▶ We are able to punctuate direct speech correctly, taking a new line for a new speaker.

▶ We are also able to use a range of reporting verbs for 'said.'

2 Student Book teaching notes and grammar exercise answers

Model how direct speech should be written, with the following rules:

▶ Speech marks are placed round what is actually said, stopping and starting again if necessary. Confirm that a comma is used to mark off one section of speech from the next.

▶ The reporting clause can be placed at the beginning of the sentence, the middle, or the end.

▶ Exclamation and question marks go inside the speech marks.

Read out the summary explanation regarding a new speaker, new line, and use of precise verbs and adverbs.

A

In pairs, students read the paragraph together and identify when a new line should be taken, and what verbs could be used instead of 'said.' Students could also be encouraged to add more exclamation marks.

Answers (showing new lines for new speakers only):

"I want to go swimming," said Soo Young. "I can't stand staying indoors all day."

"I thought you had homework to do," said Mum.

"Oh, Mum," said Soo Young. "I've almost finished it. Can't I just take an hour off?"

"Yes," said Mum. "But only when you've finished your work."

"But the pool will be closed if I don't go soon!" said Soo Young.

"Then you'd better get going," said Mum.

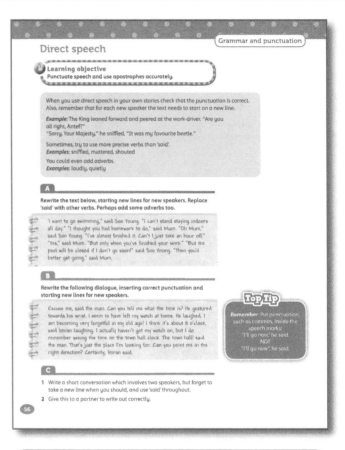

B

Students work alone, and then swap their answers with a partner. Read out the required corrections to the class and clarify any incorrect answers and elicit any queries relating to the use of direct speech.

Answers:

"Excuse me," said the man. "Can you tell me what time it is?" He gestured towards his wrist. "I seem to have left my watch at home," he laughed. "I am becoming very forgetful in my old age!"

"I think it's about 8 o'clock," said Imran, laughing. "I actually haven't got my watch on, but I do remember seeing the time on the town hall clock."

"The town hall!" said the man. "That's just the place I'm looking for. Can you point me in the right direction?"

"Certainly," Imran said.

C

Check students' attempts at the punctuation exercise before they give it to their partner. Ask that the corrected examples are handed in for assessment purposes.

3 Top Tip

Remind students that the placement of question marks with quotes follows logic. If a question is in quotation marks, the question mark should be placed inside the quotation marks.

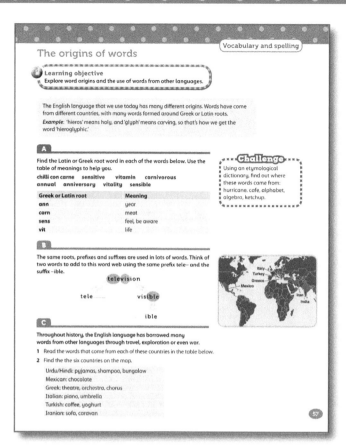

The origins of words

Vocabulary and spelling

Learning objective
Explore word origins and the use of words from other languages.

The English language that we use today has many different origins. Words have come from different countries, with many words formed around Greek or Latin roots.
Example: 'hieros' means holy, and 'glyph' means carving, so that's how we get the word 'hieroglyphic.'

A

Find the Latin or Greek root word in each of the words below. Use the table of meanings to help you.

chilli con carne   sensitive   vitamin   carnivorous
annual   anniversary   vitality   sensible

Greek or Latin root	Meaning
ann	year
carn	meat
sens	feel, be aware
vit	life

B

The same roots, prefixes and suffixes are used in lots of words. Think of two words to add to this word web using the same prefix tele– and the suffix –ible.

television

tele ——— visible

ible

C

Throughout history, the English language has borrowed many words from other languages through travel, exploration or even war.

1 Read the words that come from each of these countries in the table below.
2 Find the the six countries on the map.

Urdu/Hindi: pyjamas, shampoo, bungalow
Mexican: chocolate
Greek: theatre, orchestra, chorus
Italian: piano, umbrella
Turkish: coffee, yoghurt
Iranian: sofa, caravan

Challenge
Using an etymological dictionary, find out where these words came from:
hurricane, cafe, alphabet, algebra, ketchup.

57

Learning objective

(4)

Explore word origins and the use of words from other languages.

Students learn more Latin and Greek roots, and about words which originate in other countries

Remember to display the child-friendly learning objective to the class along with the child-friendly checklist that students can use to assess how well they achieve it.

We know that we have achieved this because:

▶ **We know how Latin and Greek roots are used to form words.**

▶ **We can recognize words that have derived from other languages.**

(5) Student Book teaching notes and vocabulary exercise answers

Read the explanation of how the English language comes from many different sources. Explain that one reason for this is the high number of different people who have invaded Great Britain and come to live there. *Example:* The Celts, Romans, Danish, German, French. This makes for a high number of borrowed words. Explain that as learning and writing increased in the 15th and 16th centuries, many Latin and Greek roots were adopted.

A

Once students have finished the exercise they could add more examples of words using these roots.

Answers:

ann – annual, anniversary

carn – chilli con carne, carnivorous

sens – sensitive, sensible

vit – vitamin, vitality

B

Use the example given to demonstrate how a word web works.

Explain that the prefix tele– makes you think of another word beginning with tele–, like television. These could have been 'telegraph, telegram, telephone', which would have taken the web in a different direction. However, 'television' takes us into another group of words which use, 'vision' such as 'visionary'. We could then go off onto another word web and think of words which end in 'ary', but as we have chosen 'visible' (which means can be seen), it means that we need to go on to another word web on words ending in 'ible' such as 'sensible' and 'invisible.'

C

Read through the list of words from other countries. Ask students to copy out the world map on one whole side of A4 or in their note books, and then help them place the words on the map. More could be added.

(6) Challenge

Direct students to use an etymological dictionary. Explain that this will give information about where words come from, and how word meanings have changed over the years.

Answers:

hurricane Caribbean

cafe France

alphabet Greece

algebra Arabic/Middle East

ketchup China

Learning objective

① Recognize key characteristics of a non-fiction historical text.

Students answer questions on a non-fiction historical text, and learn to assess features of structure and new vocabulary.

Remember to display the child-friendly learning objective to the class along with the child-friendly checklist that students can use to assess how well they achieve it.

We know that we have achieved this because:

▶ We are able to answer questions on historical information.

▶ We are able to determine how structure has been used to help the reader access this information.

▶ We can assess how new language is introduced.

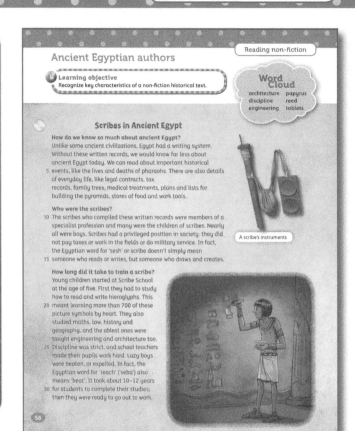

Ancient Egyptian authors

Learning objective
Recognize key characteristics of a non-fiction historical text.

Word Cloud
architecture   papyrus
discipline   reed
engineering   tablets

Scribes in Ancient Egypt

How do we know so much about ancient Egypt?
Unlike some ancient civilizations, Egypt had a writing system. Without these written records, we would know far less about ancient Egypt today. We can read about important historical
5 events, like the lives and deaths of pharaohs. There are also details of everyday life, like legal contracts, tax records, family trees, medical treatments, plans and lists for building the pyramids, stores of food and work tools.

Who were the scribes?
10 The scribes who compiled these written records were members of a specialist profession and many were the children of scribes. Nearly all were boys. Scribes had a privileged position in society: they did not pay taxes or work in the fields or do military service. In fact, the Egyptian word for 'sesh' or scribe doesn't simply mean
15 someone who reads or writes, but someone who draws and creates.

A scribe's instruments

How long did it take to train a scribe?
Young children started at Scribe School at the age of five. First they had to study how to read and write hieroglyphs. This
20 meant learning more than 700 of these picture symbols by heart. They also studied maths, law, history and geography, and the ablest ones were taught engineering and architecture too.
25 Discipline was strict, and school teachers made their pupils work hard. Lazy boys were beaten, or expelled. In fact, the Egyptian word for 'teach' ('seba') also means 'beat'. It took about 10–12 years
30 for students to complete their studies; then they were ready to go out to work.

68

② Reading non-fiction notes

Refer to the CD-ROM or read the text while students follow in their books. Ask students to raise their hand when a word they are not familiar with comes up. Check to see if it is defined in the glossary or Word Cloud. If not, list the words on the board for students to research themselves. Read that sentence again, giving students the opportunity to contextualize the meaning. Ask students to read through the text again and to note down key pieces of information from each paragraph. These notes should be compared with a partner. Do they have the same information? Can they agree? Students decide on three facts they find the most interesting and join up with another pair and share their ideas.

③ Word Cloud definitions

Refer to the CD-ROM for pronunciation help. Expect students to be already familiar with papyrus, reed and tablets from previous work. Students could be asked to explain these, to confirm understanding.

architecture the art or practice of designing and constructing buildings

discipline the practice of training people to obey rules or a code of behaviour

engineering the branch of science and technology concerned with the design, building, and use of engines, machines, and structures

papyrus material used in sheets throughout the ancient world for writing on

reed tall, slender-leaved plant which grows in water or on marshy ground

tablets flat slabs of stone, clay, or wood, used especially for inscriptions

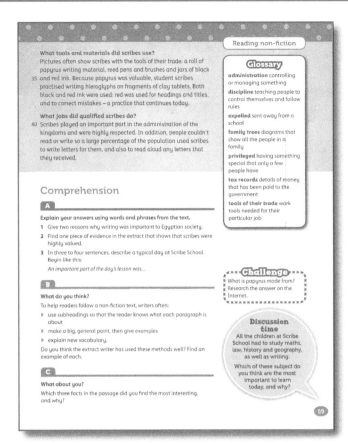

B

Explain that general sentences followed by examples are often the topic – or key – sentence in a paragraph. Ask students to identify the key sentences in each paragraph, i.e. the sentences which essentially sum up what the paragraph is about. **Example:** 'Unlike some ancient civilisations, Egypt had a writing system' (line 2); the scribes who compiled these written records were members of a specialist profession and many were the children of scribes (lines 11–12). Explain that there may be more than one topic and general sentence in each paragraph. Tell students that rhetorical questions can also act as key sentences. **Example:** 'What was recorded?'

Provide students with examples of subheadings, such as: How do we know much about ancient Egypt? Who were the scribes? How long did it take to train a scribe? What tools and materials did scribes use? What jobs did qualified scribes do?

Point out the reference to the word 'sesh' (line 14), and that the Egyptian word for 'teach' (seba), also means 'beat'.

C

Students could go back to their original list of interesting facts. They now know the text much better. Is there anything they would want to remove – or add?

4 Student Book teaching notes and comprehension answers

First, direct students' attention to the glossary. Students can either copy these definitions down, or be taken through them. Students should know — or understand — the words well enough so they are able to recognize them in the text.

A

Students locate the necessary information in the text. Then they compare their answers in pairs.

Answers:

1 To record important historical events; legal contracts; tax records; family trees; medical treatments; plan and lists for building the pyramids; stores of food and works tools, etc.
2 They did not pay taxes or work in the fields or do military service (lines 12–13); they played an important part in the administration (line 40) and were highly respected (line 41).
3 Students should make notes on what information they should include. **Example:** how to read and write hieroglyphics; studied maths, law, history, and geography (possibly engineering and architecture); strict discipline; worked hard/could not be lazy. Each set of information could possibly constitute one of the sentences.

5 Discussion time

Take feedback on what subjects students think are important to learn today. Using selected students, tease out some of the reasons for their choices. Explain that writing is still important. Many professions — doctors, nurses, teachers — will need to write handwritten reports so that they can communicate. Point out that the move towards technology means more and more information is typed. **Ask:** *Do they think handwriting will die out? What would be lost if that happened?*

6 Challenge

Students work in groups to research and a write a step by step guide on how to make paper from papyrus. Students should draw the process in a comic strip frame. Display in class and elicit discussion on which guides are the clearest and why.

Learning objective

(1)

Revise different word classes.

Students revisit and consolidate knowledge and understanding of non-finite verbs – past/present participle and infinitive.

Remember to display the child-friendly learning objective to the class along with the child-friendly checklist that students can use to assess how well they achieve it.

We know that we have achieved this because:

▶ We can identify infinitive, present and past participle verbs.

▶ We can use these appropriately in sentences.

(2) Student Book teaching notes and grammar exercise answers

Read the explanatory box explaining that non-finite verbs have no subjects, and can be used to make your writing more interesting. Make sure that students understand there is nothing wrong with using finite verbs, but they now need to be aware that there is a choice. Students could go through the 'The King's Visit' and the 'Scribe' text locating different kinds of verbs, both finite and non-finite.

Using the infinitive form in sentences should be fairly straightforward. You may want to encourage students to use them at the beginning of a sentence.

This exercise encourages students to use the present participle in the beginning and middle of a sentence. When used in the beginning, students need to be reminded that a comma is necessary. ***Example:*** 'Running, he reached forward.' Alternatively, the participle could be extended into a non-finite clause. ***Example:*** 'Running furiously, he just made it to the shop in time.'

Students may struggle a little with the correct tense. Sentences should be read aloud, so that this can be checked.

Students should see that they need to make the past participle into a verb phrase using the verb form 'to be'. ***Example:*** 'I have eaten a large meal; The trees have fallen to the ground; I have given you everything I have.' The infinitive forms given could also be used in a sentence, again varying the position.

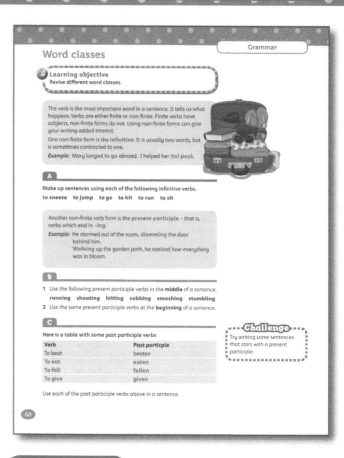

(3) Challenge

Students use one of each type of non-finite verb in a short paragraph of writing: infinitive, present participle, and past participle.

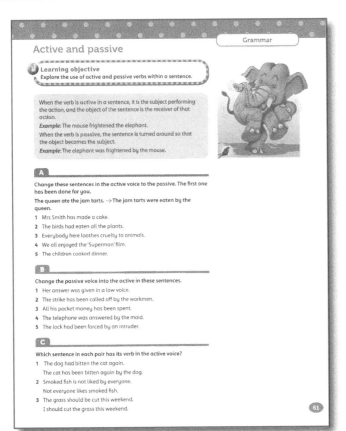

Active and passive

Grammar

Learning objective
Explore the use of active and passive verbs within a sentence.

When the verb is active in a sentence, it is the subject performing the action, and the object of the sentence is the receiver of that action.
Example: The mouse frightened the elephant.
When the verb is passive, the sentence is turned around so that the object becomes the subject.
Example: The elephant was frightened by the mouse.

A
Change these sentences in the active voice to the passive. The first one has been done for you.
The queen ate the jam tarts. → The jam tarts were eaten by the queen.
1 Mrs Smith has made a cake.
2 The birds had eaten all the plants.
3 Everybody here loathes cruelty to animals.
4 We all enjoyed the 'Superman' film.
5 The children cooked dinner.

B
Change the passive voice into the active in these sentences.
1 Her answer was given in a low voice.
2 The strike has been called off by the workmen.
3 All his pocket money has been spent.
4 The telephone was answered by the maid.
5 The lock had been forced by an intruder.

C
Which sentence in each pair has its verb in the active voice?
1 The dog had bitten the cat again.
  The cat has been bitten again by the dog.
2 Smoked fish is not liked by everyone.
  Not everyone likes smoked fish.
3 The grass should be cut this weekend.
  I should cut the grass this weekend.

61

Learning objective

④

Explore the use of active and passive verbs within a sentence.

Students learn another variation of verbs – verbs written in either the active or passive voice.

Remember to display the child-friendly learning objective to the class along with the child-friendly checklist that students can use to assess how well they achieve it.

We know that we have achieved this because:

▶ **We can identify the active or passive voice in a text.**
▶ **We understand when and why the active or passive voice is used in writing.**

⑤ Student Book teaching notes and grammar exercise answers

Read the information in the grammar box, and ask students to read the example aloud. Point out that who is doing and receiving the action changes. Explain that passive voice is often used in reports or more formal writing when doing the action is either understood (The chemical was dissolved in water) or not important (A new school will be built in the town).

 A

Working in pairs, students complete the exercise then answers are shared with the class.

Answers:

1 A cake was made by Mrs Smith.
2 All the plants were eaten by the birds.
3 Cruelty to animals is loathed by everyone here.
4 The 'Superman' film was enjoyed by all of us.
5 The dinner was cooked by the children.

Note how the words from 'by' onwards could be omitted and the sentences would still be in the passive voice. Ask students what they notice about the verb form used in the passive voice. Explain that the passive forms of a verb are created by combining a form of the 'to be' verb with the participle of the main verb. Other helping verbs are also sometimes present. *Example:* could have been; will have been; are being; were being; etc.

 B

Working alone, students complete the exercise then answers are shared with the class. Clarify any queries and confirm the explanation of the change from passive to active voice.

Answers:

1 She gave her answer in a low voice.
2 The workmen called off the strike.
3 He spent all his pocket money.
4 The maid answered the telephone.
5 The intruder forced the lock.

C

Working in pairs, students complete the exercise then answers are shared with the class.

Answers:

The dog had bitten the cat again. (active)

The cat has been bitten again buy the dog. (passive)

Smoked fish is not liked by everyone. (passive)

Not everyone likes smoked fish. (active)

The grass should be cut this weekend. (passive)

I should cut the grass this weekend. (active)

⑥ Extension

Students collect examples of the passive voice from notices around the school, and school textbooks. Arrange on a display board under the headings 'active' and 'passive'.

① Learning objective

Explore how poets manipulate and play with words and their sounds.

Students identify the use of kennings and alliteration in three poems and comment upon their effect.

Remember to display the child-friendly learning objective to the class along with the child-friendly checklist that students can use to assess how well they achieve it.

We know that we have achieved this because:

▶ We know what kennings are.
▶ We understand kennings and their impact on meaning and effect.
▶ We understand how alliteration is used to emphasize the impact of a kenning.

② Teaching notes on the poem

Read the explanatory box, and confirm that students understand how a kenning poem is constructed.

Refer students to the words in the glossary before reading the poem, and ask them to find these words in the poem. Confirm that a 'historian' is someone who studies the past, so all the kennings in the poem will obviously refer to this. Refer students again to the hyphen and how it has been used like a chain to link two very different words together into one new word. It is a very economical way of expressing ideas and feelings — especially for poets!

Explain the slightly more difficult kennings before the poem is read. Explain that 'villain-hounder' means a hunter of villains/evil characters; 'parchment-keeper' (keeps paper/records); 'alphabet-reader' (reader of letters/words/books); 'stone-saver' (a sword that can cut through stone).

Refer to the CD-ROM or read the text while students follow in their books. Ask students to highlight those kennings they do not understand.

Time-detective: someone who uses clues to find out the truth.

Bone-collector: someone who is interested in skeletons because they provide information.

Hero-maker: promotes certain people as heroes and heroines.

Grave-digger: writes about people's deaths.

Fact-hunter: hunts for facts so as to find what happened in the past.

Story-sharer: shares stories about the past.

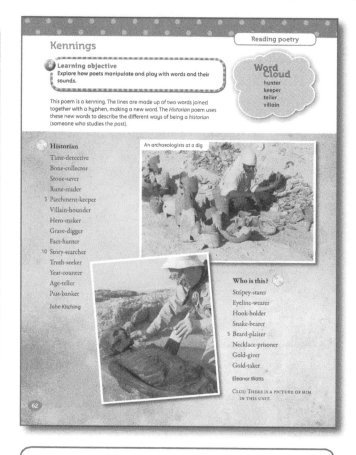

Truth-seeker: always wants to show a true past, or history.

Year-counter: focused on events year by year, and the passage of time.

Age-teller: tells about society, people getting older.

Past-banker: likes to hold on to the past, a bit like a banker does with money.

Point out to students how the '–er' ending is used to show action.

③ Word Cloud definitions

Ask students to work through what the Word Cloud words mean, and then compare their answers with a partner. Confirm that the answers are correct or clarify with the definitions provided. Refer to the CD-ROM for help with pronunciation.

hunter a person searching for something
keeper a person who manages or looks after something or someone
teller a person who tells something
villain a wicked or evil person

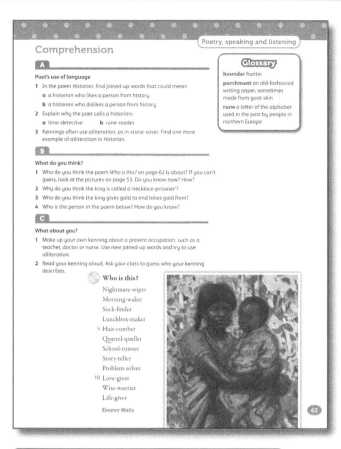

Comprehension

A

Poet's use of language

1 In the poem *Historian*, find joined-up words that could mean:
   a a historian who likes a person from history
   b a historian who dislikes a person from history
2 Explain why the poet calls a historian:
   a time-detective   b rune-reader
3 Kennings often use alliteration, as in stone-saver. Find one more example of alliteration in *Historian*.

Glossary

hounder hunter

parchment an old-fashioned writing paper, sometimes made from goat-skin

rune a letter of the alphabet used in the past by people in northern Europe

B

What do you think?

1 Who do you think the poem *Who is this?* on page 62 is about? If you can't guess, look at the pictures on page 53. Do you know now? How?
2 Why do you think the king is called a 'necklace-prisoner'?
3 Who do you think the king gives gold to and takes gold from?
4 Who is the person in the poem below? How do you know?

C

What about you?

1 Make up your own kenning about a present occupation, such as a teacher, doctor or nurse. Use new joined-up words and try to use alliteration.
2 Read your kenning aloud. Ask your class to guess who your kenning describes.

Who is this?

Nightmare-wiper
Morning-waker
Sock-finder
Lunchbox-maker
5 Hair-comber
Quarrel-queller
School-runner
Story-teller
Problem-solver
10 Love-giver
Wise-worrier
Life-giver

Eleanor Watts

63

4 Student Book teaching notes and comprehension answers

A

1 Students can complete this activity in pairs. Check the answers with the whole class.

Answers:

a hero-maker
b villain-hunter

Confirm that the words 'hero' and 'villain' are opposites (antonyms).

2 Confirm that students understand the meaning of the words: detective (a person, especially a police officer, whose occupation is to investigate and solve crimes); rune (a symbol with mysterious significance).

Answers:

a Studies the passage of time.
b Uses clues like a detective.

3 Confirm students understanding of alliteration. (The occurrence of the same letter or sound at the beginning of adjacent or closely connected words.)

Answers:

Rune-reader; Story-searcher

B

1 Give students a clue at a time, so that they are steered towards the answer of Tutankhamun.

What Egyptian statue/artefact have they come across in the chapter that was:

▶ decorated in stripes
▶ wearing eyeliner
▶ wearing a necklace round the neck
▶ covered in gold?

Answer:

Tutankhamun

2 Explain that a prisoner is someone who is kept in, unable to be free. **Ask:** *How could Tutankhamun's neck be like a prisoner because he has a necklace on?* (His neck is not free, trapped by the necklace – which is very big.)

3 Remind students of why pharaohs would have valuable and gold items in their tombs. (To have wealth and power available in the afterlife.) The gold would have been taken from the people through taxes and other means. Pharaohs would have had incredible wealth.

4 Read the poem aloud with the whole class. Explain that a 'quarrel-queller' will be someone who stops or quietens and keeps in check any arguments or disagreements. **Ask:** *Who is this?* (Mother.) **Ask:** *Which kenning do they think best sums up what a mother is?* (Love-giver; Life-giver.)

Confirm how the one-word lines give the poem bounce and rhythm, particularly with the repeated '–er' endings.

C

1 Students base their kenning on the model of 'Who is this?'. Specify the number of lines, and how the poem has range across the mundane and trivial to the big and important. *Example:* 'Pen-giver' to 'Friend-lover.'

2 Ask for volunteers to read their kenning aloud to the class. As the class guesses the subject of each kenning, write the key words used on the board.

5 Extension

Write a kenning on a particular occupation. *Example:* a builder, teacher, doctor, dentist. Can other students guess what this is?

① Learning objective

Understand aspects of narrative structure.

Students examine the narrative structure used in the extract, and then apply it to their own writing.

Remember to display the child-friendly learning objective to the class along with the child-friendly checklist that students can use to assess how well they achieve it.

We know that we have achieved this because:

▶ We are able to distinguish different features of narrative structure.

② Writing workshop teaching notes

Books open. Students read out the explanation of story structure. Reinforce this structure with the plot of a well-known fairy tale or film plot.

Model writing

Explain that these questions will be used to consider how the narrative (story) about the king's visit has been developed. Confirm that students are going to use this structure in their writing.

1 **Ask:** *Where is the story set?* (Egypt.) Ask students what difference it would make if the setting was in a part of the countryside close to where the students live, and the weather was bad or the setting some very busy town. This should make clear how much setting makes a difference to what the story is going to be about. Explain that the writer will drop in hints which lets the reader know where it is and when it is taking place. *Example:* 'pyramid, carved lions in the temple...' Even the 'shaded chair' and 'sizzling sand' lets readers know it is hot, without directly telling us. In effect, we have showing, not telling.

2 **Ask:** *Who are the main characters?* (The King, Antef (in disguise) and the Boat Gang.) Explain that all characters have a function — a job to do — in the story. The King is the representative of power and status, who must not be upset; otherwise there could be terrible consequences. Antef is a young girl who we do not want to be found out; she is the heroine of the story, and whose side the audience is on. Antef — the original — was a bully, so he would have been the villain. Confirm that sometimes characters can have the function of a messenger, or a supporter or carer, so that they can give characters help and support when needed. The main characters are those that drive the plot along. ⇨

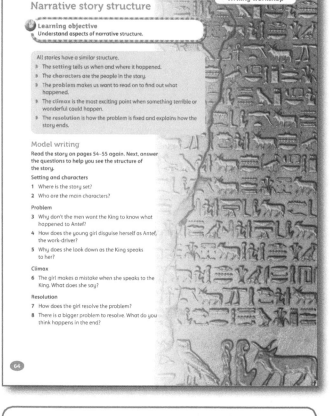

3 They don't want the King to find out that the original Antef has been killed. They would all be in trouble.

4 Dramatic tension is created by how the young girl tries to disguise herself — wig, beard, even trying to adopt the bullying manner of the original Antef. The reader perpetually wonders if she will be found out.

5 There is more tension when the King calls her over to speak to her. The reader will be thinking: what happens when he sees her close up? Will he realise the truth? She looks down when the King speaks to her as she does not want her face to be seen too closely. This is dramatic irony — when the reader knows something that the characters don't.

6 This is when the tension is stretched to its ultimate point. We think that it can't get any worse when she says, 'We don't want any more accidents.'

7 Readers need to end the story or extract with some sense that any conflict has been resolved. Here the girl tries to resolve her immediate problem by saying that the accident concerned a crushed beetle. But it only saves her for the moment.

8 The reader realizes that there is a much bigger problem to resolve: that is whether the girl is going to get found out. She got away with it on this occasion, but not very well, and she cannot keep pretending to be Antef forever. What about people who know him? Surely the King will find her out? This makes the reader want to keep on reading. They would expect the ultimate

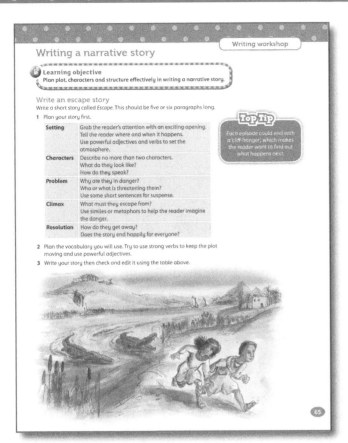

The setting should be suggested not told. So, if it was a hot place in Egypt, students should not tell the reader that it is hot, but describe it. ***Example:*** 'The glare of the midday sun shone fiercely on yellow sand. Drips of sweat dripped from my forehead.'

Characters

Confirm that readers need to be able to see characters. Ask students to copy a formula character thumbnail sketch: Orlando Ferez, 14 years old, scruffy, with a wide grin and shoes that didn't quite fit, raced across the prison compound. 'Come on' he whispered loudly. 'We need to go this way. Follow me.'

Problem

The character may be in danger because he did not want to be seen during the escape or they are just about to escape and something goes wrong. A problem must happen no later than the second paragraph.

Climax

This is where the problem gets worse. ***Example:*** Just as they are about to escape, someone sees them, or someone falls down and cannot get up?

Resolution

Explain that no matter what happens, the characters should be allowed to succeed — perhaps simply by escaping and running towards freedom.

2 Students should be deterred from using verbs such as went, got and did, etc., and routine adjectives such as good, nice and well. You may wish to provide synonym lists or word banks.

3 Students write their story. Factor in lesson time and homework time for students to complete their story. In their evaluation and proof reading task, students should focus on:

▶ Short sentences
▶ Paragraphs
▶ Range of vocabulary (word bank used)
▶ Any errors in syntax/grammar. ***Example:*** words missed out, or subject verb agreement not correct
▶ Setting and characters described appropriately
▶ Narrative tension built up through problem, climax and resolution.

A proof reading card with these prompts on it could be provided, so as to help with the peer assessment.

Learning objective

Plan plot, characters and structure effectively in writing a narrative story.

Students use the defined narrative structure in their own writing.

Remember to display the child-friendly learning objective to the class along with the child-friendly checklist that students can use to assess how well they achieve it.

We know that we have achieved this because:

▶ **We know how to apply the features of narrative structure in our own writing and to sustain these appropriately.**

4 Writing workshop teaching notes

Write an escape story

1 Explain that students can work on this exercise over the space of several lessons. The aim of the exercise is to employ a compelling narrative structure and plot, not just a lengthy tale.

Setting

Take students through the planning format. Explain that an opening could be made exciting through direct speech. This lets the reader know exactly what is happening. ***Example:*** 'Quick! Let's make a run for it, before the guards see us!'

5 Top Tip

Explain to students 'cliff hanger' is an idiom meaning 'a situation that is both dramatic and uncertain'.

End of Unit Test

Question Paper

Reading: fiction

Read the extract and answer the questions.

Percy is in trouble

The end of his journey was close — almost right under his feet. But how could that be? There was nothing on the hilltop.

The wind changed. Percy caught the sour scent of reptile. A hundred yards down the slope, something rustled through the woods — snapping
5 branches, crunching leaves, hissing.

Gorgons.

For the millionth time, Percy wished their noses weren't so good. They always said they could *smell* him because he was a demigod – the half blood son of some old Roman god. Percy had tried rolling in mud, splashing
10 through the creeks, even keeping air freshener sticks in his pocket so he'd have that new car smell, but apparently demigod stink was hard to mask.

He scrambled to the west side of the summit. It was too steep to descend. The slope plummeted eighty feet, straight to the roof of an apartment complex built into the side of the hill. Fifty feet below that, a highway
15 emerged from the base of the hill and wound its way toward Berkley.

Great. No other way off the hill. He'd managed to get himself cornered. He cursed and pulled his pen from his pocket. The pen didn't look like much, just a regular cheap ballpoint, but when Percy uncapped it, it grew into a glowing bronze sword.

From *Heroes Of Olympus: The Son of Neptune* by Rick Riordan

Glossary
scent a distinctive smell
uncapped took the lid off

Comprehension

A

Give evidence from the extract to support your answers.

1 What is Percy? Tick the correct box.

   a demigod   ☐

   b Gorgon   ☐

   c god   ☐

   d soldier   ☐   [1]

2 Is Percy at the end or the beginning of his journey?

_____ [1]

3 Who does Percy identify as his enemy?

_____ [1]

4 What did Percy do to hide his smell?

_____ [1]

5 What action does Percy perform to turn the ballpoint into a bronze sword?

_____ [1]

B

Give evidence from the extract to support your answers.

1 Find two different words which show that Percy is on a hill.

_____ [2]

2 How do we know Gorgons have a good sense of smell?

_____ [1]

3 _'Great. No other way off the hill. He'd managed to get himself cornered.'_ Underline the words in these sentences which show Percy was unable to get down the hill. [1]

4 The extract combines the action Percy is involved in and what he is thinking. Find one example of Percy thinking, rather than acting.

_____ [1]

C

Give evidence from the extract to support your answers.

1 What three verbs describe the noises made by the Gorgons?

_____

_____ [1]

2 The writer often uses short sentences. Find one example of this and explain why short sentences are used.

_____

_____ [3]

3 Which adjective suggests that the bronze sword might be a special weapon?

_____ [1]

Reading: non-fiction

Read the extract and answer the questions.

Greek gods

The Ancient Greeks believed in a wide variety of gods and goddesses. Many of these may originally have had a connection with nature or natural phenomena. Zeus, for example, was a sky god, whose main weapon, the thunderbolt, was clearly connected with thunder and lightning. They also
5 had characteristics to do with their role in human life. Zeus was also the god with responsibility for justice and order.

The Greeks believed in a number of major gods who were thought to live on Mount Olympus. These are often referred to as the Olympian gods – but there were also many other lesser gods and also some very minor spirits. For
10 example, the many nymphs who lived in streams, trees and mountains.

Worship of gods and goddesses took place in sacred places, usually containing a temple in which the god was thought to live, but with the worship actually taking place ***outside*** the temple. You could also worship gods in sacred places or shrines in the countryside, at home or in the city.
15 Small offerings such as wine or milk were made on an everyday basis.

Of course, there was a great deal of variety in the ways in which the ancient Greeks believed in their gods. For many ordinary Greeks, the minor gods were much more important because they were relevant to the day to day life they led.

Adapted from www.britishmuseum.org/

Glossary
phenomena facts or situations that happen, especially those whose explanation is in question

Comprehension

A

Give evidence from the extract to support your answers.

1 Which god was connected with thunder and lightning and with justice and order?

_____ [1]

2 Were nymphs Olympian gods? Explain your answer.

_____

_____ [3]

3 Who were most important to the Greeks — major or minor gods? Explain your answer.

_____

_____ [3]

B

Give evidence from the extract to support your answers.

1 Do all Greek gods have a connection with nature? Find a quotation from the text which supports your answer and explain why.

_____

_____ [3]

C

Give evidence from the extract to support your answers.

1 What punctuation mark is used to signal that not all gods are Olympian gods?

_____ [2]

2 Why has the word 'outside' been written in bold in the text? Tick the correct box.

a To make it more interesting. ☐

b To show this is unusual. ☐

c To help the reader remember it. ☐ [1]

3 Find a connecting phrase which introduces an example.

_____ [2]

Writing: fiction

Percy is a 12-year-old boy who discovers his father is the Greek God Poseidon, the god of the sea. The Gorgons are three sisters who had hair of living, poisonous snakes. Anyone who looked at them turned into stone. Continue the fiction extract. Please use a separate sheet of paper.

Remember!

Develop the dramatic tension, stopping at an exciting point.

Write four to five paragraphs.

[30]

Writing: non-fiction

Summarize the non-fiction extract in no more than 100 words. Please use a separate sheet of paper.

To do this, you should:

- Note down the main points.
- Join these up so that they are in connected sentences.
- Remove unnecessary words or phrases so that you are left with 100 words.

[20]

5 Spies and mystery

① Warm up objective

Begin to develop awareness that the context in which the writer is writing and the context in which the reader is reading can impact on how the text is understood.

Students learn the meaning of context and its impact on both fiction and non-fiction texts.

Remember to display the child-friendly learning objective to the class along with the child-friendly checklist that students can use to assess how well they achieve it.

We know that we have achieved this because:

▶ We are able to understand the meaning of context.

▶ We understand how context is used by the writer.

5 Spies and mystery

Speaking and listening

Alex Rider, a teenage spy and hero of many adventures, such as in the film, *Stormbreaker*

"Life is a struggle and a good spy goes in there and fights."
Harriet the Spy

The *Spy Kids* movies are popular all over the world.

Let's Talk

1 A spy wears a disguise so they are not recognized. If you were a spy, what could you change about how you look, move and speak so that no one knew it was you?

2 What genre do you think the Alex Rider spy books belong to?

66

② Unit warm up

Write the unit title on the board. **Ask:** *What is a spy?* (A person who secretly collects and reports information about an enemy or competitor.) Explain that countries will sometimes use spies, but businesses and large corporations will also spy on competitors to find out information about their products. **Ask:** *How would being a spy involve mystery?* Explain that spies gather information in secret. Often they are in disguise and use hidden gadgets to obtain information such as a miniature tape recorder or camera. All of these factors create mystery.

Books open. Explain that spies pretend to be absolutely normal people, just like Alex Rider, the 14-year-old school boy featured in the photographs.

Before focusing students' attention on the photographs, explain that *MI High* is a children's television spy adventure series, and continues with the Alex Rider series of *Stormbreaker* books and films. The series follows the adventures of three secondary school pupils who work as undercover spies. The spies are led by an agent, Frank London, who works undercover as the school caretaker.

Direct students' attention to the illustration of what most people think spies look like. Explain that if they did look like this, it would probably make them more noticeable! An ordinary school boy and school caretaker are much less likely to be noticed and found out.

Read the quote. Explain that *Harriet the Spy* is the title of a book about a girl called Harriet who spies on her classmates and writes down what she thinks about them as she is too afraid to tell them personally. In the end, the truth comes out.

Elicit students' understanding of the word 'fight' (battle, war, argue, etc.) and 'struggle' (effort, hard work) and write these on the board. Read the quote again. **Ask:** *Which meaning most closely fits the words in the quote?* Explain that it means that life is hard work. A good spy will be battling undercover on the side of good – rather like a secret soldier.

③ Let's Talk

1 **Ask:** *What could you do to change your appearance?* Elicit responses such as changing hair colour and style, putting on or taking off glasses, wearing scarves and hats, etc. Ask students to describe their suggestions in detail to a partner.

2 In pairs, students list different genres: romance, adventure, fantasy, mystery, horror, spy thrillers, etc. List responses on the board. Explain that the *Alex Rider* books are spy thrillers. Point out that genres sometimes overlap. **Example:** the spy genre also incorporates mystery and adventure.

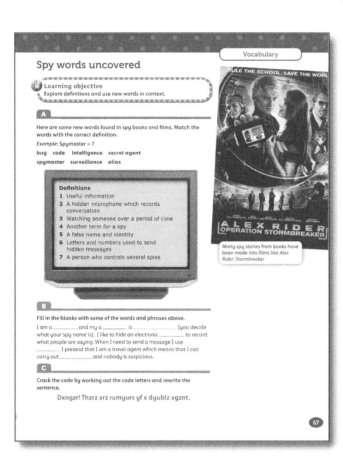

Spy words uncovered

Learning objective
Explore definitions and use new words in context.

A

Here are some new words found in spy books and films. Match the words with the correct definition.

Example: Spymaster = 7

bug   code   intelligence   secret agent

spymaster   surveillance   alias

Definitions
1 Useful information
2 A hidden microphone which records conversation
3 Watching someone over a period of time
4 Another term for a spy
5 A false name and identity
6 Letters and numbers used to send hidden messages
7 A person who controls several spies

Many spy stories from books have been made into films like *Alex Rider: Stormbreaker*

B

Fill in the blanks with some of the words and phrases above.

I am a _____ and my a _____ is _____ [you decide what your 'spy name' is]. I like to hide an electronic _____ to record what people are saying. When I need to send a message I use _____ . I pretend that I am a travel agent which means that I can carry out_____ and nobody is suspicious.

C

Crack the code by working out the code letters and rewrite the sentence.

Dxngzr! Thzrz xrz rumyurs yf x dyublz xgznt.

67

Learning objective

Explore definitions and use new words in context.

Students will recognize words associated with spies and mystery, and understand what they mean.

Remember to display the child-friendly learning objective to the class along with the child-friendly checklist that students can use to assess how well they achieve it.

We know that we have achieved this because:
▶ We are able to understand the meaning of words associated with spies and mystery.
▶ We can recognize the surrounding context of these words.

⑤ Student Book teaching notes and vocabulary exercise answers

A

Elicit students' understanding of the words surveillance, bug, intelligence, double agent, and alias. Correct any issues relating to the meanings and ask students to complete the exercise.

Answers:
1 intelligence
2 bug
3 surveillance
4 secret agent
5 alias
6 code
7 spymaster

B

Students complete the gap fill exercise with a partner. Read the correct text to the class and ask students to swap with another pair and check their completed exercise.

Answers:
I am a **secret agent** and my **alias** is [you decide what your 'spy name' is]. I like to hide an electronic **bug** to record what people are saying. When I need to send a message I use **code**. I pretend I am a travel agent which means I can carry out **surveillance** and nobody is suspicious.

C

Ask students to make up their own messages using codes. Highlight how other possible codes could be used, such as exchanging letters for numbers, writing words back to front or missing specific letters out of words.

Answer:
Danger! There are rumours of a double agent.

① Learning objective

Comment on the writer's use of language, demonstrating awareness of its impact on the reader.

Students will understand how language is used to build up interest and tension.

🔘 Remember to display the child-friendly learning objective to the class along with the child-friendly checklist that students can use to assess how well they achieve it.

We know that we have achieved this because:

▸ We are able to identify words and phrases which build up interest and tension.

② Reading fiction notes 🔘

Read through the summary. Write 'villain' on one side of the board. **Ask:** *What is a villain?* (A character whose evil actions or motives are important to the plot.) **Ask:** *What are the characteristics of a villain?* (Clearly on the side of bad/evil, and against the forces of good.) **Ask:** *Who is the villain in the Stormbreaker series?* (Herod Sayle.) On the other side of the board write characters on the side of the good: Blunt, Mrs Jones and Alex.

Select students to read out the definitions given in the glossary. Ask students to find these phrases in the text. Refer to the CD-ROM or read the text while students follow in their books.

③ Word Cloud definitions 🔘

Ask students to focus on the two nouns agent and assignment. **Ask:** *Which one means to act on behalf of someone else?* (Agent.) *Which one means a job or duty?* (Assignment.) **Ask:** *Which would students prefer to be described as 'resourceful' or 'preposterous'?* For those who choose 'preposterous' explain that this would mean they were ridiculous and silly. Those who choose 'resourceful' would be the ones who can think of clever ways to get out of difficulties!

Direct students attention to the sentence, "Why don't you ask this Felix Lester to <u>snoop</u> around for you?" **Ask:** *What would be the effect if 'observe', 'spy', 'find out' were used instead?* Explain that 'snoop' is more intrusive than these words and it looks and sounds like it, with the thin 'sn' consonants and long 'oo' sound! Refer to the CD-ROM. To 'snoop' means to poke into people's private lives to find out things about them. Confirm that's why Alex uses the word, as he thinks spying is associated with negative behaviour. Another negative activity

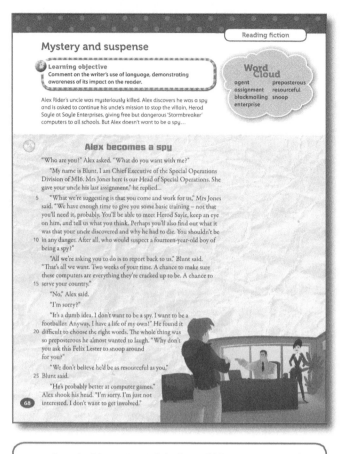

Alex becomes a spy

"Who are you?" Alex asked. "What do you want with me?"

"My name is Blunt, I am Chief Executive of the Special Operations Division of MI6. Mrs Jones here is our Head of Special Operations. She gave your uncle his last assignment," he replied…

5 "What we're suggesting is that you come and work for us," Mrs Jones said. "We have enough time to give you some basic training – not that you'll need it, probably. You'll be able to meet Herod Sayle, keep an eye on him, and tell us what you think. Perhaps you'll also find out what it was that your uncle discovered and why he had to die. You shouldn't be

10 in any danger. After all, who would suspect a fourteen-year-old boy of being a spy?"

"All we're asking you to do is to report back to us," Blunt said. "That's all we want. Two weeks of your time. A chance to make sure these computers are everything they're cracked up to be. A chance to

15 serve your country."

"No," Alex said.

"I'm sorry?"

"It's a dumb idea. I don't want to be a spy. I want to be a footballer. Anyway, I have a life of my own!" He found it

20 difficult to choose the right words. The whole thing was so preposterous he almost wanted to laugh. "Why don't you ask this Felix Lester to snoop around for you?"

"We don't believe he'd be as resourceful as you,"

25 Blunt said.

"He's probably better at computer games." Alex shook his head. "I'm sorry. I'm just not interested. I don't want to get involved."

68

associated with spying is 'blackmail' (threatening to do something to someone unless a demand is met). Blunt tells Alex that if he doesn't agree to become a spy, he will not be allowed to live in the house his uncle has left him or have access to money. **Ask:** *Do you think this will have an impact on what Alex decides to do?*

agent a person who works secretly to obtain information for a government or official body

assignment the allocation of a task or a job

blackmailing threatening to do something to someone unless a demand is met

enterprise a project or undertaking, especially a bold or complex one

preposterous contrary to reason or common sense; utterly absurd or ridiculous

resourceful having the ability to find quick and clever ways to overcome difficulties

snoop investigate, or look around secretly in an attempt to find out something

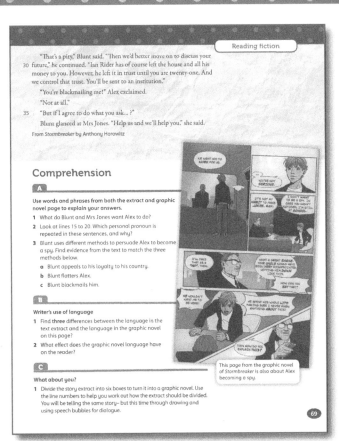

The student book page (page 69) reads:

"That's a pity," Blunt said. "Then we'd better move on to discuss your
30 future," he continued. "Ian Rider has of course left the house and all his
money to you. However, he left it in trust until you are twenty-one. And
we control that trust. You'll be sent to an institution."

"You're blackmailing me!" Alex exclaimed.

"Not at all."

35 "But if I agree to do what you ask...?"

Blunt glanced at Mrs Jones. "Help us and we'll help you," she said.

From Stormbreaker *by Anthony Horowitz*

Comprehension

A

Use words and phrases from both the extract and graphic
novel page to explain your answers.

1 What do Blunt and Mrs Jones want Alex to do?

2 Look at lines 15 to 20. Which personal pronoun is
repeated in these sentences, and why?

3 Blunt uses different methods to persuade Alex to become
a spy. Find evidence from the text to match the three
methods below.
a Blunt appeals to his loyalty to his country.
b Blunt flatters Alex.
c Blunt blackmails him.

B

Writer's use of language

1 Find **three** differences between the language in the
text extract and the language in the graphic novel
on this page?

2 What effect does the graphic novel language have
on the reader?

C

What about you?

1 Divide the story extract into six boxes to turn it into a graphic novel. Use
the line numbers to help you work out how the extract should be divided.
You will be telling the same story– but this time through drawing and
using speech bubbles for dialogue.

*This page from the graphic novel
of* Stormbreaker *is also about Alex
becoming a spy.*

69

④ Student Book teaching notes and comprehension answers

A

1 Students use the vocabulary learnt and references
from the text to support their answers. Confirm
students understand that this question sets up
the story and clearly explains what Alex has to do.

Answers:
They want Alex to spy on Herod Sayle, find out why his
uncle discovered and why he died, and to find out
more about the Stormbreaker computers. (Lines 7–8)

2 Remind students that personal pronouns refer to
people without saying their proper names.

Answers:
'I', because Alex is emphasizing what he wants to do.

3 Reinforce students understanding of this task with
drama work. Working in pairs, one student has to
persuade the other to do something by appealing
to their national loyalty, flattering them and then,
using blackmail.

Answers:

Appeal to national loyalty	Flattery	Blackmail
EVIDENCE		
'A chance to serve your country.'	'We don't believe he'd be as resourceful as you.'	'You'll be sent to an institution.'

B

1 Students read the text and the extract from the
graphic novel then complete the grid below, with
references and supporting evidence.

Answers:

Differences between the story extract and graphic novel	
Story	*Graphic novel*
The reader has to create the pictures with their imagination.	There is an artistic representation of the characters.
Characters are shown to be talking by the use of speech marks around spoken text.	Speech bubbles are used for dialogue. The words characters say can be seen coming out of their mouths.
We are not told anything about the physical appearance of the characters.	This gives a clear idea of what they look like, but leaves little to the reader's imagination.
Descriptions, sentence structure and information are the tools used to represent time and plot development.	Boxes are used to represent time passing and the plot developing.

2 The language in the graphic novel is supported by
the illustration which immediately involves the
reader in the dramatic tension and narrative.
Supported by the speech bubbles, the emotions
and feelings of the characters are visually
apparent to the reader.

C

Students summarize in six sentences what has
happened in the story extract. Ask for volunteers to
share these with the whole class. Pick up on overlong
sentences, or surplus information, and show how
these should be cut so that the sentence is
straightforward and simple.

Remind students to use: speech bubbles; a range of
facial expressions; details of characters' appearance.

① Learning objective

Revise different word classes.

Students revisit what different word classes are and how they are used in sentences.

 Remember to display the child-friendly learning objective to the class along with the child-friendly checklist that students can use to assess how well they achieve it.

We know that we have achieved this because:

▶ We are able to recognize different word classes and understand their function.

▶ We are also able to use different word classes to improve our writing.

② Student Book teaching notes and grammar exercise answers

Give students a quick test on the word classes listed in A. Elicit students' understanding by asking them to give two examples of each. Extend this by asking them to write out a definition of each word class. This will provide assessment information so that you can target word classes where student knowledge is insecure.

A

1 Working in pairs ask students to stand back to back and tell their partner what they did last weekend. They should be discouraged from using 'and' in between sentences. Explain that they have to say 'full stop' at the end of each sentence and 'new sentence' when they start a new one. They should then write these sentences down. Next, they check whether they have the range of word clauses, adding these as necessary. When they have finished, students should read their sentences to their partner. Do they sound the same as the first six sentences?

Answers:

Common noun: uncle, training, spy, country, footballer, words, games, etc.

Proper noun: Alex, Blunt, Mrs Jones, Felix Lester

Verb: are, asked, want, is, am, gave, replied, are suggesting, come to work, etc.

Adjective: chief, last, special, two, right, dumb, computer

Personal pronoun: I, his, your, me, our, us, you, we, he, she, her, etc.

Preposition: of, on, in, up, at, etc.

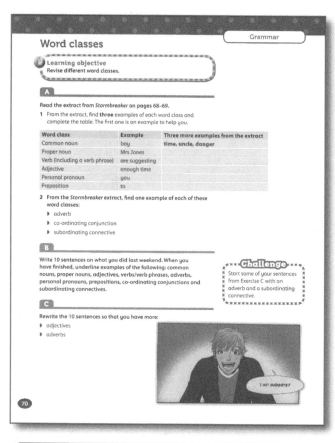

2 Students read the extract from *Stormbreaker* on page 68 again, and find an example for each.

Answers:

adverb: 'He's <u>probably</u> better at computer games.'

co-ordinating conjunction: '<u>But</u> if I agree …'

subordinating connective: '<u>What</u> we are suggesting is that you …'

Students' own answers should be based on previous experience. Tell students to refer back to A to help in defining word classes.

Students could be told how many adjectives or adverbs they have to add. When they have finished they should read their sentences to a partner. **Ask:** *What difference did the additional adjectives and adverbs make to the sentences?* (Adjectives add increased emphasis to the nouns; provide the reader with more detailed information. Additional adverbs heighten the readers' sense of time, place, or stance.)

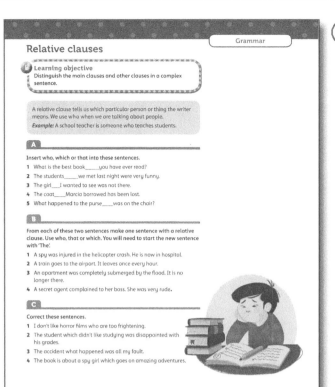

Relative clauses

Grammar

Learning objective
Distinguish the main clauses and other clauses in a complex sentence.

A relative clause tells us which particular person or thing the writer means. We use who when we are talking about people.
Example: A school teacher is someone who teaches students.

A

Insert who, which or that into these sentences.
1 What is the best book_____ you have ever read?
2 The students_____ we met last night were very funny.
3 The girl___I wanted to see was not there.
4 The coat____Marcia borrowed has been lost.
5 What happened to the purse____was on the chair?

B

From each of these two sentences make one sentence with a relative clause. Use who, that or which. You will need to start the new sentence with 'The'.
1 A spy was injured in the helicopter crash. He is now in hospital.
2 A train goes to the airport. It leaves once every hour.
3 An apartment was completely submerged by the flood. It is no longer there.
4 A secret agent complained to her boss. She was very rude.

C

Correct these sentences.
1 I don't like horror films who are too frightening.
2 The student which didn't like studying was disappointed with his grades.
3 The accident what happened was all my fault.
4 The book is about a spy girl which goes on amazing adventures.

71

Learning objective

Distinguish the main clauses and other clauses in a complex sentence.

Students learn how to differentiate between relative clauses which use 'who, which' and 'that'.

Remember to display the child-friendly learning objective to the class along with the child-friendly checklist that students can use to assess how well they achieve it.

We know that we have achieved this because:
▶ We understand why who, which and that are used differently to introduce relative clauses.
▶ We can construct relative clauses using these connectives.
▶ We can recognize when they have been used incorrectly.

④ Student Book teaching notes and grammar exercise answers

A

Students complete the exercise on their own. Then they swap answers with a partner and mark and correct with the whole class.

Answers:
1 What is the best book <u>which/that</u> you have ever read?
2 The students <u>who</u> we met last night were very funny.
3 The girl <u>who</u> I wanted to see was not there.
4 The coat <u>which/that</u> Marcia borrowed has been lost.
5 What happened to the purse <u>which/that</u> was on the chair.

B

Refer students to the grammar reference box for an explanation on the use of relative clauses. Students complete this task on their own.

Answers:
1 A spy <u>who</u> was injured in the helicopter crash is now in hospital.
2 The train <u>that/which</u> goes to the airport leaves once every hour.
3 An apartment <u>that/which</u> was completely submerged by the flood is no longer there.
4 The secret agent <u>who</u> complained to her boss was very rude.

C

Students rewrite the sentences using the correct relative clause.

Answers:
1 I don't like horror films <u>which</u> are too frightening.
2 The student <u>who</u> didn't like studying was disappointed with his grades.
3 The accident <u>that</u> happened was all my fault
4 The book is about a spy girl <u>who</u> goes on amazing adventures.

⑤ Extension

1 Give students a list of occupations (teacher, doctor, farmer, actress, etc.) and ask them to write what they do using a relative clause introduced by 'who'.
2 Give students a list of things (table, car, train, classroom, etc.) and ask them to write an explanation of what each is, using a relative clause introduced by 'that' or 'which'.

1 Learning objective

Analyse how paragraphs and chapters are structured and linked.

Students investigate how a text has been structured to make the development of information clear for the reader.

Remember to display the child-friendly learning objective to the class along with the child-friendly checklist that students can use to assess how well they achieve it.

We know that we have achieved this because:

- We are able to identify how and why the text has been structured.
- We are able to identify how pictures are used to complement the development and organisation of a text.

2 Reading non-fiction notes

Explain that gadgets are electronic devices (often very small) that enable us to do things better and more quickly than we could do ourselves. ***Example:*** an electric nail clipper or voice recognition on an iPhone. Elicit examples of gadgets students use and write them on the board. **Ask:** *Why is it important for a spy to have gadgets?* (They are small so they won't be seen; can get information quickly and secretly; can help spies to do things without being seen.) Explain that the non-fiction extract gives them more details about some very clever gadgets that could be used by spies. Explain that James Bond (known by his code name of 007) was a fictional character created in 1953 by writer Ian Fleming. Direct students attention to the glossary. Ask students to find the glossary words in the second and third paragraphs. Select one or two students to read the sentences out with these words, inserting their meanings.

Refer to the CD-ROM or read the text while students follow in their books. Ask students to write down three things they have learned from reading the extract. In small groups ask students which fact they found the most interesting and why. The groups then share their responses with the class.

All about spy gadgets

Learning objective
Analyse how paragraphs and chapters are structured and linked.

Reading non-fiction

Word Cloud
compass   ingenious
constructing   sprinkled
devices

Spy gadgets

All spies use clever devices called gadgets. In the James Bond movies the character 'Q' designs all the spy gadgets. He is based on a real man, Charles Fraser-Smith, who created some of the most amazing gadgets during World War II. [5]

The past

During the war, Fraser-Smith thought up ingenious solutions to difficult problems. As a small compass sewn into clothes could be detected, he decided to put magnetized [10] needles inside matchsticks. The match could be dropped in a pool of water and point north, acting exactly like a compass.

The future

Gadgets and devices have become more [15] important in spying. How we spy will change in future as human agents can be easily seen and caught, but machines and gadgets can be made to destroy themselves if discovered. It also helps that gadgets are very tiny. Nanotechnology is the science of constructing microscopic machines, called 'nanobots' (tiny robots). These could be sprinkled like dust [20] over electronic equipment and into rooms to send back information.

A submarine disguised as a crocodile

Glossary
magnetized turned into a magnet (a piece of metal that attracts iron and steel towards it)

microscopic not visible with the human eye; only seen through a microscope

When wet, the top layer of these playing cards can be peeled back to show a map.

72

3 Word Cloud definitions

Focus students' attention on the Word Cloud and refer to the CD-ROM. Direct them to the second paragraph and the word 'compass.' From what is written ask students to explain what a compass is. Then check if it matches with the teacher's (previously hidden) definition on the board. Which word do they think means clever? (Ingenious.) Point out that although there is similarity to 'genius' (someone exceptionally clever), it has a different spelling. Give an example sentence, 'I sprinkle sugar on my cereal' to lead students to what 'sprinkled' means (scatter over something). Tell them that 'devices' almost means the same as 'gadgets', but is generally something made to do a particular task. **Ask:** *Does 'constructing' mean 'building' or 'using'?*

compass an instrument for determining direction

constructing building or making something

devices things made or adapted for a particular task, especially electronic equipment

ingenious cleverly and originally devised and well suited to its purpose

sprinkled scatter small drops or particles over something

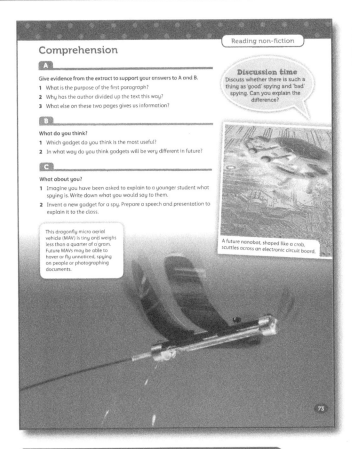

Comprehension

A

Give evidence from the extract to support your answers to A and B.
1 What is the purpose of the first paragraph?
2 Why has the author divided up the text this way?
3 What else on these two pages gives us information?

B

What do you think?
1 Which gadget do you think is the most useful?
2 In what way do you think gadgets will be very different in future?

C

What about you?
1 Imagine you have been asked to explain to a younger student what spying is. Write down what you would say to them.
2 Invent a new gadget for a spy. Prepare a speech and presentation to explain it to the class.

Discussion time
Discuss whether there is such a thing as 'good' spying and 'bad' spying. Can you explain the difference?

This dragonfly micro aerial vehicle (MAV) is tiny and weighs less than a quarter of a gram. Future MAVs may be able to hover or fly unnoticed, spying on people or photographing documents.

A future nanobot, shaped like a crab, scuttles across an electronic circuit board.

73

(4) Student Book teaching notes and comprehension answers

A

1 Explain that the purpose of the first paragraph is to introduce the topic of gadgets, and to acquaint students with the name of a famous gadget-maker. Having been introduced to him in paragraph 1, the reader will be keen to go on reading and find out more. Explain that we will find out more detail about Fraser-Smith in paragraph 2.

2 The author has divided up the text into three parts. The introduction serves as an overview of the topic. The use of historical narrative in paragraph 2 serves to reinforce the importance of past experience. The final paragraph focuses on future developments. This structure lets the reader know how gadgets have developed over time. The text also ends with a particular gadget rather than reference to lots of gadgets, so that the reader has something to focus upon. Subheadings have been used to make the development of the text clear.

3 Ask students to feedback their suggestions on other sources of information on the page. Point out that pictures offer an accessible way of providing a lot of information quickly. It means the reader doesn't have to read too much to get key information.

⇨

B

1 Write the answers on the board and ask students to vote on which they consider to be the most useful.

2 Encourage a class discussion on how gadgets of the future may evolve. Direct students to focus on size, shape, mobility, technology, etc.

C

1 Ask students to create a list of the positive and negative points of spying. As they write their descriptions remind them of the structure and focus of the paragraphs in *Spy gadgets,* and how a similar structure will both engage and inform a reader of their work.

2 Working in pairs, students invent and present a new spy gadget. Explain that their invention must have a very clear purpose. They need to be able to say what it is for and how it would help a spy. Each invention should be drawn. Students explain their gadget to another pair. Does it make sense? After any questions have been answered students prepare a larger scale drawing with suitable labels. Each pair should then present their invention to the class, using their descriptions and illustrations to clearly explain its function.

(5) Discussion

As a class discuss the differences between 'good' and 'bad' spying. Elicit responses that suggest students understand how 'good' spying would mean a spy remains incognito on a mission. 'Bad' spying would suggest that a spy's cover or alias is easily detectable.

Learning objective

Understand and use dashes and brackets.

Students learn how commas, dashes and brackets separate phrases and clauses for different emphatic effect.

 Remember to display the child-friendly learning objective to the class along with the child-friendly checklist that students can use to assess how well they achieve it.

We know that we have achieved this because:

▶ We know when to use commas, dashes and brackets to separate off a phrase or clause.

▶ We know how to then use these different punctuation marks in our own writing.

2 Student Book teaching notes and punctuation exercise answers

A

Remind students that dashes are used to emphasize and brackets are used to clarify and separate information.

Answers:

1 Alex took a coin — all he had in his pocket — and passed it to his friend.
Alex took a coin (all he had in his pocket) and passed it to his friend.

2 Complete the form in ink— not pencil — and give it to the teacher.
Complete the form in ink (not pencil) and give it to the teacher.

3 The spy moved — very suddenly — towards me.
The spy moved (very suddenly) towards me.

B

Answers:

1 Charles Dickens (1812–1870) is a famous writer.
2 For this recipe you need 2 kilograms of (finest) flour.
3 I need to borrow five hundred dollars ($500) from the bank.
4 She finally answered (after taking five minutes to think about it) that she didn't understand the question.

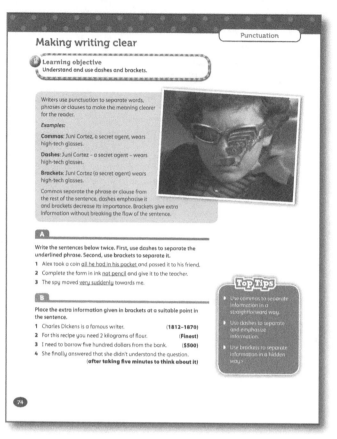

Making writing clear

Learning objective
Understand and use dashes and brackets.

Writers use punctuation to separate words, phrases or clauses to make the meaning clearer for the reader.

Examples:

Commas: Juni Cortez, a secret agent, wears high-tech glasses.

Dashes: Juni Cortez – a secret agent – wears high-tech glasses.

Brackets: Juni Cortez (a secret agent) wears high-tech glasses.

Commas separate the phrase or clause from the rest of the sentence, dashes emphasise it and brackets decrease its importance. Brackets give extra information without breaking the flow of the sentence.

A

Write the sentences below twice. First, use dashes to separate the underlined phrase. Second, use brackets to separate it.

1 Alex took a coin all he had in his pocket and passed it to his friend.
2 Complete the form in ink not pencil and give it to the teacher.
3 The spy moved very suddenly towards me.

B

Place the extra information given in brackets at a suitable point in the sentence.

1 Charles Dickens is a famous writer. (1812–1870)
2 For this recipe you need 2 kilograms of flour. (Finest)
3 I need to borrow five hundred dollars from the bank. ($500)
4 She finally answered that she didn't understand the question. (after taking five minutes to think about it)

Top Tips
▶ Use commas to separate information in a straightforward way.
▶ Use dashes to separate and emphasize information.
▶ Use brackets to separate information in a hidden way.

74

3 Top Tip

To reinforce the information, ask students to find examples of the three points in the *Spy Gadgets* extract.

4 Extension

Tell students that the single dash can also be used to emphasize a sudden or dramatic pause in a sentence.

Before me I saw a — mouse!

Please let me give you — oh no, I've lost my purse.

Ask students to write three sentences showing how a single dash is used in this way.

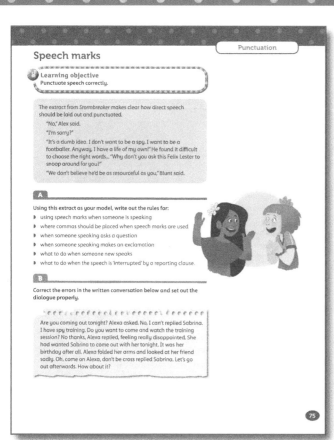

Speech marks

Learning objective
Punctuate speech correctly.

The extract from *Stormbreaker* makes clear how direct speech should be laid out and punctuated.

"No," Alex said.

"I'm sorry?"

"It's a dumb idea. I don't want to be a spy. I want to be a footballer. Anyway, I have a life of my own!" He found it difficult to choose the right words... "Why don't you ask this Felix Lester to snoop around for you?"

"We don't believe he'd be as resourceful as you," Blunt said.

A

Using this extract as your model, write out the rules for:
▸ using speech marks when someone is speaking
▸ where commas should be placed when speech marks are used
▸ when someone speaking asks a question
▸ when someone speaking makes an exclamation
▸ what to do when someone new speaks
▸ what to do when the speech is 'interrupted' by a reporting clause.

B

Correct the errors in the written conversation below and set out the dialogue properly.

Are you coming out tonight? Alexa asked. No, I can't replied Sabrina. I have spy training. Do you want to come and watch the training session? No thanks, Alexa replied, feeling really disappointed. She had wanted Sabrina to come out with her tonight. It was her birthday after all. Alexa folded her arms and looked at her friend sadly. Oh, come on Alexa, don't be cross replied Sabrina. Let's go out afterwards. How about it?

75

Learning objective

(5)

Punctuate speech correctly.

Students revisit and revise the rules for the laying out of direct speech and how it should be punctuated.

Remember to display the child-friendly learning objective to the class along with the child-friendly checklist that students can use to assess how well they achieve it.

We know that we have achieved this because:
▸ **We are able to punctuate speech correctly.**
▸ **We can explain why specific punctuation is used to identify direct speech.**

(6) Student Book teaching notes and punctuation exercise answers

A

Students read this extract, or other examples from fiction texts in other units, to identify the rules of punctuation.

Answers:
1 Round the beginning and end of the speech.
2 Before the reporting clause.
3 Inside the speech marks.
4 Inside the speech marks.
5 Start a new line.
6 Stop and start the speech marks, but don't start a new line unless there is a new speaker.

B

"Are you coming out tonight?" Alexa asked.
"No, I can't," replied Sabrina. "I have spy training.
Do you want to come and watch the training session?"
"No thanks," Alexa replied, feeling really disappointed.
She had wanted Sabrina to come out with her tonight. It was her birthday after all. Alexa folded her arms and looked at her friend sadly.
"Oh, come on Alexa. Don't be cross," Sabrina pleaded.
"Let's go out afterwards. How about it?"

(7) Extension

Choose one sentence from the extract from *Stormbreaker* and write it as reported speech, not direct speech.

Learning objective

Explore how the poet manipulates and plays with words and their sounds.

Students identify the ways in which the poet has manipulated words and sounds in the poem in order to emphasize its meaning.

Remember to display the child-friendly learning objective to the class along with the child-friendly checklist that students can use to assess how well they achieve it.

We know that we have achieved this because:

We understand how language and sound has been manipulated in the poem.

We can answer questions about features of language and sound.

② Student Book teaching notes and comprehension answers

Books closed. Explain that spies are usually very good at what they do because they have to be — otherwise they would get found out very quickly. However, the poem — by Ken Nesbitt — is about a boy whose dad is a secret agent, who isn't very good at one thing.

Before the poem is read for the first time, direct students to the glossary and explain that these are all terms for a detective.

Read through the poem once, building in a dramatic pause before the final revolution of the 'keys'. You can also refer to the CD-ROM. Point out how the lines are the same length; the verses are the same number of lines; words are repeated at the beginning of lines; alternate lines rhyme. Emphasize that all these features contribute towards the easy-to-read, humorous, and rhythmic effect of the poem.

A

1 Sleuth, private eye, snoop, secret agent.
2 Best detective; perfect private eye; unrivalled at detecting; eyesight like an eagle, etc.
3 The poet saves the punch line until the end; it's the point of the poem — dad can do extraordinary, but not ordinary things.

B

1 Review the techniques listed with the class to confirm their understanding of poetic techniques. Explain that alliteration is a literary device in which two or more consecutive words (or words that are nearby in the same sentence) start with

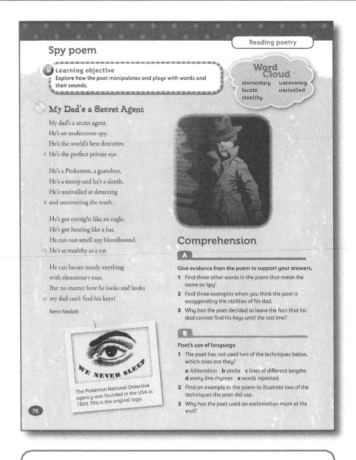

the same letter. Using repetition of words in a poem reinforces the point and gives it power. Similies directly compare two different things. Line length in poetry provides contrast or rhythm.

In some poems rhythm will help to direct the reader to important points and build momentum. In this poem the rhyme influences the pace and adds to the humour.

Answers:
d Only alternate lines rhyme
e Words repeated
2 The use of similes such as 'hearing like a bat' and 'stealthy as a cat', helps to personify the phrase. The similes rhyme too, which influences the pace and adds to the humour.
3 The exclamation mark emphasizes the importance

③ Word cloud definitions

Refer to the CD-ROM. Ask students what the prefix 'un' means at the beginning of a word? (Not.) Can students work out what 'unrivalled' and 'uncovered' mean? Explain that 'elementary' in the poem means that the dad can find out and discover things with no trouble at all. Explain that 'locate' means to discover the exact position or place of something.

elementary straightforward and uncomplicated
locate discover the exact position of something
stealthy cautious and secretive
uncovering revealing, exposing
unrivalled no one can rival him; the best there is

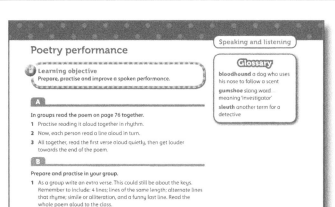

to look out for what you are doing to make the reading more effective. ***Example:*** regular bouncy pace, drawing attention to the rhyme, enunciating consonants and vowels, emphasizing alliteration, similes, repetition, growing more enthusiastic and exaggerating as the poem goes on, so that the 'keys' incident in the last line is made more humorous.

A

1 Tell students to create rhythm by lightly tapping their feet or hands in unison, and to read the poem aloud together.

2 When reading their line aloud in turn, students could stand in a particular shape — straight line, circle, triangle — and given numbers, so that the student at the front says line 1, and the student at the back says line 2. Ensure students use all the features demonstrated by you in your reading of the poem.

3 Help 'conduct' the collective reading of the poem so that the students become progressively louder. Encourage them to stop just before 'keys' (a count of two), and to then emphasize it.

B

Ask students to consider additional words for 'spies' or 'sleuths', and rhyming words for 'keys', which may help in creating an additional verse.

Students practise their extended poems and present them to the class. Remind them of the key points practised in A to ensure the reading is entertaining.

C

The assessment criteria could be agreed with the students. This could focus on how clear their voices were in pronouncing words; keeping a steady rhythm; comparative volume; dramatic features e.g. emphasis of alliteration, rhyme; dramatic pause, etc.

Learning objective

4 **Prepare, practise and improve a spoken performance.**

Students prepare the poem, practise it, and then improve it.

Remember to display the child-friendly learning objective to the class along with the child-friendly checklist that students can use to assess how well they achieve it.

We know that we have achieved this because:

▶ We have prepared and practised reading the poem for performance.

▶ We have received feedback so can improve our reading for performance.

▶ We can perform effectively for an audience.

5 Student Book teaching notes and speaking exercise answers

Explain to students that if they enjoy reading a poem they can share this enjoyment with an audience, by reading a poem aloud.

Read the poem to the class in a deliberately bad way — quickly, falteringly, monotone, etc. Point out how a poor reading can destroy a poem for an audience. Read the poem again, asking the students

6 Extension

Ask students to learn a poem off by heart and recite it at home in front of their family and friends.

Learning objective

①

Use mystery genre as a model for writing. Develop some imaginative detail through careful use of vocabulary and style

Students create characters that can be used to move a plot along in the beginning of a mystery story.

Students incorporate imaginative detail in order to make their characters and plot interesting for the reader.

Remember to display the child-friendly learning objective to the class along with the child-friendly checklist that students can use to assess how well they achieve it.

We know that we have achieved this because:

▶ We are able to construct to contrasting characters.

▶ We are able to incorporate them into the beginning of a narrative.

▶ We can incorporate imaginative detail.

Heroes and villains

Writing workshop

Learning objectives
Use the mystery genre as a model for writing.
Develop some imaginative detail through careful use of vocabulary and style.

You are the hero/heroine
Write a description of yourself as the hero or heroine. You are going to be quite ordinary in comparison to the villain. You will need to write about yourself in the third person.

Example:

Name:	Description:
	He/she has a large mop of untidy hair and a small, inquisitive nose. The hair looked as if it hadn't been combed in a long, long time. It reminded people who saw him/her of an old bird's nest.

78

---

② Writing workshop teaching notes

You are the hero/heroine

Read out the example description. Draw attention to how physical features are described in the first sentence, and more detail concerning the hair is given in the second sentence. Highlight the use of metaphor in the third sentence when compared with *'an old bird's nest'.*

Ask students to copy this formula as they go on to create their own description of themselves. Students read these to the class. Discuss what the most effective examples are and elicit reasons why.

Remind students of third person pronouns: *he, she, it, they, him, her, them,* etc. Ask students to consider adjectives to describe heroes such as: courageous, strong, selfless, determined, compassionate, brave, etc. As the heroes will be quite ordinary in comparison to the villains, what tools can they use in their descriptions to reinforce important character traits or seemingly innocuous physical features? (Alliteration, similes, etc.)

③ Extension

Students create a 'Wanted' poster which will visually represent a villain that they have created. Explain that any descriptions they have written should be drawn on the poster. ***Example:*** a round, bald head, missing teeth, large ears, etc.

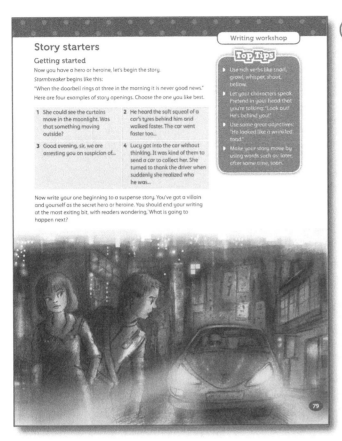

1 Once students have finished their stories they can use word processing packages to type them up. Encourage them to illustrate their stories as well. If students are proficient with ICT they could use clip art, or royalty free images from the Internet. Students can otherwise print out the story and illustrate it by hand.

2 Alternatively, students can design and create a front cover for their story. Encourage them to think about how they can relay the theme and intended audience for the story by their use of fonts and illustrations, etc. They can research covers by looking online or in the school library. Again those proficient with ICT should be encouraged to do this on a computer.

3 In addition, students can select part of their story, illustrate it and write it as a page from a graphic novel, using the example on page 78 as a guide.

④ Writing workshop teaching notes

Getting started

Explain to students that the first line of a story is very important, a good one will create interest and suspense and hook the reader in, making them want to read more. Refer students to the Top Tips list to inspire them to use description and dialogue to create imaginative beginnings.

Now students have their beginnings they have to think about plot and structure, and how to bring the story to an effective climax. Suggest some settings to students who may be struggling with a plot. Keep these simple such as school, or the park, and encourage students to be creative with plot lines for what are normally quite mundane situations.

End of Unit Test

Question Paper

Reading: fiction

Read the extract and answer the questions.

The passenger

Two hours later, a man in a blond wig, wearing sunglasses and holding a huge bunch of flowers, boarded the Eurostar train to Paris. Zeljan Kurst hated these disguises, but it was something else he had learned in his long career. If you're trying not to be seen, it often helps to make yourself as prominent as possible. The
5   flowers and the wig were ridiculous, but although the police and MI6 were looking for him all over London, they certainly wouldn't associate them with him.

As he settled into his pre-booked seat in first class and sipped his complimentary glass of champagne, Kurst's mind focused on the problem he had been given. The shoot-out at the museum was already forgotten. The question
10 was – who would be the best person to handle this quite interesting business of the Elgin Marbles? There were now twelve members of Scorpia, including him, and he mentally went over them one by one...

There was a blast of a whistle and the train moved off. Kurst took out his mobile phone – encrypted, of course – and dialled a number. The train
15 slid down the platform and picked up speed, and as they left St Pancras International, Kurst permitted himself the rare luxury of a smile. Yes. Razim was perfect. He would bring his unique talents to this new assignment. Kurst was sure of it. He had chosen exactly the right man.

From *Scorpia Rising* by Anthony Horowitz

Glossary
encrypted conceal data in (something) by converting it into a code

Comprehension

A

Give evidence from the extract to support your answers.

1 What did Zeljan Kurst do to disguise his appearance?

_____ [1]

2 Why did Zeljan Kurst need to change his appearance?

_____ [1]

3 What had happened at the museum?

_____ [1]

4 What transport did Kurst take to leave London? Tick the correct box.

   a bus   ☐

   b train   ☐

   c car   ☐

   d aeroplane   ☐   [1]

5 Who does Kurst think is the right person to handle the business of the Elgin Marbles?

   _____ [1]

B

Give evidence from the extract to support your answers.

1 Why did Kurst use a disguise that made him look as prominent as possible?

   _____ [1]

2 Give the names of two members of Scorpia.

   _____ [1]

3 Kurst is on the run from the police and MI6. Find evidence in the extract that shows he predicts he is going to get away.

   _____ [2]

4 Which phrase in the last paragraph clearly shows that Kurst is a spy?

   _____ [1]

C

Give evidence from the extract to support your answers.

1 Is Kurst a serious man? Explain your answer.

   _____

   _____ [2]

2 Is the text written in the first, second or third person?

   _____ [1]

3 There are three paragraphs in the extract. Match a title (a–c) to the paragraphs (1–3).

   a Decision _____

   b Thought _____

   c Disguise _____   [2]

Reading: non-fiction

Read the extract and answer the questions.

Sherlock Holmes

Sherlock Holmes is the famous fictional detective created by Sir Arthur Conan Doyle. Doyle wrote four novels and 56 short stories about the detective, with the first novel published in 1887. Working from his apartment at 221b Baker Street, London, Holmes solves many perplexing cases simply
5   through using his clever powers of observation and reasoning. His friend and assistant Doctor Watson helped him with many cases, although it was always Holmes who solved the crime!

Doctor Watson narrates all but four stories, describing how Holmes picked up on clues that no one else noticed — not even Watson! Sherlock
10   Holmes was an instant hit when Doyle first created him, and when he had him killed in 1891 by his arch enemy, Moriarty, the public even insisted Doyle bring him back to life again! Among the most famous stories are 'A Study in Scarlet' (1887) and 'The Hound of the Baskervilles' (1902).

Nancy Drew

Nancy Drew is an American 18-year-old fictional detective and star of the
15   Nancy Drew Mystery stories, a series of stories for children. The first book in the series, 'The Secret of the Old Clock' was published in April 1930. All the stories are ghost-written under the name, Carolyn Keene, although many different authors have written them.

Nancy does not attend school or have a job. Instead, she spends all her
20   time solving mysteries. Her two best friends Bess Marvin and Georgia (George) Fayne often help her.

Adapted from www.capstonekids.com/characters/Damian.../spykit_detectives

Glossary
perplexing completely baffling; very puzzling

Comprehension

A

Give evidence from the extract to support your answers.

1 Who wrote the following books: *A Study in Scarlet* and *The Secret of the Old Clock*?

_____

_____ [2]

2 Which detective series was written first: Sherlock Holmes or Nancy Drew?

_____ [2]

B

Give evidence from the extract to support your answers.

1 Give two differences between the detectives, Sherlock Holmes and Nancy Drew.

_____

_____ [3]

2 Give two similarities between the detectives, Sherlock Holmes and Nancy Drew.

_____

_____ [3]

3 Find evidence in the extract which shows that Sherlock Holmes was popular.

_____ [2]

C

1 Write a title summarizing both non-fiction extracts.

_____ [3]

Writing: fiction

Imagine you are on the same train as Zeljan Kurst, and are able to observe him closely. Write an email to a friend afterwards telling them what you observed, and what suspicions you had. Please use a separate sheet of paper.

Remember!

Develop the dramatic tension.

Consider sentence length.

Use effective punctuation.

Write three to four paragraphs.

[30]

Writing: non-fiction

Write about a fictional character you admire. Please use a separate sheet of paper.

Write three paragraphs. Consider these questions.

1 What is their name? What do they do?

2 What questions would you like to ask them?

3 Why will other people be interested in them?

[20]

6

Extreme Earth

1 Warm up objective

Help to move group discussion forward.
Example: by clarifying, summarizing.

Students ask questions to develop understanding.

Remember to display the child-friendly learning objective to the class along with the child-friendly checklist that students can use to assess how well they achieve it.

We know that we have achieved this because:

▶ We are able to ask questions to confirm discussion ideas and opinions.

▶ We are able develop discussions using summaries.

2 Unit warm up

Books closed. Write the unit title on the board and ask students to explain the meaning of 'extreme.' Confirm that it means three things: reaching a high degree of heat or cold; not usual; exceptional. This all points to the unit being about severe and exceptional events and conditions on Earth.

Ask students to name two places that have extreme weather all the time. *Example:* the Sahara desert and the Arctic. Point out that in the Sahara the summer temperatures can be greater than 50 °C, and in the Arctic winter temperatures can drop below −50 °C. Ask students what extreme Earth conditions they have experienced, or know of. These experiences could be written as an 'extreme Earth' mind map. These could include: floods, storms, dense fog, volcanic eruptions, typhoon, tornado, excessive heat, landslide, and avalanche. Explain that extreme events often result in chaos and destruction for human beings.

Although many geographical terms come up in the Word Cloud on page 81, you may want to go through some of these explanations with students now.

Books open. Working in groups, ask students to explain their understanding of the quote. Confirm that the quote says that nature and its extreme forces contributes to the beauty of Earth.

Ask students to make up a quote bubble which tells us to see extreme weather as a creative element, changing our environments and shaping our surroundings.

6 **Extreme Earth**

Volcanic lava cooled and hardened

Satellite picture of a tornado

Let's Talk

Look at the examples of Extreme Earth in the pictures.

1 What has happened in the volcanic photo?
2 What is about to happen to the town in the large photo?
3 What extreme weather or events have happened in your country? Explain them to a partner.

"Should you shield the canyons from the windstorms you would never see the true beauty of their carvings."
Elizabeth Kubler-Ross

80

3 Let's Talk

Focus students' attention on the photos and ask them to describe what they see. Question 3 asks the students to focus on extreme weather or disasters in their own country.

4 Extension

Split students into groups and ask each to research one of the following natural events: volcano, earthquake, tsunami, and avalanche. Ask students to describe what they are and why they occur. Students should be concise in their definitions and use only four sentences in their responses. Each group then presents their definitions to the class.

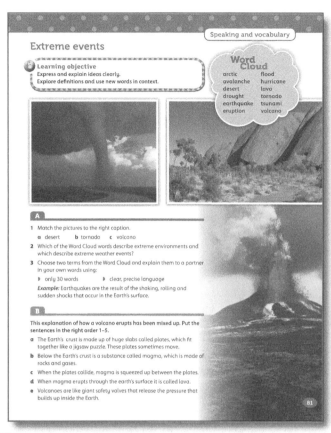

Answers:

1 **a** top right **b** top left **c** bottom right

2 Show the area of the Arctic on a globe. Explain that the Arctic also has many icebergs and glaciers. Explain that these are big chunks of ice. A comparison could be made of the coldest winter day in the students' community, with a typical Arctic day −40 °C. Show the Sahara desert on the globe and explain it is the world's largest hot desert, where during the hottest months temperatures can exceed 50 °C. Explain that because of these extreme conditions both plant and animal life are sparse.

Answers:

Extreme environment: arctic, desert

Extreme weather: flood, hurricane, tornado

3 Students work in pairs to answer the question and write down their definitions. Ask for volunteers to read their definitions to the class. Write the key points of each on the board.

 B

Students could be given some help with this exercise. For example, you can tell them which sentence would work as number 1 or number 5. Alternatively, discuss and order the sentences as a class.

Example answer:

1 a, **2** e, **3** b, **4** c, **5** d

Learning objective

Express and explain ideas clearly.

Explore definitions and use new words in context.

Students find out new words and their definitions, which they then explain to someone else, using language that is clear and concise.

Remember to display the child-friendly learning objective to the class along with the child-friendly checklist that students can use to assess how well they achieve it.

We know that we have achieved this because:

▶ **We are able to understand new words and their meanings.**

▶ **We are able to explain new words and their meanings.**

 Student Book teaching notes and speaking exercise answers

A

1 Students should be able to complete the caption matching exercise following on from the Word Cloud definitions.

Word Cloud definitions

Direct students attention to the Word Cloud.

arctic area around the North Pole

avalanche an excessive amount of snow sliding down a mountainside

desert a dry, barren area of land

drought no rain for a long time

earthquake the shaking, rolling, or sudden shock of the Earth's surface

eruption the sudden outpouring of a particular substance from somewhere, such as a volcano

flood excess water from heavy rain

hurricane strong winds at speeds of 75–200 mph

lava hot molten or semi-fluid rock erupted from a volcano or fissure, or solid rock resulting from cooling of this

tornado a violent rotating column of air

tsunami a large ocean wave

volcano an opening in the Earth's crust

Learning objective

1

Consider writer's use of language and how characters and settings are presented.

Students consider how language is used to create distinct characters and setting.

Remember to display the child-friendly learning objective to the class along with the child-friendly checklist that students can use to assess how well they achieve it.

We know that we have achieved this because:

▶ We can identify language which depicts character and setting.

▶ We can answer questions about language, character and setting.

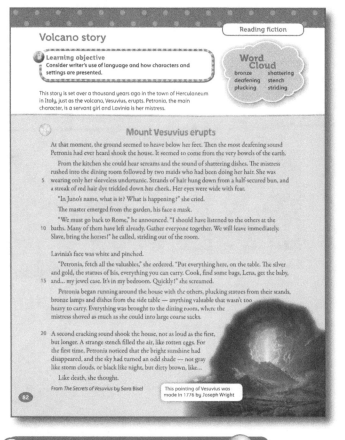

Reading fiction

Volcano story

Learning objective
Consider writer's use of language and how characters and settings are presented.

This story is set over a thousand years ago in the town of Herculaneum in Italy, just as the volcano, Vesuvius, erupts. Petronia, the main character, is a servant girl and Lavinia is her mistress.

Word Cloud
bronze   shattering
deafening   stench
plucking   striding

Mount Vesuvius erupts

At that moment, the ground seemed to heave below her feet. Then the most deafening sound Petronia had ever heard shook the house. It seemed to come from the very bowels of the earth.

From the kitchen she could hear screams and the sound of shattering dishes. The mistress rushed into the dining room followed by two maids who had been doing her hair. She was
5 wearing only her sleeveless undertunic. Strands of hair hung down from a half-secured bun, and a streak of red hair dye trickled down her cheek. Her eyes were wide with fear.

"In Juno's name, what is it? What is happening?" she cried.

The master emerged from the garden, his face a mask.

"We must go back to Rome," he announced. "I should have listened to the others at the
10 baths. Many of them have left already. Gather everyone together. We will leave immediately. Slave, bring the horses!" he called, striding out of the room.

Lavinia's face was white and pinched.

"Petronia, fetch all the valuables," she ordered. "Put everything here, on the table. The silver and gold, the statues of Isis, everything you can carry. Cook, find some bags, Lena, get the baby,
15 and... my jewel case. It's in my bedroom. Quickly!" she screamed.

Petronia began running around the house with the others, plucking statues from their stands, bronze lamps and dishes from the side table — anything valuable that wasn't too heavy to carry. Everything was brought to the dining room, where the mistress shoved as much as she could into large coarse sacks.

20 A second cracking sound shook the house, not as loud as the first, but longer. A strange stench filled the air, like rotten eggs. For the first time, Petronia noticed that the bright sunshine had disappeared, and the sky had turned an odd shade — not gray like storm clouds, or black like night, but dirty brown, like...

Like death, she thought.

From The Secrets of Vesuvius by Sara Bisel

82

This painting of Vesuvius was made in 1776 by Joseph Wright

Reading fiction notes

2

Read the overview. Explain that the story starts at the precise moment the volcano erupts, so beginning the story very directly, 'At that moment, the ground seemed to heave below her feet.'

Read the extract. Ask students to track and note signs of the volcano. (Shattering dishes, a second cracking sound, a strange stench, and the sky had turned an odd shade, etc.) Explain how these signs — combined with the reaction of Lavinia and the master — build up the tension and interest. Emphasize their respective behaviour. **Ask:** *How do we know Lavina is afraid and anxious?* (Her eyes were wide with fear; her face was white and pinched; her eyes wide with fear, etc.) Details, such as 'She was wearing only her sleeveless undertunic' and her hair was in 'a half-secured bun' show the extent of her disarray.

Lavinia is focused on taking valuable items; the master is focused on making arrangements to get his family to safety. The servants have to carry out their orders.

Refer to the CD-ROM or read the text while students follow in their books. Stop as glossary words come up, and explain these.

Word Cloud definitions

3

Refer to the CD-ROM. Focus students' attention on the Word Cloud and ask them to locate the word 'stench'. Can they explain what it is? **Ask:** *What other words can be used to describe 'smell'?* (Reek, pong, odour, whiff.) Then they locate the rest of the words.

bronze a yellowish-brown alloy of copper with up to one-third tin

deafening a noise so loud as to make it impossible to hear anything else

plucking taking (something) and quickly removing it from its place

shattering breaking suddenly and violently into pieces

stench a strong and very unpleasant smell

striding walking with long, decisive steps in a specified direction

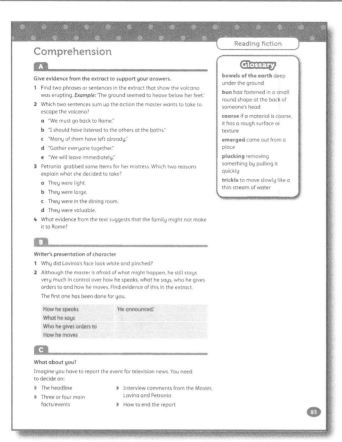

4 Student Book teaching notes and comprehension answers

A

1 Remind students of what a volcano does. Ask students to scan the text for changes in sound, movement, light and smell.

Answers: (two out of the following)

'the most deafening sound Petronia had ever heard'; 'A second cracking sound'; 'A strange stench filled the air'; 'bright sunshine had disappeared; the sky had turned an odd shade...dirty brown'.

2 Emphasize that the focus of the question is not on the master's reflections or thoughts, but on **action.** Direct students to the section where the master speaks; the focus should be on how he sees the situation, reacts, makes a decision and then takes action quickly.

Answers:

d Gather everyone together.

e We will leave immediately.

3 **Ask:** *Which phrase suggests that large items will not be taken?* ('everything you can carry'). Direct students' attention to the mention of 'silver and gold' and 'jewel case'. This suggests that the items taken will be valuable.

Answers:

a They were light.

d They were valuable.

4 On one side of the board, write down reasons why the household might make it to Rome: everything is organized quickly; they have servants and horses so can access immediate help and transport. On the other side, write negative points: the second cracking sound; the stench and darkening sky, which suggests the volcano is actually erupting. It is unlikely they can escape the speed and force of that. There is also the final prophetic phrase, 'Like death'. The ellipsis suggests a dramatic pause…

B

1 **Ask:** *What does a 'white face' usually signify?* (Illness, fear, anxiety.) Explain that as a verb 'pinch' means to squeeze, and that this meaning is then carried into the adjective 'pinched' — meaning Lavina's face is squeezed, little, and mean.

2 Ask students to re-read the lines where the master speaks. **Ask:** *Where is the one example of his fear expressed?* (His face a mask.) Explain that, 'His face a mask' is an idiom which means that someone's face is as white as a mask. It could also mean that it was without any expression of emotion. The master is able to hide his fears by keeping a front up (unlike Lavina) and acting decisively.

Answers:

What he says: 'We must go back to Rome', 'Gather everyone together', 'We will leave immediately.'
Who he gives orders to: 'Slave, bring the horses!'
How he moves: 'striding'.

C

Ask students to work in groups of four, and to imagine they work for national television, and have been asked to report on what has happened in the extract for the television news. The slot available is only two minutes. The group will need to decide on the presenter, and cast the characters.

Explain that a headline should sum up the story to make the reader want to hear more about it. Features such as alliteration, simile, rhetorical question, and emotive words should be used.

Working in a group, each student suggests a headline, and the group decides which one to use. Ask students to consider what they think the main four events to be. Point out how news reports tell the reader or viewer the story, and then fill it in with comments from those involved. In order to include the voices of Lavinia and the master, students will need to change the direct speech into indirect speech and back to direct speech again. Petronia does not actually speak, so students will need to work out what she would say. The report should end with where the family are now.

Learning objective

Revise language conventions and grammatical features of different types of texts.

Students learn how question marks, exclamation marks and ellipsis are used in fiction to help emphasize characters' feelings.

 Remember to display the child-friendly learning objective to the class along with the child-friendly checklist that students can use to assess how well they achieve it.

We know that we have achieved this because:

▶ **We are able to add question marks, exclamation marks and ellipses to a fiction extract in order to emphasize the emotions and feelings of the characters for the reader.**

② Student Book teaching notes and grammar exercise answers

Read the explanation with the class, and the example given. Explain how the exclamation mark and question mark have been used to convey Lavinia's fear and anxiety. Explain that the exclamation mark can be used to depict a range of emotions: fear, wonder, happiness, etc. Tell students that question marks indicate a question being asked, but can give a more realistic feel because the voice rises on the end of the sentence. Point out that if more than one question is asked quickly it can suggest an agitated state of mind.

A

Working in pairs, ask students to read the dialogue in monotone voices. Then, ask students to decide where exclamation and question marks can be added. They repeat the dialogue — this time adding emotion. Explain that an ellipsis means the omission of a word or words. It is a punctuation device that can be used to show that the speaker is unable to go on with a sentence because they feel emotional, sad, or worried.

Select pairs to read their paragraphs aloud, correcting any overuse or marks placed incorrectly.

Answer:

'Oh, no! What's happening?' cried Ahmed. 'Why are all those rocks falling from the mountain? Oh no! It's a landslide … We're trapped! We're trapped! We can't get out!'

'Keep calm!' Fatima ordered.

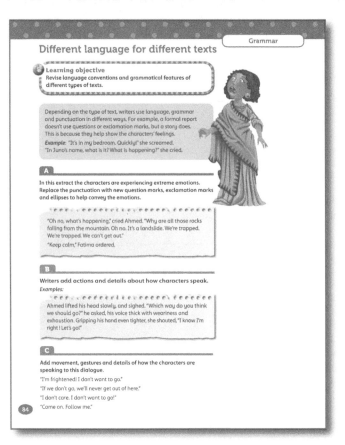

Grammar

Different language for different texts

Learning objective
Revise language conventions and grammatical features of different types of texts.

Depending on the type of text, writers use language, grammar and punctuation in different ways. For example, a formal report doesn't use questions or exclamation marks, but a story does. This is because they help show the characters' feelings.
Example: "It's in my bedroom. Quickly!" she screamed.
"In Juno's name, what is it? What is happening?" she cried.

A

In this extract the characters are experiencing extreme emotions. Replace the punctuation with new question marks, exclamation marks and ellipses to help convey the emotions.

"Oh no, what's happening," cried Ahmed. "Why are all those rocks falling from the mountain. Oh no. It's a landslide. We're trapped. We can't get out."
"Keep calm," Fatima ordered.

B

Writers add actions and details about how characters speak.
Examples:

Ahmed lifted his head slowly, and sighed. "Which way do you think we should go?" he asked, his voice thick with weariness and exhaustion. Gripping his hand even tighter, she shouted, "I know I'm right! Let's go!"

C

Add movement, gestures and details of how the characters are speaking to this dialogue.
"I'm frightened! I don't want to go."
"If we don't go, we'll never get out of here."
"I don't care. I don't want to go!"
84 "Come on. Follow me."

B

Working in pairs. Ask students to read the dialogue and to think about what the characters say and how they speak. *Example:* shouting, crying, sobbing, wailing, etc. Ask students to consider what body language is used in various situations and how our emotions effect the pitch and tone of our voices.

C

Work in pairs. Ask students to read the dialogue and to consider their physical reactions to the text. Ask students to consider how they might feel and what they might do in a tense situation. Would they run or walk slowly? Would they be looking at the ground or quickly scanning all around them?

Students write their dialogues. Ask for volunteers to read theirs out to the class.

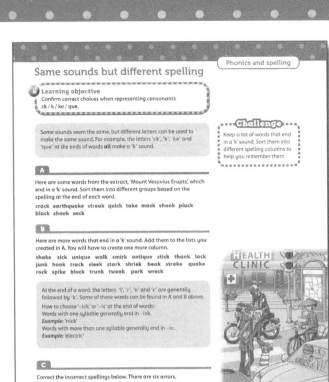

Phonics and spelling

A

Confirm with students that there should be three columns, with the word endings as follows: ke, ck, k.

Answers:

ke: earthquake, take

ck: crack, quick, pluck, black, sack

k: streak, mask, shook

B

Students should be encouraged to fulfil the Challenge at this point, adding as many words as they can to each column. Then make this into a timed quiz. It is imperative that students 'verify' all the words added to the columns with a dictionary.

Answers:

ck: sick, stick, lack, track, rock, block, wreck

que: unique, antique

k: walk, smirk, thank, junk, hook, sleek, stark, shriek, beak, trunk, tweak, park

ke: shake, stroke, quake, spike

C

Students read the text and identify the incorrect spellings and correct them. Ask students to swap answers with a partner and mark them as a class to elicit any incorrect answers or confusion as to the spelling rules.

Answers:

clinike/clinic

panick/panic

terrificke/terrific

traffick/traffic

dramtique/dramatic

horrifik/horrific

Learning objective

Confirm correct choices when representing consonants ck/k/ke/que.

Students know how to differentiate between different consonant letter endings of words with a 'k' sound.

Remember to display the child-friendly learning objective to the class along with the child-friendly checklist that students can use to assess how well they achieve it.

We know that we have achieved this because:

▶ We know how to distinguish between an 'ick' and 'c' sound.

▶ We are able to correct errors of the spellings of words with the 'ick/ic' sounds.

④ Student Book teaching notes and phonics exercise answers

Read the introductory explanation which explains that although words ending in a 'k' sound the same, their spellings are very different. Provide initial examples such as, 'stock, book, make.' Ask students to add other examples to the list. Explain that the exercises which follow will help students to remember which ending to use.

Learning objective

Distinguish between fact and opinion in a recount.

Students to distinguish between fact and opinion in a recount text.

 Remember to display the child-friendly learning objective to the class along with the child-friendly checklist that students can use to assess how well they achieve it.

We know that we have achieved this because:

▶ We are able to distinguish fact from opinion in a recount text.

▶ We understand that fact and opinion have different functions in a recount text.

② Reading non-fiction notes

Tell students they are going to read an account by someone who has won a wildlife photography competition. Their prize is the opportunity to take more photographs in one of the most famous wildlife spots in the world — the Galápagos Islands. Show the islands on a map. Explain that the islands are very old (between 3 and 10 million years), but have been subjected to very little human interference or pollution. Explain that all animals arrived on the islands by swimming, floating or flying, so large mammals did not make it; this meant no predators, and the Giant Tortoise became the most dominant species. In 1835 the scientist Charles Darwin observed the unusual life forms and how they had adapted to the harsh environment.

Refer to the CD-ROM or read the text while students follow in their books. Explain words featured in the glossary when appropriate. On completion tell students to volunteer any other words that could have been included in the glossary or the Word Cloud.

So as to ensure overall understanding, ask students to provide a note-style summary of each paragraph.
Example:

Paragraph 1: Wildlife photographer wins competition to go to the Galápagos Islands.

Paragraph 2: Some facts about the islands and how good they are for wildlife.

Paragraph 3: Tortoises.

Paragraph 4: Marine iguanas.

Paragraph 5: Waved albatross.

Paragraph 6: Due to his experiences, writer now more interested in conservation programmes.

③ Word Cloud definitions

Refer to the CD-ROM. Focus students' attention on the Word Cloud and ask them to locate the word 'breeding'. Can they explain what it means? (The mating and production of offspring by animals.) Explain that in the text it is used as an adjective: 'breeding site.' This means a place or habitat where animals mate and produce offspring. Explain that it can be used as a verb (breeding) and a noun. Explain that the noun 'breed' means a distinctive species that has been developed by deliberate selection, such as a new breed of dog. Next, students locate the rest of the words.

aerodynamic having a shape which reduces the drag from air moving past

breeding the mating and production of offspring by animals

conservation the action of conserving something, in particular the natural environment and of wildlife

species a group of organisms/individuals that are similar

unique being the only one of its kind; unlike anything else

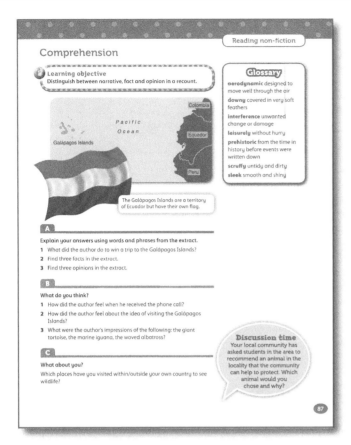

Reading non-fiction

Comprehension

Learning objective
Distinguish between narrative, fact and opinion in a recount.

Glossary
aerodynamic designed to move well through the air
downy covered in very soft feathers
interference unwanted change or damage
leisurely without hurry
prehistoric from the time in history before events were written down
scruffy untidy and dirty
sleek smooth and shiny

Colombia
Pacific Ocean
Ecuador
Galápagos Islands
Peru

The Galápagos Islands are a territory of Ecuador but have their own flag.

A
Explain your answers using words and phrases from the extract.
1 What did the author do to win a trip to the Galápagos Islands?
2 Find three facts in the extract.
3 Find three opinions in the extract.

B
What do you think?
1 How did the author feel when he received the phone call?
2 How did the author feel about the idea of visiting the Galápagos Islands?
3 What were the author's impressions of the following: the giant tortoise, the marine iguana, the waved albatross?

C
What about you?
Which places have you visited within/outside your own country to see wildlife?

Discussion time
Your local community has asked students in the area to recommend an animal in the locality that the community can help to protect. Which animal would you chose and why?

87

4 Student Book teaching notes and comprehension answers

Explain that 'fact' is something that is *known* for certain to have happened, or known to be true. Explain that an 'opinion' is what is *believed* to be true. Often, facts are disguised as opinions.

A

1 Students read the recount to elicit the answer.

Answer:

He entered a photography competition in a wildlife magazine. The assumption must be that he has won the competition.

2 Remind students that facts are certain, and that opinions are believed.

Example answer:

Charles Darwin visited the island in 1835.

3 **Ask:** *Why does there need to be a mixture of fact and opinion in a recount like this?* (Opinion gives a personal perspective and feel. If it was all facts it would not be a recount text but an information text.)

Example answer:

'What a beautiful sight'

⇨

B

These questions explore the opinion and personal side of the article.

1 Ask students to re-read the first paragraph, and find the idiom. Explain that 'I couldn't believe my ears' is an idiom meaning 'I cannot believe what I am hearing.' **Ask:** *What does this show?* (Surprise, excitement, amazement.)
2 **Ask:** *What is the 'again' the writer refers to?* (It means the opportunity to take more wildlife photos.)
3 Ask students to underline key words or phrases which present the writer's attitude towards the animals.

Example answers:

The giant tortoise: lives a leisurely life; weighs 250 kgs; sleeps up to 16 hours a day.

The marine iguana: looks fierce and prehistoric but in fact they are harmless; live off seaweed.

The waved albatross: huge wingspan of over two metres; scruffy, downy chicks.

C

Ask students if they have visited somewhere specifically to see wildlife — a zoo, national park, etc. They share what they saw and what their impressions were with the class. If some students have not made any trips, ask them to explain where they would like to go and why.

5 Discussion time

With students brainstorm what conservation means. (Preservation, protection, or restoration of the natural environment and of wildlife.) Students will need to consider why their choice of animal is important, and why its continued existence is important.

Learning objective

Know how to transform meaning with prefixes and suffixes.

Students learn about the meaning and spelling of prefixes and suffixes.

 Remember to display the child-friendly learning objective to the class along with the child-friendly checklist that students can use to assess how well they achieve it.

We know that we have achieved this because:

▶ We know what particular prefixes and suffixes mean.

▶ We know how to spell words which use particular prefixes and suffixes.

2 Student Book teaching notes and vocabulary exercise answers

Books closed. Ask students what a prefix and suffix is and give some examples: 'un, il' (not) and 'ful' (full of). Explain that in this lesson they are going to find out about more prefixes and suffixes. This will help students with their knowledge and understanding of words and their spelling. Read through the explanatory summary.

A

Ask students to identify words in the non-fiction extract about the Galápagos Islands that contain prefixes. Go through these in class, writing examples on the board. Then ask students to complete the task.

Answers:

con– conservation
bi– binoculars
inter– interference, interested

B

Read through the explanatory paragraph about suffixes with the class. Then students complete the task.

Answers:

hopeless, sleepless, harmless, homeless, lifeless, painless

C

Students could be helped by being given a matching exercise or a word search. Explain that most of the time removing –able from a word will leave a complete word. If you remove –ible from a word, you are not left with a complete word.

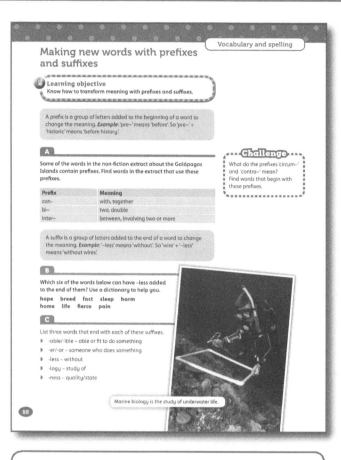

Example answers:

responsible, horrible, terrible, visible, sensible, possible

affordable, washable, readable, lockable, sociable

calculator, investigator, conductor, doctor, actor

reporter, player, fighter, listener, cleaner, diver, writer

hopeless, sleepless, harmless, homeless, painless

biology, geology, zoology, theology, archaeology

coolness, fairness, shyness, blackness, messiness

3 Challenge

Elicit answers from the class as to the meaning of the prefixes circum– (round about, around) and contra– (against, opposing). Once answers are confirmed ask students to provide examples of words starting with these prefixes. **Example:** circumstance, contraband, etc.

4 Extension

Students can extend these lists as an ongoing homework project. They should record new words in their vocabulary notebooks.

Spellings and descriptions

Vocabulary and spelling

Learning objectives
Further investigate spelling rules and exceptions, including representing unstressed vowels.
Explore definitions and shades of meaning and use new words in context.

Sometimes words have unstressed vowels in them. These are vowels (a, e, i, o, u) that are not easy to hear in words. As a result, they are often missed out in spellings.

A

All these words have unstressed vowels.
business offering familiar different easily family Wednesday interest frightening separate generous marvellous miserable generally

1 Say the words aloud several times, stressing the underlined vowel.
2 Write the words with the underlined vowels enlarged or highlighted. This will help you to remember the vowel.
3 Write sentences using each of these words, spelling them correctly.

B

To describe extreme settings, it is important to pick adjectives carefully and to think about their meanings. Read the description of the inside of a dirty house. Choose one adjective from each pair.

No one had lived in the farmhouse for years. There was a pile of (1) dusty/filthy clothes on the floor in the corner of the kitchen, and a pair of (2) muddy/untidy boots still stood next to the back door that led out into the farmyard. The kitchen was the (3) untidiest/muddiest room I'd ever seen. How had the farmer managed to find things? Magazines were piled in heaps on the table, with packets of cereal and a box of hand tools. Books lay on (4) dusty/filthy shelves and the floor was a (5) grimy/dirty brown colour. A little light came through the (6) grimy/muddy windows, which were covered on the outside with climbing plants.

C

Describe a dirty, neglected place that you know. It could be an old house or apartment building, or a garden. Use words and phrases from B.

(5) **Learning objective**

Further investigate spelling rules and exceptions, including representing unstressed vowels.

Explore definitions and shades of meaning and use new words in context.

Students learn about which have unstressed vowels, and related spelling rules and exceptions.

Remember to display the child-friendly learning objective to the class along with the child-friendly checklist that students can use to assess how well they achieve it.

We know that we have achieved this because:
▶ **We are able to spell words with unstressed words correctly.**
▶ **We are able to use new words in context.**

(6) **Student Book teaching notes and vocabulary exercise answers**

Explain the term, unstressed vowels, and what it means. (You don't actually hear them when you say the word.) Read the explanation regarding unstressed vowels. Ask students if they can provide one or two examples of such spellings.

A

1 Read the spellings aloud. With each one, pronounce it without stressing the vowel, and then stressing it, so that students can immediately see the difference and recognize what the unstressed vowel is. Ask students to repeat the unstressed word and then again with the vowel stressed.

2 Ask students to write the words in their notebooks, writing them in such a way that the unstressed vowel is emphasized. Demonstrate this on the board through enlarging, colouring, underlining, or using a different font.

3 Tell students that when they write sentences with these words, the word should be written so that the unstressed vowel is conspicuous.

B

Explain that when students are describing something or somewhere it can sometimes prove difficult for them to think of enough describing words. This can especially be the case when there is a particular descriptive focus — such as dirty, clean, untidy, etc.

Explain that the exercise is going to help students choose suitable synonyms, and to recognize that the precise use of a word is important; synonyms will have different layers and degrees of meaning.

After students complete the exercise, ask students to read their descriptions aloud and clarify and correct any inappropriate choices made.

Answers:

1 filthy, 2 muddy, 3 untidiest, 4 dusty, 5 dirty

C

With the description of a dirty, neglected place that they know, encourage students to structure their answer based on examples of the following:

▶ Focus on just one room. *Example:* the kitchen, their bedroom, the garage, etc.

▶ Focus on a waste ground, starting at the back and moving forward.

▶ Focus on certain places. *Example:* the kitchen sink, the bedroom window, the dining table, etc.

▶ Include something very big, something very small, something that smells, something of an unusual colour, something that shines, something that protrudes into the air.

▶ Write in the style of a running commentary. 'Would you like to see a really dirty, neglected garden? Well, come with me. Firstly, here on our right we have…'

① Learning objective

Read and interpret poems in which meanings are implied or multi-layered.

Students analyse how the poet has used words and sounds to convey the key message and central imagery of the poem.

Remember to display the child-friendly learning objective to the class along with the child-friendly checklist that students can use to assess how well they achieve it.

We know that we have achieved this because:

▶ We understand that the poem is about the metaphoric effects of rain on land.

▶ We can see that the poet has used a range of techniques and sound effects to convey the effect of heavy rain on the land.

▶ We can identify these techniques and comment upon them.

② Student Book teaching notes and comprehension answers

Refer to the CD-ROM or read through the poem once with the class. Ensure students are secure in their understanding of the poem and that the ending is imaginary.

A

1 Ask students to pick out a land-related word from each verse of the poem. *Example:* hills, street's, pavement, traffic-lights. This should enforce the idea that the poem is about the effect of flooding on the land.

Answer:

b The poem describes the land after there has been a flood.

2 Explain that rain has fallen so hard the poet feels the street has become like a river, and then a sea. The land and sea are mixed up in his imagination.

Answers:

cars founder and sink, buses crawl laden as ocean liners.

B

Explain that 'rising mark' and 'gleaming shallows' are not participles because they are being used as adjectives. 'Gleaming' would be a verb if the sentence was 'Gleaming like a new pin, the polished car sat proudly on the road.'

Explain that the present participle 'ing' ending is used to give a sense that things are actually happening although they are still in the poet's imagination.

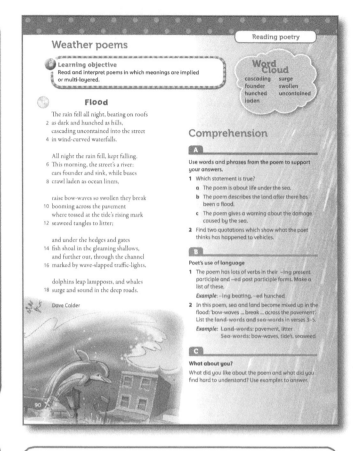

Reading poetry

Weather poems

Learning objective
Read and interpret poems in which meanings are implied or multi-layered.

Word Cloud
cascading   surge
founder   swollen
hunched   uncontained
laden

Flood

The rain fell all night, beating on roofs
2 as dark and hunched as hills,
  cascading uncontained into the street
4 in wind-curved waterfalls.

  All night the rain fell, kept falling.
6 This morning, the street's a river:
  cars founder and sink, while buses
8 crawl laden as ocean liners,

  raise bow-waves so swollen they break
10 booming across the pavement
  where tossed at the tide's rising mark
12 seaweed tangles to litter;

  and under the hedges and gates
14 fish shoal in the gleaming shallows,
  and further out, through the channel
16 marked by wave-slapped traffic-lights,

  dolphins leap lampposts, and whales
18 surge and sound in the deep roads.

Dave Calder

Comprehension

A

Use words and phrases from the poem to support your answers.

1 Which statement is true?
  a The poem is about life under the sea.
  b The poem describes the land after there has been a flood.
  c The poem gives a warning about the damage caused by the sea.

2 Find two quotations which show what the poet thinks has happened to vehicles.

B

Poet's use of language

1 The poem has lots of verbs in their –ing present participle and –ed post participle forms. Make a list of these.
  Example: –ing beating, –ed hunched.

2 In this poem, sea and land become mixed up in the flood: 'bow-waves ... break ... across the pavement'. List the land-words and sea-words in verses 3–5.
  Example: Land-words: pavement, litter
             Sea-words: bow-waves, tide's, seaweed.

C

What about you?
What did you like about the poem and what did you find hard to understand? Use examples to answer.

90

Answers:

beating, cascading, falling, booming

hunched, slapped, tossed, marked

Answers:

Land roofs, rain, hills, street, cars, buses, pavement, litter, hedges, gates, traffic lights, lampposts.
Sea/river waterfalls, river, ocean liners, bow-waves, tide, seaweed, channel, wave-slapped, dolphins, whales.

C

Students work in pairs and to write their ideas on paper. Collect the responses and discuss as a class. Which examples did students struggle to understand? Clarify these with the class, and confirm their understanding.

③ Word Cloud definitions

Refer to the CD-ROM or read the poem as a class, pausing at words from the Word Cloud. Read the definition and discuss how the word adds to the meaning or atmosphere.

cascading pouring down in great amounts
founder fill up with water and sink
hunched bent over
laden loaded with or full of
surge move forward suddenly
swollen full of liquid so bigger and rounder
uncontained not stopped or slowed down

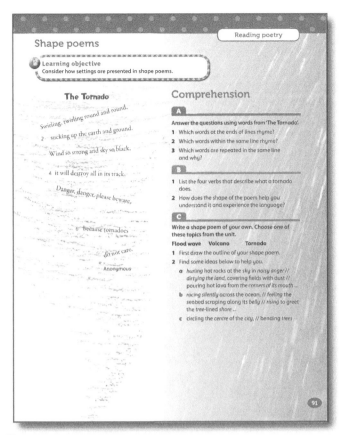

Shape poems

Reading poetry

Learning objective
Consider how settings are presented in shape poems.

The Tornado

Swirling, twirling round and round.

2   sucking up the earth and ground.

Wind so strong and sky so black.

4   it will destroy all in its track.

Danger, danger, please beware,

8   because tornadoes

do not care.

Anonymous

Comprehension

A
Answer the questions using words from 'The Tornado'.
1   Which words at the ends of lines rhyme?
2   Which words within the same line rhyme?
3   Which words are repeated in the same line and why?

B
1   List the four verbs that describe what a tornado does.
2   How does the shape of the poem help you understand it and experience the language?

C
Write a shape poem of your own. Choose one of these topics from the unit.
Flood wave   Volcano   Tornado
1   First draw the outline of your shape poem.
2   Find some ideas below to help you.
    a   hurling hot rocks at the sky in noisy anger // dirtying the land, covering fields with dust // pouring hot lava from the corners of its mouth ...
    b   racing silently across the ocean, // feeling the seabed scraping along its belly // rising to greet the tree-lined shore ...
    c   circling the centre of the city, // bending trees

91

key words such as: swirling, twirling, sucking, strong, black, destroy, danger.' Ask students to repeat the reading, and build in same emphasis. A second reading could focus on the power and might of the tornado building up.

1   Students can complete this activity in pairs.

Answers:

round, ground, black, track, beware, care.

2   Confirm that students understand how the use of internal rhyme puts emphasis on the two words that rhyme, it also quickens the pace of the line.

Answers:

swirling, twirling

3   Confirm that students understand the use of repetition in poetry to reinforce an idea or to emphasize a feeling, emotion, or sense.

Answers:

round and round; Danger, danger

1   Explain to students that the use of verbs helps the reader experience the action of the poem in their imagination.

Answers:

swirl, twirl, suck, destroy

2   Discuss how the sloping lines give a sense of the chaos and movement in the poem (as if the words are being blown around in the tornado).

1   Students work individually, and choose a topic. They draw their outline of the shape poem. Check that they are big or clear enough for students to work on.
2   Read out the three lines supplied as examples. Point out how participle verbs start each line, and the average number of words in each line. Tell students they will need to follow this pattern. Suggest their respective last lines should be about the destructive power of the flood, volcano, or tornado. Perhaps students could have the last two lines rhyming? Students should then be asked to read their shape poems, taking care to emphasize verbs and key words.

(4) **Learning objective**

Consider how settings are presented in shape poems.

Students learn that a shape poem is written so the lines form a shape related to the subject of the poem.

Remember to display the child-friendly learning objective to the class along with the child-friendly checklist that students can use to assess how well they achieve it.

We know that we have achieved this because:

▶   We understand the structure and impact of shape poems.

▶   We can write shape poems about specific subjects.

(5) **Student Book teaching notes and comprehension answers**

Books closed. Tell students that the poem in the Student Book is shaped as a tornado. Ask students to draw the shape for: a flower, a fire, and the wind. They then show these to the class. Can students work out what they are meant to be? Stress that the shape must be clear enough for the reader to recognize, and allow enough 'space' to fit in the words of the poem.

Read through the shape poem, 'Tornado', emphasizing ⇨

(6) **Extension**

Ask students to write a shape poem based on the patterns given in 'Tornado' i.e. rhyming couplets; repetition within the first and penultimate lines; alliteration in the third line.

① Learning objective

Combine narrative, facts and opinions into a recount.

Students to write a recount which combines narrative, opinion and fact.

 Remember to display the child-friendly learning objective to the class along with the child-friendly checklist that students can use to assess how well they achieve it.

We know that we have achieved this because:

▶ We are able to recognize narrative, facts and opinion.

▶ We know how these combine in a recount text.

▶ We understand how to combine these features in our own recount.

② Writing workshop teaching notes

Books closed. Direct students' attention back to the visit to the Galápagos Islands (page 86). Point out the combination of **fact** and **opinion** and how this helped give the account an appropriately personal slant and made the information more interesting. Confirm that the writer was also **narrating** what happened. Just like a story. Starting with the moment he hears of his competition win, then developing into an account of his experiences, culminating in the end of the trip and his subsequent reflection of what had been learned. He finishes with how this was going to impact on his future. Explain that the short extract of the recount they are now going to read from 'Expedition of a Lifetime' combines all these three elements.

Model writing

Books closed. Read aloud the extract. Working in pairs, ask students to copy down the extract and underline in pencil the narrative , opinion, and facts, sections, labelling them N,O, F respectively. Books open, students check answers against the annotation. Were they right? Elicit any questions from the class to clarify any misconceptions.

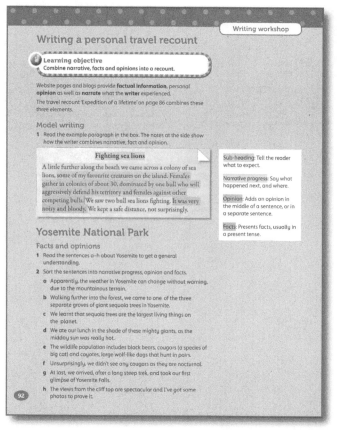

Facts and opinions

1 Read through the sentences with the class. Elicit any queries as to the meaning of the text to ensure students' understanding.

2 Working in pairs, students arrange the sentences into fact and opinion.

Answers:

Fact: a, b, c, e, f

Opinion: d, g, h

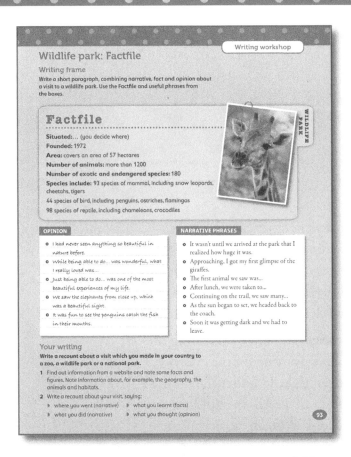

Wildlife park: Factfile

Writing frame

Write a short paragraph, combining narrative, fact and opinion about a visit to a wildlife park. Use the Factfile and useful phrases from the boxes.

Factfile

Situated:... (you decide where)
Founded: 1972
Area: covers an area of 57 hectares
Number of animals: more than 1200
Number of exotic and endangered species: 180
Species include: 93 species of mammal, including snow leopards, cheetahs, tigers
44 species of bird, including penguins, ostriches, flamingos
98 species of reptile, including chameleons, crocodiles

OPINION

- I had never seen anything so beautiful in nature before.
- While being able to do... was wonderful, what I really loved was...
- Just being able to do... was one of the most beautiful experiences of my life.
- We saw the elephants from close up, which was a beautiful sight.
- It was fun to see the penguins catch the fish in their mouths.

NARRATIVE PHRASES

- It wasn't until we arrived at the park that I realized how huge it was.
- Approaching, I got my first glimpse of the giraffes.
- The first animal we saw was...
- After lunch, we were taken to...
- Continuing on the trail, we saw many...
- As the sun began to set, we headed back to the coach.
- Soon it was getting dark and we had to leave.

Your writing

Write a recount about a visit which you made in your country to a zoo, a wildlife park or a national park.

1 Find out information from a website and note some facts and figures. Note information about, for example, the geography, the animals and habitats.
2 Write a recount about your visit, saying:
  ‣ where you went (narrative)   ‣ what you learnt (facts)
  ‣ what you did (narrative)   ‣ what you thought (opinion)

93

③ Writing workshop teaching notes

Writing frame

Explain that students are required to write their own paragraph combining narrative, fact and opinion about an imaginary visit to a wildlife park. Point out that the students have to decide where the wildlife park is. Explain that a wildlife park is a park where animals can live in natural surroundings. The animals often chosen are endangered animals which means they are threatened with extinction. It is therefore important they are given the right conditions so they can thrive and breed.

Read through the facts, turning each prompt into a question which the students have to answer. **Ask:** *When was this wildlife park founded?* (1972) Explain that a hectare is equal to 100 acres, or 10 m². Point out that vast amounts of land will be needed for the animals: they will need space to roam, and to search for food. Read the list of the number of species. Explain that exotic species mean animals from foreign countries.

Ask selected students to read out the opinion comments. Confirm that students remember what constitutes opinion. (What is believed to be true, rather than what is actually true.) Point out the emotive, descriptive words and phrases such as: beautiful, wonderful, what I really loved was, one of the most beautiful experiences, it was fun to see, etc.

Read through the narrative phrases. Confirm that these tell the reader the story of what the writer saw and did.

Tell students to write out the narrative comments in the order they are in the box and to then to carry on into facts and opinions. Students could underline, or write the different components in different colours.

Ask selected students to read their paragraphs aloud. The class could be asked to identify which parts are opinions, narrative, or fact.

Your writing

Inform students that they are now going to write their own recount of a visit to a wildlife park, national park or zoo. If some students have had no experience of this, they could focus on a zoo or park they would like to go to.

Ask students to put forward their choice of place, and those written on the board. Students choosing the same place can be placed together in groups.

1 Explain that students will need to do their own fact finding and complete their own fact file, using the same prompts as on the previous task. Other prompts could be added, such as: how the animals are looked after; the most unusual animal there; how visitors are managed; what the geography of the park is like, etc.
2 Students use the prompts to write their recounts. Split the class into two groups: group one asks for information, group two provides information. Students in group one ask questions that will elicit the responses written in the recounts by the students in group two.

End of Unit Test

Question Paper

Reading: fiction

Read the extract and answer the questions.

The storm

A storm broke over the island that night, such a fearsome storm, such a
thunderous crashing of lightning overhead, such a din of rain and wind that sleep
was quite impossible. Great waves roared from the ocean, pounding on the beach,
and shaking the ground beneath me. I spread out my sleeping mat at the very back
5 of the cave. Stella lay down beside me and huddled close. How I welcomed that.

It was fully four days before the storm blew itself out, but even during the
worst of it, I would find my fish and fruit breakfast waiting for me every
morning under my tin, which he had now wedged tight in under the same
shelf of rock. Stella and I kept to the shelter of our cave. All we could do was
10 watch as the rain came lashing down outside. I looked on awestruck at the
power of the vast waves rolling in from the open sea, curling, tumbling, and
exploding as they broke on to the beach, as if they were trying to batter the
island into pieces and then suck us all out to sea. I thought often of my
mother and father and the *Peggy Sue*, and wondered where they were. I just
15 hoped the typhoon — for that was what I was witnessing — had passed them by.

Then, one morning, as suddenly as the storm had begun, it stopped. I
ventured out. The whole island steamed and dripped. I went at once up Watch
Hill to see if I could see a ship, perhaps blown off course, or maybe sheltering in
the lee of the island. There was nothing there.

From *Kensuke's Kingdom* by Michael Morpurgo

Glossary
huddled to crowd together with other people for warmth or comfort

Comprehension

A

Give evidence from the extract to support your answers.

1 List three things that happened during the storm.

_____ [2]

2 Find two quotations in the first paragraph which show that the storm broke out at night.

_____

_____ [2]

3 How long did the storm last?

_____ [1]

B

Give evidence from the extract to support your answers.

1 The writer does not leave the cave during the storm. Explain how he gets food.

_____ [1]

2 How do we know that the writer's parents are not on the island with him?

_____ [2]

3 What would make the island steam? Tick the correct box.

a heat ☐

b smoke ☐

c wind ☐

d fire ☐ [1]

4 Why might the writer want to see if a ship had been blown on to the island?

_____ [2]

C

Give evidence from the extract to support your answers.

1 List three verbs which show the terrible force of the storm.

_____ [1]

2 What other word or phrase could be used instead of 'ventured'?

_____ [1]

3 How do we know that the extract has been written in the first person?

_____
_____ [2]

Reading: non-fiction

Read the extract and answer the questions.

> ### Antarctica Cruises
>
> Mysterious and vast, Antarctica — the 'white continent' at the bottom of the world — is like no other place on Earth. A land of glittering ice, majestic peaks and dazzling beauty, it is the only continent with no native population. Instead, it has been a haven for millions of years for migratory
> 5   birds, whales, seals, and other marine mammals.
>
> When you choose an Antarctic expedition, you step into a world so removed from your own, you may feel you've landed on the moon, or stepped into a fairy tale. Here the sun neither rises nor sets. Icebergs drift. Curious penguin chicks waddle past you. Humpback whales surface metres away.
>
> 10   Quark Expeditions has been the world leader in personal polar adventures for over two decades. We know these waters like nobody else. When you're ready for the best Antarctic cruise in the world, call us!
>
> If you visit in the **early spring** (beginning in November), you'll see countless penguins marching from the sea to their inland nests. You'll also see
> 15   great numbers of other seabirds arriving at their southern breeding grounds. If you come in **high-to-late summer**, you'll still see plenty of seabirds, along with whales and more seals than you ever thought possible!
>
> Although Antarctic weather is extremely changeable, summer temperatures hover just above the freezing mark, comparable to a warm
> 20   winter's day in North America. The 24-hour sunlight warms air in sheltered areas, so there is some heat. Either way, don't worry. Our Expedition Leaders will make sure you're perfectly comfortable.
>
> Adapted from www.quarkexpeditions.com
>
> ---
>
> **Glossary**
> **haven** a place of safety or refuge

Comprehension

A

Give evidence from the extract to support your answers.

1 How long has Quark Expeditions been organizing Antarctic cruises?

_____ [2]

2 Would you expect to find villages and towns in the Antarctic? Explain your answer.

_____

_____ [2]

B

Give evidence from the extract to support your answers.

1 Find two phrases in the extract which show that the weather in Antarctica is extremely cold.

_____

_____ [3]

2 Find two quotations which try to reassure the reader that Antarctica is not too cold.

_____

_____ [3]

C

Give evidence from the extract to support your answers.

1 Find three adjectives in the first paragraph which describe Antarctica.

_____ [3]

2 Underline the two pronouns in the quote below.

'When you're ready for the best Antarctic cruise in the world, call us'! [2]

Writing: fiction

Write four paragraphs describing an extreme weather event. Please use a separate sheet of paper.

Consider this structure.

Paragraph 1: Show how the extreme weather is building up.

Paragraph 2: Describe the increasing force of the weather, reaching a climax.

Paragraph 3: Show how the extreme weather is dying down.

Paragraph 4: Explain what the environment looks like afterwards. [30]

Writing: non-fiction

Imitating the style of the Antarctica Cruises non-fiction extract, write an advertisement which tries to persuade travellers to visit a very cold or a very hot part of the world. Please use a separate sheet of paper.

Remember!

Explain all the positive features and think of ways to convince travellers that the weather will not be a problem! [20]

7 Performance art

1 Warm up objective

Discuss your own experience of performance.

Students talk about performances they have seen, or been part of.

Remember to display the child-friendly learning objective to the class along with the child-friendly checklist that students can use to assess how well they achieve it.

We know that we have achieved this because:

▶ We can explain our role in a performance/or reason for watching a performance.

2 Unit warm up

Books closed. Write the unit title on the board and ask students to explain its meaning. Confirm that it refers to the act of showing a dramatic, musical, or any other form of show to an audience. An effective performance will engage, interest, and entertain an audience. The 'art' refers to the skills and talents of the performers; they need to be very good at what they do. Explain that as they study this unit, they will come across a huge range of different performers such as clowns, musicians, and jugglers.

Explain that the stage picture (photo 2) is a replica of the original Globe theatre in London where the plays of William Shakespeare were performed in the 16th century. Confirm that Shakespeare is one of the most famous playwrights in the world, writing plays such as 'Romeo and Juliet'. Explain that in the 16th century, the audience would stand around the stage to see the play. Those with more money could sit in seats, and shelter from the weather. There was no indoor lighting so plays could only be performed during the day. Women were not allowed to be actresses so teenage boys would play the parts of girls!

Books open. Read the quote and ask students to repeat it chorally. Tell students that Charlie Chaplin was a 20th century comedy actor, famous for his silent films. **Ask:** Why do we like to know or watch someone who is funny? (They brighten up the day, and make us see the funny rather than the serious side of things.) Although television and film can make us laugh, it is always good to create laughter ourselves. Explain the difference between laughing at someone — which can be quite cruel — and laughing with someone, when the laughter is shared. Ask students to recount funny incidents or lines from popular television programmes or films.

3 Let's Talk

1 Focus students' attention on the photos. Ask which students have:

▶ Taken part in a performance?

▶ Seen acrobats/dancers/musicians perform?

▶ Been to the theatre or circus?

Ask students to share their experiences with the class. **Ask:** What makes for a good performance? (Skill, talent, engagement with the audience, spectacular, etc.)

2 **Ask:** What would you expect to see at a circus? (Clowns, acrobats, animals performing tricks, jugglers, fire eaters, etc.) Explain that circus performers are often colourful and larger than life, but with an extremely high level of skill and talent. Circus audiences expect something extraordinary. Confirm that the photograph of the clown is from a circus. Explain that a clown is a performer who pretends to be a fool and exaggerates this in order to amuse his audience. The clown's character is created by the use of makeup, as well as his costume. Once the clown establishes this 'face', it becomes his trademark, and no other clown may copy it.

116

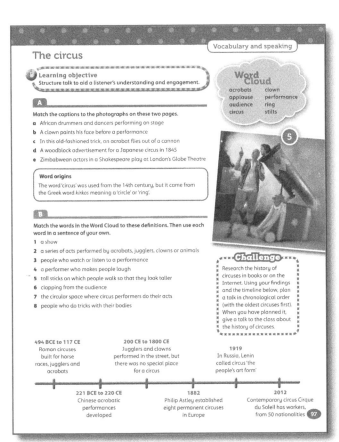

The circus

Learning objective
Structure talk to aid a listener's understanding and engagement.

A

Match the captions to the photographs on these two pages.
a   African drummers and dancers performing on stage
b   A clown paints his face before a performance
c   In this old-fashioned trick, an acrobat flies out of a cannon
d   A woodblock advertisement for a Japanese circus in 1845
e   Zimbabwean actors in a Shakespeare play at London's Globe Theatre

Word origins
The word 'circus' was used from the 14th century, but it came from the Greek word *kirkos* meaning a 'circle' or 'ring'.

B

Match the words in the Word Cloud to these definitions. Then use each word in a sentence of your own.
1   a show
2   a series of acts performed by acrobats, jugglers, clowns or animals
3   people who watch or listen to a performance
4   a performer who makes people laugh
5   tall sticks on which people walk so that they look taller
6   clapping from the audience
7   the circular space where circus performers do their acts
8   people who do tricks with their bodies

Word Cloud
acrobats   clown
applause   performance
audience   ring
circus   stilts

Challenge
Research the history of circuses in books or on the Internet. Using your findings and the timeline below, plan a talk in chronological order (with the oldest circuses first). When you have planned it, give a talk to the class about the history of circuses.

494 BCE to 117 CE
Roman circuses built for horse races, jugglers and acrobats

200 CE to 1800 CE
Jugglers and clowns performed in the street, but there was no special place for a circus

1919
In Russia, Lenin called circus 'the people's art form'

221 BCE to 220 CE
Chinese acrobatic performances developed

1882
Philip Astley established eight permanent circuses in Europe

2012
Contemporary circus Cirque du Soleil has workers, from 50 nationalities

97

Answers:

1 e   **2** e   **3** b   **4** d   **5** c

Explain that in Latin the word *circum*, also means 'around'. Can students think of a mathematical word which uses this root? (Circumference.) Point out that circuses can also be traced back to Roman times where horse races and gladiator fights were held in circular arenas.

B

Students could be asked to add any more performance and circus related words, with respective definitions such as: ringmaster, trapeze artist, tightrope walker, and lion tamer.

Answers:

1   performance
2   circus
3   audience
4   clown
5   stilts
6   applause
7   ring
8   acrobats

Learning objective

Structure talk to aid a listener's understanding and engagement.

Students answer questions, research and follow a timeline on circuses so they have sufficient knowledge and understanding to inform a subsequent presentation.

Remember to display the child-friendly learning objective to the class along with the child-friendly checklist that students can use to assess how well they achieve it.

We know that we have achieved this because:
▶ We understand what happens in a circus.
▶ We know how circuses have developed.
▶ We can structure a talk on the history of the circus, and present it to our peers.

5   Student Book teaching notes and vocabulary exercise answers

A

Students share and confirm their choices with a partner. Check answers through whole class feedback.

⇨

6   Word Cloud definitions

Focus students' attention on the Word Cloud, and read them to the class.

acrobats people who do tricks with their bodies
applause clapping from the audience
audience people who watch a performance
circus a series of acts performed by acrobats, jugglers, clowns or animals
clown a performer who makes people laugh
performance a show
ring the circular space where circus performers act
stilts tall sticks on which people walk

7   Challenge

Students use the dates on the timeline, or add some dates of their own. There should be a maximum of six key dates, and three or four sentences on each.

Ask students to write the key date, followed by their sentences on a series of cards. These will inform the structure of the talk. Provide examples of linking words and phrases on the board.

Learning objective

(1)

Comment on the writer's use of language, demonstrating awareness of its impact on the reader.

Students consider how language is used to create character, setting and atmosphere.

 Remember to display the child-friendly learning objective to the class along with the child-friendly checklist that students can use to assess how well they achieve it.

We know that we have achieved this because:

▶ We can infer how language has been used to create character, setting and atmosphere.

▶ We understand how vocabulary, sentence length, and tension have been combined to create narrative interest.

(2) Reading fiction notes

Tell students that in this lesson, they will comment on the ways the writer, Noel Streatfeild, has used language, and the impact of this on the reader. This involves looking at vocabulary, sentence length, and the management of narrative tension to build up excitement and atmosphere. Explain that Peter (12) and Santa (11) are brother and sister who have been brought up by their Aunt Rebecca. When she dies, they run away to their only other relative, Uncle Gus, who works for Cobb's Circus. This extract describes the very first time they see a live circus performance.

Refer to the CD-ROM or read the text while students follow in their books. Explain that a 'parade' means the walk round the ring by the circus performers so the audience can see what fantastic acts to expect. **Ask:** *What acts are there going to be?* (Uncle Gus on stilts, horses, ponies pulling a coach with a little girl standing up dressed as a butterfly, six elephants with golden cloths on their backs.) Focus on vocabulary which may be problematic. Confirm students understanding of 'bounded' (walk or run with leaping strides); grey (the grey horse which Paula rides); cantered (a horses movement.)

Point out the first act is Paula, a performer who can stand on horses while they are moving. She starts off standing on the backs of two horses, then a third, gradually moving up to a seventh horse. Students could be asked to track this gradual increase in numbers.

Revisit the lines when Alexsis speaks. Explain that he is from Russia. **Ask:** *What difference would this make to how he speaks?* (Confused of past/present tense, sentence structure, word confusion.)

Classic fiction

This text is from a famous classic written in 1938. Peter and Santa have run away to find their Uncle Gus, who works for Cobb's Circus. This is the first time they watch the show. Their friend Alexsis, a Russian acrobat, is with them.

The Circus Parade

The parade went by. There were clowns in all imaginable garments. Gus was dressed as a sailor and was striding along on immense stilts. There were horses. They wore colourful harnesses. The ponies pulled a little coach with a girl standing up in it dressed as a butterfly. The six elephants were magnificent with golden cloths on their backs. They held each other by the tail. On the front one, dressed all in gold, sat a man whom the children guessed must be Kundra. There were groups of people wearing fantastic clothes. When they had gone, it was quite odd to see the ring was still sprinkled with sawdust. It would not have been surprising to see that it had turned to gold...

"This is Paula," Alexsis whispered.

Paula had the same red hair as Alexsis. She was wearing a jade-green velvet tunic and cap. She was standing on the backs of two of the greys. One foot on each. She rode round the ring. Then, just as she passed the entrance, in bounded a third grey. He passed under her legs and as he went she caught a silk rein looped on his back, and drove him before her. Round the three horses went until they were again past the entrance; then a fourth grey cantered in, passed under her legs and was again caught and driven in front of her. Santa was terrified.

"Oh, goodness, won't she fall off?"

Alexsis laughed. "No. She have rode this since she is little."

"How many horses is she going to drive in the end?" asked Peter.

"Seven," Alexsis explained. "Then there are the two she stand on. That makes nine."

The children began to count. Five. Six. They were terribly afraid she would miss the ribbon on the seventh. But no, she caught it, and drove her team out amidst roars of applause.

From *Circus Shoes* by Noel Streatfeild

98

Reading fiction

Word Cloud

fantastic   sprinkled
immense   striding
magnificent velvet

(3) Word Cloud definitions

Ask students to identify words which have been used to emphasize how wonderful and visually stunning the parade must have appeared to Peter and Santa. (Fantastic, magnificent.) You can also refer to the CD-ROM.

dragging pulling (someone or something) along forcefully, or with difficulty

fantastic imaginative or fanciful

immense extremely large or great, especially in scale or degree

magnificent impressively beautiful, elaborate, or extravagant

sprinkled scatter over a surface

striding walking with long, decisive steps

velvet a closely woven fabric of silk

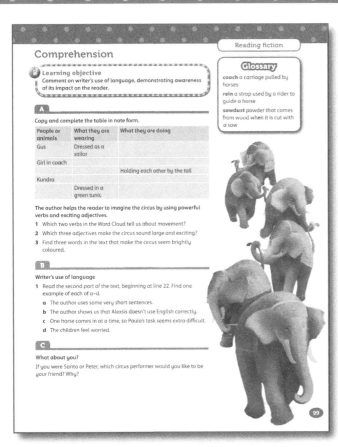

Answers:

1 bounded, cantered
2 immense, magnificent, fantastic
3 colourful, butterfly, golden, gold, jade-green

Confirm that students understand the tension that is building in the extract. The author has used short sentences to create the tension and build interest in the story.

Possible answers:

a The children began to count.
b "No. She have rode this since she is little." / "Then there are the two she stand on."
c 'Five. Six. They were terribly afraid she would miss the ribbon on the seventh.'
d 'They were terribly afraid. . .'

C

Write on the board a range of circus performers and acts. Encourage volunteers to give reasons for their choice.

 Student Book teaching notes and comprehension answers

A

Students to do this exercise individually. Use whole class feedback to confirm the answers.

Answers:

People or animals	What they are wearing	What they are doing
Gus	Dressed as a sailor	Walking with stilts
Girl in coach	Dressed as a butterfly	Driving a coach led by six horses
Kundra	Dressed all in gold	Riding the front elephant
Paula	Dressed in a green tunic	Rides nine horses

Remind students that a verb is a word class that represents an action or a state of being. Ask students to identify the verbs in the first six sentences (went, were, was dressed, was striding, were, wore, pulled, standing, dressed.)

Ask: *What is an adjective?* (A word that gives more information about a noun.) *What are the adjectives in lines 1–6?* (Imaginable, immense, colourful, little, six, magnificent, golden.)

Extension

Ask students to draw and colour an image from the circus scene and then describe what they have drawn in two or three sentences. They could add a thought bubble, and describe what the performer might be really feeling.

119

1 Learning objective

Continue to learn words, apply patterns and improve accuracy in spelling.

Students learn that the 'ou' and 'au' letters make different sound phonemes.

 Remember to display the child-friendly learning objective to the class along with the child-friendly checklist that students can use to assess how well they achieve it.

We know that we have achieved this because:

▶ We are able to recognize the different sounds made by the letters 'ou' and 'au'.

▶ We are also able to spell words correctly which use the 'au' and 'ou' sounds

2 Student Book teaching notes and phonics exercise answers

Read the explanatory summary concerning the 'ou' sound. Explain that in writing, each word is made up of letters, and in speech a word is made up of a series of phonemes. The phonemes in a word do not correspond to the letters with which we write it. Read the examples in the summary box and ask students to repeat them chorally.

 A

1 Students sort the words into the correct groups. Confirm answers with the whole class and elicit any problems the students found.

Answers:

'or'	'ow'	'o'	'uh'
your	shout	boulder	double
bought	about		could
	shoulder		tough
			colourful

 B

1 Read the summary with the class. Confirm answers with the whole class and elicit any problems the students found.

Answers:

aunt, draught, laugh

2 Ask students to read their sentences aloud. Check pronunciation and correct where required.

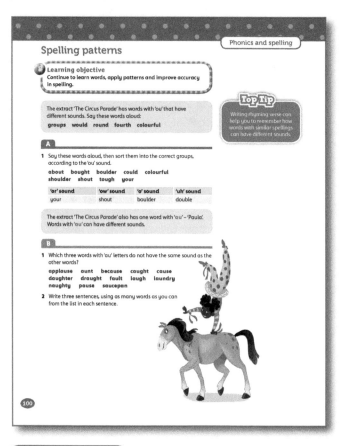

Spelling patterns

Learning objective
Continue to learn words, apply patterns and improve accuracy in spelling.

The extract 'The Circus Parade' has words with 'ou' that have different sounds. Say these words aloud:

groups   would   round   fourth   colourful

A

1 Say these words aloud, then sort them into the correct groups, according to the 'ou' sound.

about   bought   boulder   could   colourful
shoulder   shout   tough   your

'or' sound	'ow' sound	'o' sound	'uh' sound
your	shout	boulder	double

The extract 'The Circus Parade' also has one word with 'au' – 'Paula'. Words with 'au' can have different sounds.

B

1 Which three words with 'au' letters do not have the same sound as the other words?

applause   aunt   because   caught   cause
daughter   draught   fault   laugh   laundry
naughty   pause   saucepan

2 Write three sentences, using as many words as you can from the list in each sentence.

Top Tip
Writing rhyming verse can help you to remember how words with similar spellings can have different sounds.

100

3 Top Tip

Ask students to write a short verse using some of the words with similar spellings and different sounds they have looked at in this unit.

4 Extension

Ask students to add more words with 'ou' and 'au' sounds to the list of words, sorting these into different columns.

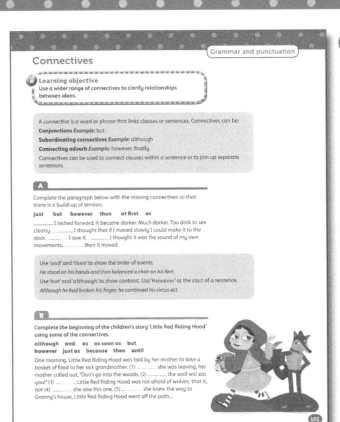

Connectives

Learning objective
Use a wider range of connectives to clarify relationships between ideas.

A connective is a word or phrase that links clauses or sentences. Connectives can be:
Conjunctions *Example:* but
Subordinating connectives *Example:* although
Connecting adverb *Example:* however, finally
Connectives can be used to connect clauses within a sentence or to join up separate sentences.

A

Complete the paragraph below with the missing connectives so that there is a build-up of tension.

| just | but | however | then | at first | as |

_____ I inched forward, it became darker. Too dark to see clearly. _____, I thought that if I moved slowly I could make it to the door. _____ I saw it. _____ I thought it was the sound of my own movements. _____ then it moved.

Use 'and' and 'then' to show the order of events.
He stood on his hands and then balanced a chair on his feet.
Use 'but' and 'although' to show contrast. Use 'However' at the start of a sentence.
Although he had broken his finger, he continued his circus act.

B

Complete the beginning of the children's story 'Little Red Riding Hood' using some of the connectives.

| although | and | as | as soon as | but |
| however | just as | because | then | until |

One morning, Little Red Riding Hood was told by her mother to take a basket of food to her sick grandmother. (1) _____ she was leaving, her mother called out, "Don't go into the woods, (2) _____ the wolf will eat you!" (3) _____, Little Red Riding Hood was not afraid of wolves, that is, not (4) _____ she saw this one. (5) _____ she knew the way to Granny's house, Little Red Riding Hood went off the path...

101

---

6 Student Book teaching notes and grammar exercise answers

A

Read the definition of connectives with the class. Confirm students understanding.

Answers:

<u>As</u> I inched forward, it became darker. Much darker. Too dark to see clearly. <u>However</u>, I thought that if I moved slowly I could make it <u>just</u> to the door. <u>Then</u> I saw it. <u>At first</u> I thought it was the sound of my own movements, <u>but</u> then it moved.

B

In pairs, students to read their sentences aloud to each other.

Answers:

1 Just as
2 because
3 However
4 until
5 Although

7 Extension

Give students a photocopied extract from a fiction text where tension is built up. Ask students to list or highlight the connectives and to then compare with a partner. Do they have the same list?

Learning objective

Use a wider range of connectives to clarify relationships between ideas.

Students learn how to use a range of connectives between and within sentences.

Remember to display the child-friendly learning objective to the class along with the child-friendly checklist that students can use to assess how well they achieve it.

We know that we have achieved this because:

▶ We understand that connectives are required to link sentences and clauses.
▶ We can link sentences and clauses using connectives.

Learning objective

Recognize the key characteristics of an information text.

Students learn how to identify a non-fiction information text, based on content and structure.

Remember to display the child-friendly learning objective to the class along with the child-friendly checklist that students can use to assess how well they achieve it.

We know that we have achieved this because:

▶ **We can identify the features and content of an information text.**

▶ **We can identify how paragraphs are structured in an information text.**

② Reading non-fiction notes

Ask students to quickly scan the text. **Ask:** *How can they tell it is a non-fiction text?* (Information/facts; history of circuses, with suggestions how they could develop in the future; introduces many new terms; does not have any main characters, setting or plot as in fiction.) Confirm that circuses are performances where the audience expect extraordinary things to happen. Generate discussion by asking which act mentioned in the text students would like to see? Tell students that Cirque du Soleil (Circus of the Sun) is Canadian, and made up of circus styles from around the world. It has been seen by 90 million people.

Refer to the CD-ROM or read the text while students follow in their books. In pairs or small groups, read it again and complete thought maps on what they now know about circuses.

Refer to the glossary and ask students to repeat the word 'saltimbanco'. Explain that the word is derived from Italian and means acrobat or entertainer. However, it is now the term given to a type of Cirque show which probably has lots of acrobatics! Explain that a 'theme-based story' (line 8) means a show based on a particular subject.

③ Word Cloud definitions

Focus students' attention on the Word Cloud and refer to the CD-ROM. **Ask:** *Which words have a prefix meaning back or again?* (Revolution, reinvented.) Explain that the Russian revolution took place in 1917. **Ask:** *What do the words review, redo and revisit mean?* (Assess something formally with the intention

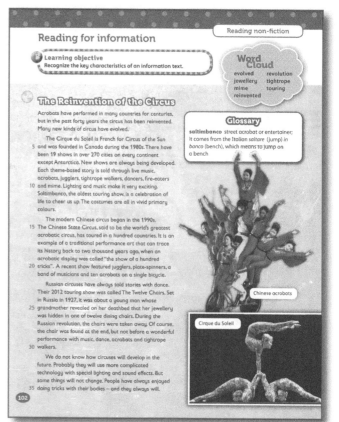

Reading non-fiction

Reading for information

Learning objective
Recognize the key characteristics of an information text.

Word Cloud
evolved   revolution
jewellery   tightrope
mime   touring
reinvented

The Reinvention of the Circus

Acrobats have performed in many countries for centuries, but in the past forty years the circus has been reinvented. Many new kinds of circus have evolved.

5 The Cirque du Soleil is French for Circus of the Sun and was founded in Canada during the 1980s. There have been 19 shows in over 270 cities on every continent except Antarctica. New shows are always being developed. Each theme-based story is told through live music, acrobats, jugglers, tightrope walkers, dancers, fire-eaters
10 and mime. Lighting and music make it very exciting. Soltimbanco, the oldest touring show, is a celebration of life to cheer us up. The costumes are all in vivid primary colours.

The modern Chinese circus began in the 1990s.
15 The Chinese State Circus, said to be the world's greatest acrobatic circus, has toured in a hundred countries. It is an example of a traditional performance art that can trace its history back to two thousand years ago, when an acrobatic display was called "the show of a hundred
20 tricks". A recent show featured jugglers, plate-spinners, a band of musicians and ten acrobats on a single bicycle.

Russian circuses have always told stories with dance. Their 2012 touring show was called The Twelve Chairs. Set in Russia in 1927, it was about a young man whose
25 grandmother revealed on her deathbed that her jewellery was hidden in one of twelve dining chairs. During the Russian revolution, the chairs were taken away. Of course, the chair was found at the end, but not before a wonderful performance with music, dance, acrobats and tightrope
30 walkers.

We do not know how circuses will develop in the future. Probably they will use more complicated technology with special lighting and sound effects. But some things will not change. People have always enjoyed
35 doing tricks with their bodies – and they always will.

102

Glossary
saltimbanco street acrobat or entertainer; it comes from the Italian *saltare* (jump) *in banco* (bench), which means to jump on a bench

Chinese acrobats

Cirque du Soleil

of instituting change if necessary; do (something) again or differently; come back to or visit again.)

Point out that the idiom 'to walk a tightrope' means to be very careful about decision making or considering someone's feelings.

evolved develop gradually from a simple to a more complex form

jewellery items of personal decoration made of precious metals and set with gems

mime gesture and movement without words

reinvented change (something) so much that it appears to be entirely new

revolution a forcible overthrow of a government or social order for a new system

tightrope rope stretched tightly high above the ground, on which acrobats walk across

touring visiting several different places

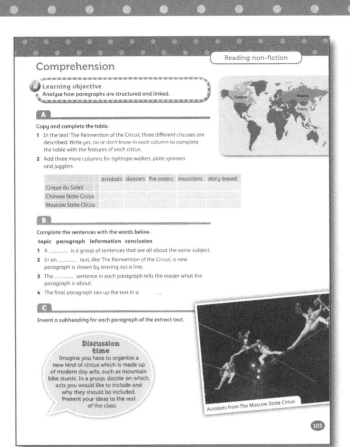

Reading non-fiction

Comprehension

Learning objective
Analyse how paragraphs are structured and linked.

A

Copy and complete the table.
1 In the text 'The Reinvention of the Circus', three different circuses are described. Write *yes, no* or *don't know* in each column to complete the table with the features of each circus.
2 Add three more columns for *tightrope walkers, plate-spinners* and *jugglers.*

	acrobats	dancers	fire-eaters	musicians	story-based
Cirque du Soleil					
Chinese State Circus					
Moscow State Circus					

B

Complete the sentences with the words below.
topic paragraph information conclusion
1 A _____ is a group of sentences that are all about the same subject.
2 In an _____ text, like 'The Reinvention of the Circus', a new paragraph is shown by leaving out a line.
3 The _____ sentence in each paragraph tells the reader what the paragraph is about.
4 The final paragraph ties up the text in a _____

C

Invent a subheading for each paragraph of the extract text.

Discussion time
Imagine you have to organize a new kind of circus which is made up of modern day acts, such as mountain bike stunts. In a group, decide on which acts you would like to include and why they should be included. Present your ideas to the rest of the class.

Acrobats from The Moscow State Circus

103

(4) **Learning objective**

Analyse how paragraphs are structured and linked.

Students will scrutinize the content of paragraphs and how they are structured.

Remember to display the child-friendly learning objective to the class along with the child-friendly checklist that students can use to assess how well they achieve it.

We know that we have achieved this because:
▶ We can scrutinize the content of different paragraphs.
▶ We can identify how paragraphs are structured in an information text.

(5) **Student Book teaching notes and comprehension answers**

Tell students that the learning objective for the lesson is focused on the analysis of how paragraphs are structured and linked. Students will elicit the information provided in each paragraph and determine what functions paragraphs have.

A

1 Students work on this task individually, with responses then confirmed as a whole class. Provide an example on the board to model how ⇨

students should complete the table. Students could be asked to head each column with initials or a small drawing, so as to create more room.

Answers:

	Acrobats	Dancers	Fire-eaters	Music	Story-based
Cirque du Soleil	Y	Y	Y	Y	Y
Chinese State Circus	Y	N	N	Y	N
Moscow State Circus	Y	Y	N	Y	Y

2 Students develop the table used in 1.

Answers:

	Tightrope	Plates	Jugglers
Cirque du Soleil	Y	N	Y
Chinese State Circus	N	Y	Y
Moscow State Circus	Y	N	N

Explain that each paragraph has a clear topic sentence. This is the sentence that tells the reader what the paragraph is going to be about. The rest of the paragraph will then go on to expand on and explain the topic sentence.

Answers:
1 paragraph
2 information
3 topic
4 conclusion

Ask: *What purpose do the headings serve?* (They summarize the information given in the paragraphs.) Remind students that headings should engage the reader and make them want to continue reading. They should also give a clear indication as to what the paragraph is about.

(6) **Discussion time**

Students brainstorm other acts that could be included. **Example:** BMX and skateboard tricks, gymnastics, cheerleading, break dancing, etc. In a group presentation, each student is required to put forward an act and justify why it should be included. Conduct a poll where students select six acts for the new 'Children's Circus'.

1 Learning objective

Know how to transform meaning with prefixes and suffixes.

Students learn how to form new words using prefixes.

🔘 Remember to display the child-friendly learning objective to the class along with the child-friendly checklist that students can use to assess how well they achieve it.

We know that we have achieved this because:

▶ We know the meanings of particular prefixes.

▶ We are able to form new words using prefixes and suffixes.

2 Student Book teaching notes and vocabulary exercise answers

Read the explanation of a prefix, and cite the example given. Point out that students should be very familiar with what prefixes are by now!

Students complete the exercise on their own. Confirm correct answers with the whole class. To extend the activity ask students to find three more words which use each of these prefixes. They can use dictionaries.

Answers:

1 c (underdog, underachieve, underwater)
2 d (overcook, overpay, overdone)
3 a (return, rethink, redo)
4 b (unlock, untie, undo)

Students can complete this exercise in pairs. If students are struggling, provide the answers and ask students to fit them in the right space.

Answers:

1 undercharged
2 replay
3 overreact

Read the explanation of a suffix, and cite the example given. Elicit any queries and confirm students understanding.

Answers:

1 overeating
2 redevelopment
3 unimaginable

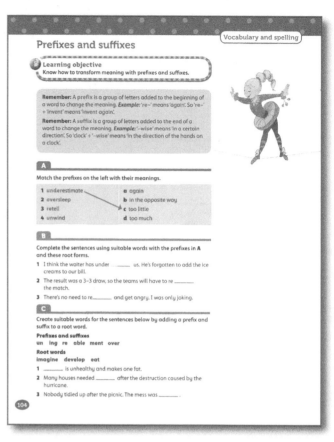

3 Extension

1 Ask students to identify words in the non-fiction extract 'The Reinvention of the Circus' that contain prefixes. Go through students' lists in class, writing examples on the board (performed, reinvented, developed, performance, display, revealed, etc.)

2 Students could be helped by being given a matching exercise or a word search. Spelling games such as Hangman could help consolidate the learning of spellings. Remind students that most of the time removing –able from a word, will leave a complete word. If you remove –ible from a word, you are not left with a complete word.

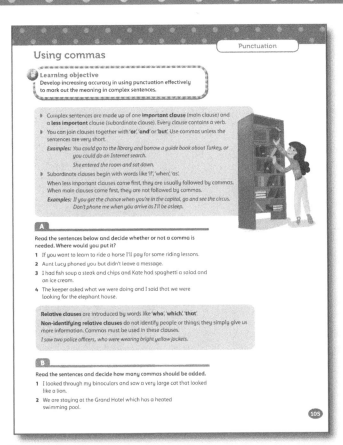

Answers:

1 If you want to learn to ride a horse, I'll pay for some riding lessons for you.
Subordinate clause comes first, so comma required.

2 Aunt Lucy phoned you, but didn't leave a message.
'But' is usually preceded by a comma, particularly in a longer sentence.

3 I had fish soup, a steak and chips, and Kate had spaghetti, a salad, and an ice cream.

4 The keeper asked what we were doing, and I said that we were looking for the elephant house.
Longer sentence, so comma required before the 'and'.

Read the explanation on identifying and non-identifying relative clauses. Explain that the connective can do the work of telling the reader which person or thing the writer is referring to. **Example:** 'The woman who lives next door is a doctor' the connective 'who' is very clearly referring to the woman so does not require a comma to help the reader. However, sometimes the connectives 'who, which, that' are used where they do identify the person or thing. In these instances, a comma has to be used to help the reader. **Example:** 'My brother, who is a doctor, lives in America.'

Answers:

1 No comma
2 Comma

(6) **Extension**

Ask students to write five sentences about where they live and who lives next door to them, using commas to separate clauses. If they find this difficult, they could 'copy' some of the sentences in the exercise, and change the vocabulary so that it fits their own scenario.

(4) **Learning objective**

Develop increasing accuracy in using punctuation effectively to mark out the meaning in complex sentences.

Students learn how to separate clauses with commas.

Remember to display the child-friendly learning objective to the class along with the child-friendly checklist that students can use to assess how well they achieve it.

We know that we have achieved this because:

▶ We know the function of a comma.
▶ We are able to use commas to separate clauses.

(5) **Student Book teaching notes and punctuation exercise answers**

A

Tell students they are going to find out when they should use commas to separate off clauses or phrases. Explain that sometimes a comma is not necessary. Read out the explanation, writing the exemplar sentences on the board so that teaching points can be emphasized.

① Learning objective

Analyse the success of writing in evoking particular moods.

Students investigate particular words and features of rhythm and rhyme.

Remember to display the child-friendly learning objective to the class along with the child-friendly checklist that students can use to assess how well they achieve it.

We know that we have achieved this because:

▸ We understand the poem is about celebration, but also incorporates excitement and fear.

▸ We can see that it uses rhythm and rhyme to simulate dance.

▸ We can point out the words and images which would have an impact on the reader.

② Teaching notes on the poem

Explain that every Chinese New Year Parade ends with a Dragon Dance, considered to be the highlight of the festivities. The Dragon represents wisdom, power, and wealth, and it is said that the dance scares away evil spirits. During the Dance, performers will hold the dragon up on poles, raising and lowering it so as to make him appear to dance to the accompaniment of horns, drums, and gongs. Although the dragon can appear frightening and bold, it is intended to be kind, and giving. Point out that the Chinese New Year begins according to the Chinese calendar so the New Year can begin anytime between late January and mid-February.

Explain that the poem describes the dance of the giant dragon at the dragon parade. Direct students to the illustration — the huge head, colourful, exaggerated mask and decoration. Ask students to tap a steady rhythm as a background to your first reading of the poem. Repeat the reading, this time asking students to join in on the last word of each line. This will emphasize the rhyming couplets. You can also refer to the CD-ROM.

Books closed. Ask students to write down a word or phrase that they remember from the poem. Write these on the board. Explain that the dragon is both joyful and frightening.

Books open. **Ask:** *Which words show the frightening aspect of the dragon?* (fearsome head, ferocious tail, smoke puffing from his head, bulging eyes are blazing red, fearful mask.) *Which words show the joyful, entertaining aspect of the dragon?* (dancing on its Chinese feet, twists and twirls, prancing shoe, fun, gongs.) *Which words focus on noise?* (BANG, explode, shout, squeal, gongs, din.)

Reading poetry

Dragon performance

Learning objective
Analyse the success of writing in evoking particular moods.

During Chinese New Year celebrations, performers take on the costume of a dragon or lion and dance through the streets.

Dragon Dance

A Chinese dragon's in the street
And dancing on its Chinese feet
With fearsome head and golden scale
And twisting its ferocious tail.
5 Its bulging eyes are blazing red
While smoke is puffing from its head
And well you nervously might ask
What lies behind that fearful mask.
It twists and twirls across the road
10 While BANG the cracker strings explode.
Don't yell or run or shout or squeal
Or make a Chinese dragon's meal
For, where its heated breath is fired
They say it likes to be admired.
15 With slippered joy and prancing shoe
Why, you can join the dragon too.
There's fun with beating gongs and din
When dragons dance the New Year in.

Max Fatchen

106

③ Word Cloud definitions

Refer to the CD-ROM. Focus students' attention on the Word Cloud and ask them to locate the word 'din'. Can they explain what it is? **Ask:** *What other words can be used to describe noise?* (Sound, racket, clatter, commotion, etc.) Then they locate the rest of the words.

bulging swelling which distorts an otherwise flat surface

din a loud, unpleasant, and prolonged noise

prancing walking around with ostentatious, exaggerated movements

puffing moving with short, noisy breaths or bursts of air or steam

scale each of the small, thin horny or bony plates protecting the skin of fish and reptiles

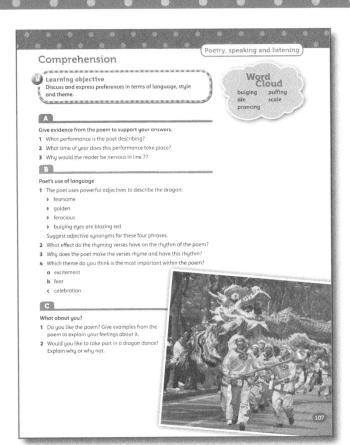

Learning objective

Discuss and express preferences in terms of language, style and themes.

Students discuss and express their preferences in terms of language, style and themes.

Remember to display the child-friendly learning objective to the class along with the child-friendly checklist that students can use to assess how well they achieve it.

We know that we have achieved this because:

▶ We can identify words which direct us to the theme of the poem.

▶ We are able to explain the use of rhythm in poetry.

5 Student Book teaching notes and comprehension answers

A

Students should provide line references to support their answers. The Chinese calendar is based on the lunar year, so the date of Chinese New Year changes every year.

Answers:

1 The performance of the Dragon Dance at the Chinese New Year parade and celebrations. (Line 18)

2 Chinese New Year. (Line 18)
3 The frightening aspects of the dragon mask have been described: 'fearsome head', 'bulging eyes that are blazing red', 'fearful mask'. (Lines 5, 6 and 8)

B

1 Remind students that a synonym is a word or phrase that means exactly or nearly the same as another word or phrase in the same language.

Answers:

1 terrifying
2 gilded
3 fierce
4 protruding eyes flaming red

2 Ask students to write down the end words of each line, and to then count the number of words in each line – generally 6, with the occasional 5. Explain that these two features combine to give the poem a steady rhyme or beat.

Answer:

Rhyming lines give the poem a steady beat.

3 Confirm that the rhythmic pattern of the poem echoes the rhythm of dance. Students read the poem aloud again, incorporating a background tapping and accentuating the last word of each line.
4 Ask students to put these themes in order of priority. Confirm it is the celebration that is important, but fear and excitement will also be integral parts.

Answer:

Celebration

C

1 Encourage students to give valid reasons for the choice.

Examples:

Like it: The Dragon looks magnificent; no need to be frightened, as only a giant mask with people underneath; smoke puffing from the mask; dancing, gongs, and fireworks all sound very exciting.

Do not like it: The Dragon is frightening; too much loud noise; idea of smoke coming out of the mask sounds really scary.

2 Elicit response to the question by hands up feedback. In groups, give students a group of lines from the poem and ask them to present a performance of these lines. Encourage them to use hands and feet to give a rhythmic accompaniment.

1 Learning objective

Argue a case in writing, developing points logically and convincingly.

Students explore how an argument is structured and built up towards a successful conclusion. They follow a paragraph plan for an argument.

Remember to display the child-friendly learning objective to the class along with the child-friendly checklist that students can use to assess how well they achieve it.

We know that we have achieved this because:

▶ We understand how an argument is structured and built up.

▶ We know what evidence we need to support an argument.

▶ We know how to divide our argument into paragraphs in a way that is helpful for the reader.

2 Writing workshop teaching notes

Read through the explanation on what is required for an effective argument. Confirm that the objective is to convince the reader that you are right. This cannot be done through simply telling the reader this; points have to be proved through evidence or example. The argument should either be totally for or against a particular proposition.

Model writing

Tell students that they are going to write their own argument, but in order to do this they are going to analyse two models of effective written arguments: one is against animals performing in circuses, the other one is for animals performing. Through 'hands up', find out what argument students initially support.

Read through the first letter, emphasizing the phrases in blue. Point out how the writer of this letter to a newspaper has expressed their feelings and argument in the first paragraph, and just in two sentences. The reader will be very clear what the letter — and argument — is going to be about.

The next two paragraphs make one point each, but use real life examples to back up each argument. One point needs to be presented at a time, and then backed up with evidence. If you can argue a point and give examples, you are more likely to convince someone than if you just keep on making lots of points.

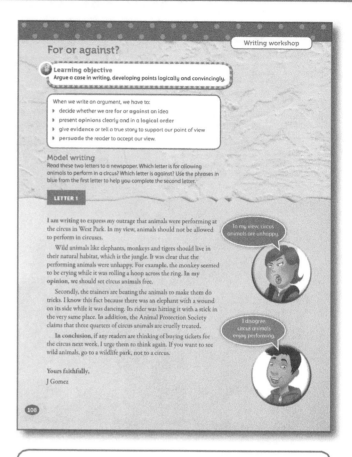

Look at how a statistic has been used at the end of the third paragraph. This can be a very effective way to convince a reader that you must be right — even if the statistic is not entirely true!

Look at the very clear way the conclusion is handled, addressing readers directly in terms of their own behaviour. As the recipient is not known personally, the signing off is 'Yours faithfully,' not 'Yours sincerely'.

Students work in pairs to choose phrases from Letter 1 for Letter 2. Compare answers as a class.

Together read through Letter 2, asking volunteers to summarize the main points.

Students could be asked what other views could have been included in these letters. Elicit students' opinions. Explain that they must support their answer with examples and / or statistics.

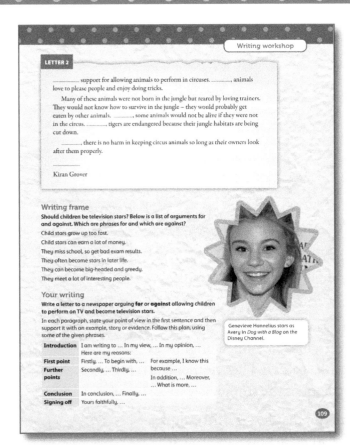

LETTER 2

_____ support for allowing animals to perform in circuses. _____, animals love to please people and enjoy doing tricks.

Many of these animals were not born in the jungle but reared by loving trainers. They would not know how to survive in the jungle – they would probably get eaten by other animals. _____, some animals would not be alive if they were not in the circus. _____, tigers are endangered because their jungle habitats are being cut down.

_____, there is no harm in keeping circus animals so long as their owners look after them properly.

Kiran Grover

Writing frame

Should children be television stars? Below is a list of arguments for and against. Which are phrases for and which are against?
Child stars grow up too fast.
Child stars can earn a lot of money.
They miss school, so get bad exam results.
They often become stars in later life.
They can become big-headed and greedy.
They meet a lot of interesting people.

Your writing

Write a letter to a newspaper arguing **for** or **against** allowing children to perform on TV and become television stars.

In each paragraph, state your point of view in the first sentence and then support it with an example, story or evidence. Follow this plan, using some of the given phrases.

Introduction	I am writing to … In my view, … In my opinion, … Here are my reasons:
First point	Firstly, … To begin with, … For example, I know this
Further points	Secondly, … Thirdly, … because … In addition, … Moreover, … What is more, …
Conclusion	In conclusion, … Finally, …
Signing off	Yours faithfully, …

Genevieve Hannelius stars as Avery in *Dog with a Blog* on the Disney Channel.

109

3 Writing workshop teaching notes

Writing frame

Explain that students are now going to move on to a new argument — whether children should be allowed to become TV or film stars. Read through the reasons given, asking students to indicate (hands up) whether these are 'for' or 'against'. Students work in pairs and list the points given in a 'for' or 'against' column and to add to these. ***Example:***

For: The money they earn could help their family live a better life; can travel the world; have beautiful houses and clothes; have lots of admiration, fans.

Against: Away from their family; can experience emotional problems adjusting to everything; never in one place for very long, so lack stability.

These could be fed back, and written on the board.

Your writing

Next, students decide whether they are going to write a letter saying they are for child stars, or against. Once they have decided, ask them to select only two points from the list. Explain that these will then need to be expanded with examples and statistics.

Ask students to write their letter using the format and linking phrases supplied. They should refer to Letters 1 and 2. This gives them additional guidance on how the paragraphs should be constructed and what 'work' each sentence needs to do.

In pairs, students read the first draft of their letter to each other. Does it have:

▶ a clear two-sentence first paragraph expressing their feelings on the subject of child stars. What is the argument?

▶ a first paragraph with one argument which is then proved through examples and statistics?

▶ a second paragraph which is then proved through examples and statistics?

▶ a final paragraph which starts with 'In conclusion' or 'Finally', and makes a direct address to the reader concerning the argument, and concludes with 'Yours faithfully . . .'?

Students then amend their first draft in accordance with the peer feedback they have received, and then hand in the final draft to the teacher to be assessed.

End of Unit Test

Question Paper

Reading: fiction

Read the extract and answer the questions.

> ### The dancer
>
> *A Russian girl, Lizinka, has joined Samantha's ballet class, and been given the main part in the production of the Nutcracker...*
>
> Only alert Naomi sensed Sam's misery. "You should have had the lead," she whispered in her ear.
>
> 5   Trying to keep the disappointment out of her face, Sam moved towards Lizinka. Her voice sounded shrill to her own ears, but she smiled brightly as she congratulated her. Nodding quickly, Samantha gathered her clothes in a little bundle as if in a hurry and quickly stepped out of the studio.
>
> Walking briskly towards home, she was thankful that it was a little dusky,
> 10 for she could no longer hold back the tears that stung her eyes and rolled down her cheeks.
>
> "I must be a good sport," she scolded herself, "Lizinka deserved the part."
>
> As she rounded the corner to her home, a sob escaped. How could she tell her mother about this? She bit her lip hard to keep back the tears.
> 15 Entering the kitchen, she saw her mother talking on the phone. Mrs Scott's smile of welcome changed to one of concern when she saw Sam's face.
>
> "I've got a little stomach-ache," Sam answered, holding her hand over her stomach and smiling weakly at her mother. "Think I'll just go to bed," she said, heading for her room.
>
> 20 She lay on her back. The pillow felt cool and smooth on her hot cheek, and the darkness enveloped her. No need to hide her disappointment now.
>
> From *Samantha on Stage* by Susan Clement Farrar
>
> ---
>
> **Glossary**
> **shrill** (of a voice or sound) high-pitched and piercing

Comprehension

A

Give evidence from the extract to support your answers.

1 Does Sam congratulate Lizinka? Explain your answer.

_____

_____ [2]

2 What did Sam do when she got home?

_____ [1]

3 Match the explanations (1–4) to the characters (a–d).

1 She noticed that the girl who did not get the part was upset.   **a** Samantha

2 She was talking on the phone.   **b** Lizinka

3 She did not get the main part in the Nutcracker.   **c** Naomi

4 She got the main part in the Nutcracker.   **d** Mrs Scott   [2]

B

Give evidence from the extract to support your answers.

1 Why was Sam thankful it was _'a little dusky'_ on the way home?

_____ [1]

2 Why does Sam tell her mother she has stomach-ache, when she hasn't?

_____ [1]

3 Find two words in the extract which show that Sam was upset and miserable.

_____ [2]

4 What do you think is most likely to happen next? Tick the correct box.

a Sam bursts into tears.   ☐

b Sam's mother asks her to go for a walk.   ☐

c Lizinka says she will give Sam the part.   ☐   [1]

C

Give evidence from the extract to support your answers.

1 Why does Sam _'quickly step out of the studio'_ and walked _'briskly towards home'_?

_____ [2]

2 What word class are _'quickly'_ and _'briskly'_? Adverbs, adjectives, nouns or verbs?

_____ [1]

3 Whose point of view is missing from this extract? How might they have felt?

_____ [2]

Reading: non-fiction

Read the extract and answer the questions.

Matilda the Musical – A review

Roald Dahl's story, 'Matilda', provides a really good starting point for the musical, as the writer always has had the ability to engage both adults and children. The story of tiny Matilda Wormwood is no exception.

5   In the production, Matilda is depicted as a little girl with big hair, and precociously intelligent — reading Charles Dickens before starting school. However, she does manage to be loveable with it, with a charming streak of naughtiness!

Matilda overcomes every disadvantage that life can throw at her. And if home life is bad, school is little better. The Academy to which Matilda is
10   sent is dominated by the manly and little girl-throwing headmistress Miss Trunchbull, portrayed with wicked glee by Bertie Carvel — a man! Comfort comes in the shape of class teacher Miss Honey, whose singing lives up to her name, and the kindly local librarian Mrs Phelps.

Throughout, the story is clearly and effectively told, while Tim Minchin's
15   really catchy tunes, including *When I Grow Up, Miracle* and *Revolting Children*, are truly memorable.

This could have been a high risk project, as it relies not only on a star who is just 11, but also a regular changeover of teams of talented youngsters. The ones we saw last night were really amazing, singing and dancing
20   perfectly. Matilda was played by Cleo Demetriou, and she was superb. She is not so much a star in the making as a star already made!

Everybody will fall in love with *Matilda*, guaranteeing a West End run that could follow the success of *Les Miserables*.

Adapted from www.britishtheatreguide.info/

Glossary
musical a play or film with music or songs

Comprehension

A

Give evidence from the extract to support your answers.

1 Who wrote the original story of Matilda?

_____ [2]

2 Find a quotation in the extract which shows that Matilda did not have a good home life.

_____ [2]

B

Give evidence from the extract to support your answers.

1 What is unusual about the part of Miss Trunchbull being played by a man?

_____ [2]

2 What word suggests Miss Honey's singing is pleasant? Explain your answer.

_____

_____ [2]

C

Give evidence from the extract to support your answers.

1 Find two adjectives which show that Matilda is small.

_____ [2]

2 The reviewer obviously enjoyed the show. Find one sentence or phrase which shows this.

_____ [2]

3 Explain the phrase 'high risk project,' using your own words.

_____

_____ [3]

Writing: fiction

**Write a diary entry in role as Sam. Describe and explain what happened.
Please use a separate sheet of paper.**

> **Organize your writing in three paragraphs.**
>
> Paragraph 1: What were you disappointed about?
>
> Paragraph 2: How did you try to hide your feelings?
>
> Paragraph 3: What did you do, and how did you feel, when you were on your own?
>
> [30]

Writing: non-fiction

Imagine your school has just run a talent competition. Your head teacher has asked you to write a review of the performance for the school magazine. Please use a separate sheet of paper.

> **Organize your writing in three paragraphs. Include:**
>
> Details about the evening and its purpose, with an overview of all the acts that were on.
>
> Commentary on performances which were not good/very good.
>
> [20]

8 Let's celebrate!

1 Warm up objective

Explore definitions and use new words in context.

Students find out new words and their definitions, which they then explain to someone else, using language that is clear and concise.

Remember to display the child-friendly learning objective to the class along with the child-friendly checklist that students can use to assess how well they achieve it.

We know that we have achieved this because:

▶ We are able to understand new words and their meanings.

▶ We are able to explain new words and their meanings.

8 Let's celebrate!

Let's Talk

1 Celebrations and festivals often include: special food, music, lights, singing and dancing, different clothes, fireworks and crowds. Find these in the pictures above.

2 Which of the celebrations in the pictures would you like to be involved in?

3 Give three reasons why people have celebrations.

4 What festivals do you have in your country?

"Celebration is a kind of food we all need in our lives, and each individual brings a special recipe or offering, so that together we will make a great feast."
Corita Kent and Jan Steward

110

2 Unit warm up

Books closed. Write the unit title on the board and ask students to explain its meaning. Explain that 'celebrate' means to mark a significant or happy day or event with a social gathering. Celebrations can be personal such as a wedding, or someone in the family coming home after a long time away. Celebrations also make us join up with others who are important to us (friends, family and community) to mark a special religious occasion. *Example:* Muslims celebrating Eid al-Adha; the Hindu festival of Diwali; the Sikh festival of Baisakhi; the Christian celebration of the birth of Jesus. Some celebrations can be about a time of the year a culture wants to celebrate, such as the onset of the Chinese New Year.

Explain that students are going to focus on vocabulary and explanations related to celebration. This can then be used to inform their subsequent writing (and presentation) of a talk on a favourite celebration to the rest of the class.

Books open. Read the quote. Explain that it is a metaphor, meaning celebration is like food, but missing out the 'like'. It means that celebrations are needed in life to give us nourishment, like food. As each person participates in a celebration, they add to it, bringing their own personal ingredient, everyone combining into the mixture of humanity that makes up any celebration. The feast (a special meal) is the combination of so many people coming together to celebrate.

Ask: *What have students celebrated in the last year? A wedding? A religious festival? Who was involved in it?*

Students share answers, and details of celebrations written on the board. This will highlight how important celebrations are to students and their community.

In groups, students brainstorm words to do with celebration such as happiness, laughter, music, etc. Write these on the board in a celebration shape such as a firework.

3 Let's Talk

1 Focus students' attention on the photos and tell them that they show different celebrations round the world. Ask students to find examples of: special food, music, lights, singing, dancing, different clothes, fireworks, and crowds.

2 Students explain which of the celebrations they would like to be involved in and why.

3 Steer students towards appropriate reasons. Write their responses on the board. *Example:* religious festivals, a new baby, etc.

4 In groups, students undertake a short research task to find out what festivals there are. Suggest each member of the group looks at a different source. *Example:* family; the Internet; books. Students should research the names of festivals, when, and why they are celebrated. Write the information into a large 'Celebration Calendar', which has dates down the side for students to write against.

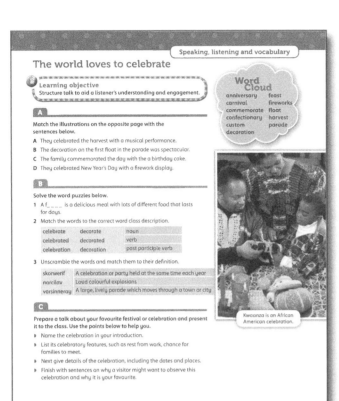

Kwaanza is an African American celebration.

Answers:

A 2 **B** 4 **C** 3 **D** 1

B

To extend the exercise ask students to write definitions of a noun, verb and past participle verb.

Answers:

1 feast

2

celebration/decoration	noun
celebrate/decorate	verb
celebrated/decorated	past participle verb

3 fireworks, carnival, anniversary

C

Ask each student to give the name of a celebration or festival, and why they like it. Use the whole class 'Celebration Calendar' to elicit more suggestions.

Use prompts to model a talk for students. Demonstrate: emphasis on key words; pace of delivery; clear enunciation; posture; eye contact with the audience.

Ask students to write out the details of the four prompts.

Select talks to be presented to the whole class.

(4) Learning objective

Structure talk to aid a listener's understanding and engagement.

Students prepare and give a talk on a particular celebration, structuring it appropriately so that it is of interest to listeners.

Remember to display the child-friendly learning objective to the class along with the child-friendly checklist that students can use to assess how well they achieve it.

We know that we have achieved this because:

▶ **We are able to structure a talk on a festival or celebration.**

▶ **We can incorporate vocabulary about celebration in our talk.**

▶ **We are able to present a talk with content that is developed to interest the listener.**

(5) Student Book teaching notes and speaking exercise answers

A

Students work in pairs and match the pictures.

(6) Word Cloud definitions

Tell students that all the words on the list are nouns, apart from one. **Ask:** *Which word is this? What part of speech?* (Commemorate/verb.)

anniversary annual date of a past event, historical, national, or personal importance

carnival a period of public celebration

commemorate remember and show respect for (someone or something) in a ceremony or festival

confectionary a collective name for sweets

custom traditional way of behaving or doing something that is accepted in a particular society

decoration items that make something attractive

feast a large meal, eaten when celebrating

fireworks devices containing gunpowder which cause spectacular explosions when set alight

float a decorated platform, on a vehicle or towed behind one

harvest a time of year when all the crops have been gathered and collected

parade a public procession

(7) Extension

Students to describe one celebration they have enjoyed over the last year using as many of the Word Cloud words as they can.

Learning objective

Consider how the author manipulates the reaction of the reader, and how characters and settings are presented.

Through a series of comprehension questions, students investigate how character and setting are presented.

 Remember to display the child-friendly learning objective to the class along with the child-friendly checklist that students can use to assess how well they achieve it.

We know that we have achieved this because:

▶ We can infer what the main characters feel, and how they behave from what they say and do.

▶ We can answer questions about the character and how he is presented to the reader.

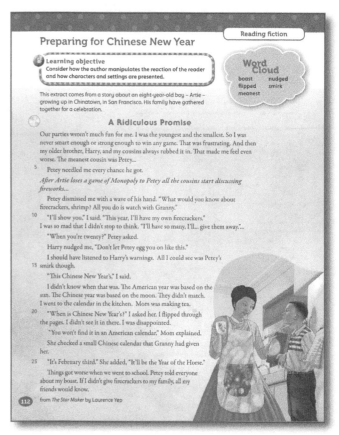

Preparing for Chinese New Year

Reading fiction

Learning objective
Consider how the author manipulates the reaction of the reader and how characters and settings are presented.

Word Cloud
boast   nudged
flipped   smirk
meanest

This extract comes from a story about an eight-year-old boy – Artie – growing up in Chinatown, in San Francisco. His family have gathered together for a celebration.

A Ridiculous Promise

Our parties weren't much fun for me. I was the youngest and the smallest. So I was never smart enough or strong enough to win any game. That was frustrating. And then my older brother, Harry, and my cousins always rubbed it in. That made me feel even worse. The meanest cousin was Petey...

5   Petey needled me every chance he got.

After Artie loses a game of Monopoly to Petey all the cousins start discussing fireworks...

Petey dismissed me with a wave of his hand. "What would you know about firecrackers, shrimp? All you do is watch with Granny."

10   "I'll show you," I said. "This year, I'll have my own firecrackers."
I was so mad that I didn't stop to think. "I'll have so many, I'll... give them away."...
"When you're twenty?" Petey asked.
Harry nudged me, "Don't let Petey egg you on like this."
I should have listened to Harry's warnings. All I could see was Petey's
15   smirk though.
"This Chinese New Year's," I said.
I didn't know when that was. The American year was based on the sun. The Chinese year was based on the moon. They didn't match. I went to the calendar in the kitchen. Mom was making tea.
20   "When is Chinese New Year's?" I asked her. I flipped through the pages. I didn't see it in there. I was disappointed.
"You won't find it in an American calendar," Mom explained. She checked a small Chinese calendar that Granny had given her.
25   "It's February third." She added, "It'll be the Year of the Horse."
Things got worse when we went to school. Petey told everyone about my boast. If I didn't give firecrackers to my family, all my friends would know.

112   from *The Star Maker* by Laurence Yep

Reading fiction notes

Tell students that they are about to read an extract from a story about a young boy called Artie who lives in Chinatown, San Francisco, USA. Explain that this is the largest Chinatown outside of Asia as well as the oldest Chinatown in North America, and one of the top tourist attractions in San Francisco. Although in America, Chinatown has its own customs, languages, places of worship, social clubs, and identity.

Explain that the beginning of the extract establishes the problem that is then going to be developed in the subsequent paragraphs; that because Artie is the youngest, he is picked on, so fights back by trying to make out that he is able to do things he can't. His brother Harry and cousin Petey push him into this by pestering and bullying him.

Confirm that the sentence in bold is to tell readers it is not like the rest of the story, but a summary of a section of the text. Confirm that firecrackers (fireworks) are used during the Chinese New Year celebrations to frighten away evil spirits. Explain that Artie's rash promise to get hold of lots of firecrackers so that he can give them away is a ridiculous (silly) idea because he is too young to go and buy them and has no way of paying for them. His problem builds when Petey tells everyone about his boast. The extract shows how a little problem can soon grow into a bigger problem. His promise is made more ridiculous by the revelation that Artie doesn't even know what the Chinese New Year is — or when it is.

⇨

Remind students that the date of the Chinese New Year changes every year with each year named after one of 12 animals, and that the calendar is based on the moon, not the sun.

Refer to the CD-ROM or read the text while students follow in their books. Ask students to confer and then answer why the extract is called 'A Ridiculous Promise'. **Ask:** *What could be another suitable title?*

Word Cloud definitions

Refer to the CD-ROM and focus students' attention on the Word Cloud. Ask students to list some negative words for laughing and smiling. If students struggle suggest words such as: grin, leer, sneer, snigger, and giggle. **Ask:** *Which word in the Word Cloud could also be used?* (Smirk.)

boast talk with excessive pride and self-satisfaction about what one has achieved

flipped turned over with a sudden quick movement

meanest unkind, spiteful, or unfair

nudged prodded (someone) gently with one's elbow in order to attract attention

smirk smug, conceited, or silly smile

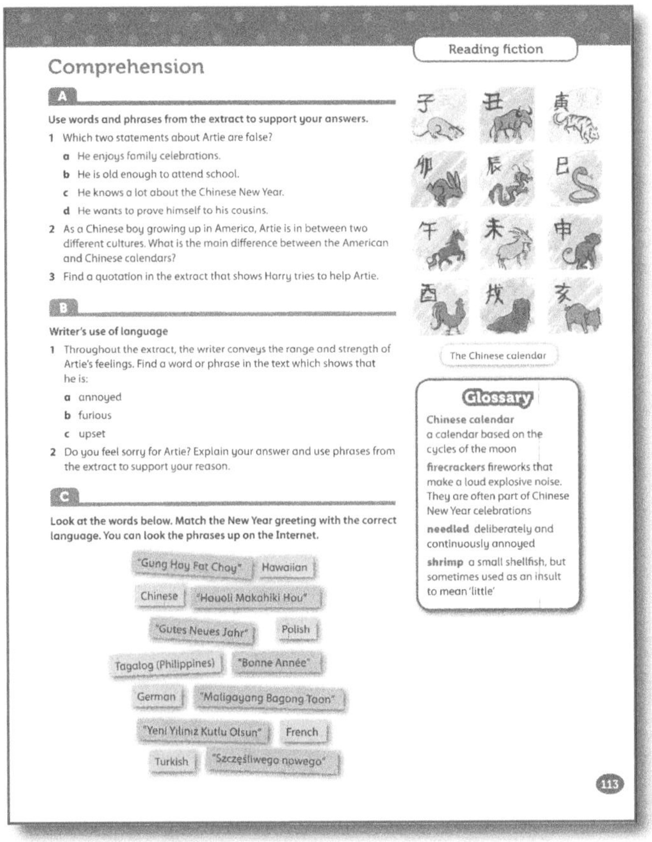
Reading fiction

Comprehension

A

Use words and phrases from the extract to support your answers.

1 Which two statements about Artie are false?
  a He enjoys family celebrations.
  b He is old enough to attend school.
  c He knows a lot about the Chinese New Year.
  d He wants to prove himself to his cousins.

2 As a Chinese boy growing up in America, Artie is in between two different cultures. What is the main difference between the American and Chinese calendars?

3 Find a quotation in the extract that shows Harry tries to help Artie.

B

Writer's use of language

1 Throughout the extract, the writer conveys the range and strength of Artie's feelings. Find a word or phrase in the text which shows that he is:
  a annoyed
  b furious
  c upset

2 Do you feel sorry for Artie? Explain your answer and use phrases from the extract to support your reason.

C

Look at the words below. Match the New Year greeting with the correct language. You can look the phrases up on the Internet.

"Gung Hay Fat Choy" | Hawaiian
Chinese | "Hauoli Makahiki Hou"
"Gutes Neues Jahr" | Polish
Tagalog (Philippines) | "Bonne Année"
German | "Maligayang Bagong Taon"
"Yeni Yiliniz Kutlu Olsun" | French
Turkish | "Szczęśliwego nowego"

The Chinese calendar

Glossary

Chinese calendar a calendar based on the cycles of the moon

firecrackers fireworks that make a loud explosive noise. They are often part of Chinese New Year celebrations

needled deliberately and continuously annoyed

shrimp a small shellfish, but sometimes used as an insult to mean 'little'

113

4 Student Book teaching notes and comprehension answers

A

1 Students should be encouraged to give reasons for the choices, and find evidence in the text to support their answers.

Answers:

a False: Artie does not enjoy family parties. (Line 1)

c False: Artie has to ask his mother to find out what it is. (Lines 19–23)

2 Answer:
The American calendar/year is based on the sun; The Chinese year is based on the moon. (Lines 17–18)

3 Direct students to read through the text again to provide evidence for their answer.

Answer:
'Harry nudged me, "Don't let him egg you on like this."' (Line 13)
'I should have listened to Harry's warnings . . .' (Line 14)

B

1 Answers:

a 'Petey needled me every chance he got' (Line 5)
'I'll show you…' (Line 10)

b 'I was so mad…' (Line 11)

c 'I didn't see it in there. I was disappointed.' (Line 21)

2 Make a list of students' responses on the board. To extend the task ask students to complete an evidence table using their responses.

Point	Evidence
Artie is too young to be getting hold of firecrackers.	'I was the youngest and the smallest.'
He is letting his feelings take over.	'I was so mad that I didn't stop to think'.

Answers:

Feel sorry for him: He is young and small, so he doesn't know any better; anyone would get annoyed by Petey's behaviour; he is only trying to show he is big and as good as the others; he has got himself into a situation and can't meet expectations.

Not feel sorry: He is only small, so shouldn't try to adopt older behaviour; he should have listened to Harry; he let himself be set up by Petey; he has promised something ridiculous; he doesn't even understand what Chinese New Year is.

C

Point out that if students are researching online they will need to ensure they use the correct spellings of the words.

Answers:

Gung Hay Fat Choy	Chinese
Bonne Année	French
Hauoli Makahiki Hou	Hawaiian
Gutes Neues Jahr	German
Maligayang Bagong Taon	Tagalog (Phillipines)
Szczęśliwego nowego	Polish
Yeni Yiliniz Kutlu Olsun	Turkish

5 Extension

Students choose a selection of greetings from C and write them on a sheet of paper. They can then decorate these and add illustrations to indicate the country or the language.

Learning objective

Explore proverbs sayings and figurative expressions.

Students learn what the terms 'idiom' and 'proverb' mean. They learn how to identify these, and to consider why they are used in writing and speech.

 Remember to display the child-friendly learning objective to the class along with the child-friendly checklist that students can use to assess how well they achieve it.

We know that we have achieved this because:

▶ We are able to recognize proverbs, idioms and slang.

▶ We are also able to understand in what contexts they should be used.

② Student Book teaching notes and vocabulary exercise answers

Explain that the extract 'A Ridiculous Promise' uses some slang terms and idioms. Explain these are common sayings that cannot always be worked out by looking the words up in a dictionary. They have meanings which people who live in that country or locality know, but are hard for people who do not speak that particular language to understand. Point out that slang terms should only be used in informal situations.

A

1 Explain that the use of idioms and slang in the extract helps to make it more realistic. Students can complete this exercise in pairs.

Answers:

Rubbed it in: made it worse.

If someone rubs it in, they keep talking about something that makes you feel embarrassed or upset

What would you know about firecrackers: you do not know anything about firecrackers.

Shrimp: small weak boy.

Explain that a shrimp is a small shellfish, so it is a slang term used as an insult.

Don't let him egg you on like this: provoke you.

Explain this idiom means to provoke or tempt.

2 Students could be required to incorporate further idioms in a humorous account of a school trip. Students could choose from: bite your tongue, a bee in her bonnet, a piece of my mind, a bad apple, as right as rain, etc. This account is then recounted to another group. Can they guess what the idioms mean?

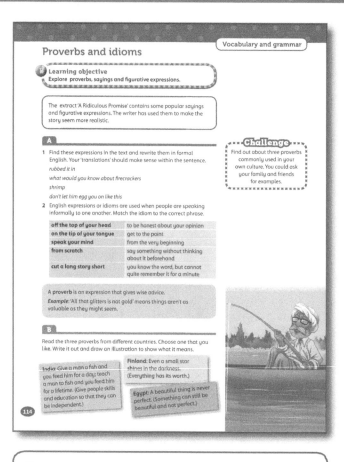

Answers:

Off the top of your head: Say something without thinking about it beforehand.

On the tip of your tongue: You know the word, but cannot remember it for a minute.

Speak your mind: To be honest about your opinions.

From scratch: From the very beginning.

Cut a long story short: Get to the point.

B

Explain what a proverb is, and read the three proverbs from different countries. Students choose and illustrate their choice so it is clear what it means.

③ Challenge

Ask students to find three proverbs that are commonly used in their own culture or community. These should be written out neatly with the explanation and pasted on to a large 'Proverb Chart'.

Ask students to read through all of these, and to choose one proverb they find personally meaningful, and to explain their choice to a partner.

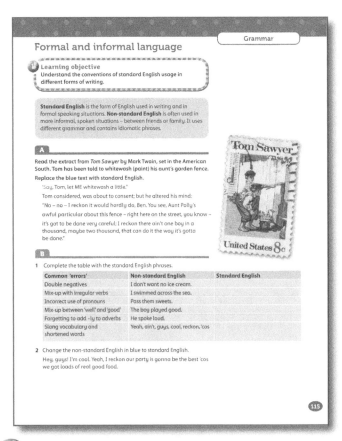

Formal and informal language

Grammar

Learning objective
Understand the conventions of standard English usage in different forms of writing.

Standard English is the form of English used in writing and in formal speaking situations. **Non-standard English** is often used in more informal, spoken situations – between friends or family. It uses different grammar and contains idiomatic phrases.

A

Read the extract from *Tom Sawyer* by Mark Twain, set in the American South. Tom has been told to whitewash (paint) his aunt's garden fence.
Replace the blue text with standard English.

'Say, Tom, let ME whitewash a little.'

Tom considered, was about to consent; but he altered his mind:

"No – no – I reckon it would hardly do, Ben. You see, Aunt Polly's awful particular about this fence – right here on the street, you know – it's got to be done very careful; I reckon there ain't one boy in a thousand, maybe two thousand, that can do it the way it's gotta be done."

B

1 Complete the table with the standard English phrases.

Common 'errors'	Non-standard English	Standard English
Double negatives	I don't want no ice cream.	
Mix-up with irregular verbs	I swimmed across the sea.	
Incorrect use of pronouns	Pass them sweets.	
Mix-up between 'well' and 'good'	The boy played good.	
Forgetting to add –ly to adverbs	He spoke loud.	
Slang vocabulary and shortened words	Yeah, ain't, guys, cool, reckon, 'cos	

2 Change the non-standard English in blue to standard English.
Hey, guys! I'm cool. Yeah, I reckon our party is gonna be the best 'cos we got loads of real good food.

115

Learning objective

(4) **Understand the conventions of standard English usage in different forms in writing.**

Students learn how to distinguish standard from non-standard forms of English, and the corresponding features of both types.

Remember to display the child-friendly learning objective to the class along with the child-friendly checklist that students can use to assess how well they achieve it.

We know that we have achieved this because:

▶ We understand the difference between standard and non-standard English.

▶ We can recognize the features of non-standard English.

▶ We can change non-standard English into standard English.

(5) **Student Book teaching notes and grammar exercise answers**

Read the definition of standard and non-standard English with the class. Confirm that students have just experienced examples of non-standard English in their work on idioms and slang.

A

Explain that Tom was a naughty, but clever, boy. He doesn't actually want to paint the fence, but instead of just saying 'yes' to Ben and thanking him for his offer to paint the fence, he makes out that it is a special privilege to painting the fence and it needs to be done to a very high standard. **Ask:** *How would this encourage Ben to want to paint the fence?* Explain that this is reverse psychology. This means that you do or say something opposite to what you believe in order to obtain a desired outcome.

Students write their 'translations' and compare them with a partner. Correct the exercise with the class. **Ask:** *What was the effect of translating the non-standard English into standard English?* Explain that some of the realistic effect is lost. With the non-standard English it feels like a real boy talking. Confirm that writers will often have their characters using idioms, slang and other forms of non-standard English to make them seem real. However, if they use too much, readers might not understand it.

Answers:

Please, Tom, let ME . . .

No – no – I think it would not be right / enough.

You see, Aunt Polly is very particular about this fence . . .
It's got to be done very carefully . . .

I think there is not one boy… .

B

Students complete the exercise. Go through the correct answers as a class. Confirm that more formal speech would not use the apostrophe for omission. Confirm that the extract used just enough informal language to suggest a real boy living in the American South. The majority of it was standard English, so would be accessible to most readers.

Answers:

1 I don't want any ice cream
   I swam across the sea.
   Pass the sweets.
   The boy played well.
   He spoke loudly.
   Yes, is/are not, you/people, good, think, because

2 Hello everyone, I am all right. Yes, I think our party is going to be the best because we have lots of excellent food.

1 Learning objective

Compare the language, style and impact of a range of non-fiction writing.

Students answer questions on the features of the non–fiction text.

Remember to display the child-friendly learning objective to the class along with the child-friendly checklist that students can use to assess how well they achieve it.

We know that we have achieved this because:

▶ **We are able to answer questions about the features of a non-fiction information text.**

▶ **We can understand why subheadings have been used.**

▶ **We are able to distinguish between facts and personal information.**

▶ **We can summarize key points.**

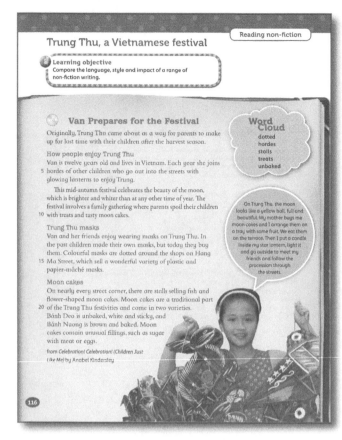

2 Reading non-fiction notes

Show students where Vietnam in on the world map.

Explain that the Trung Thu festival dates back as far as 20 000 years ago in Southeast Asia. It was celebrated after the harvest so that children could spend more time with their parents. It was held under the full moon, which represents fullness and prosperity of life. It is customary to give boxes of moon cakes. These generally have a bright yolk in the centre to represent the moon. Children parade on the streets, while singing and carrying colourful lanterns of different sizes. Some of the popular shapes include fish, stars, butterflies and a lantern that spins when a candle is inserted, representing the Earth circling the Sun. Dances include the dragon dance and the flower dance.

Refer to the CD-ROM or read the text while students follow in their books. In pairs or small groups, they read it again and write down a bullet point list of what they have learned about the Trung Thu festival. They should refer to the glossary to help them. **Ask:** *What is similar and different to an important celebration in their own culture?*

3 Word Cloud definitions

Focus students' attention on the Word Cloud and refer to the CD-ROM. Remind students that the 'un' prefix means 'not'. **Ask:** *What does 'unusual' mean in the text?* Explain that it means something that is not common. **Ask:** *Do students often have sugar with meat or eggs? What unusual foods do they eat?*

dotted scattered, spread

hordes large groups of people

stalls stands or booths, for the sale of goods in a market

treats events or items that are out of the ordinary and give great pleasure

unbaked not baked, uncooked

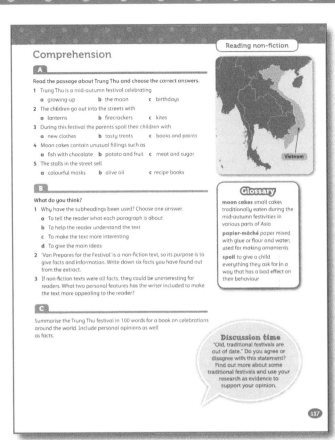

Point out that phrases like, 'brighter and whiter than any other time of the year . . .' / 'tasty moon cakes . . .' / 'Van and her friends enjoy wearing masks on Trung Thu' are all a matter of personal opinion.

3 Personal features include the references we have seen in the answers to question 2. ***Examples:*** 'Van is twelve years old and lives in Vietnam.' / 'Parents spoil their children . . .' / 'Van and her friends enjoy wearing masks on Trung Thu.'
Point out that focusing on one girl and her friends gives a personal perspective. The speech bubble focuses on Van's experience of the festival. It's personal and emotive and makes the text more real for the reader.

C

In writing a summary, students could use some of the following techniques:

▶ Create a mind map or spider diagram of the main points.
▶ Use a note grid, with 'Main points' on one side, 'Supporting detail' on the other.
▶ List key words and information in their notebooks.
▶ Summarize the text on one side of a postcard, with headings and subheadings.
▶ On a photocopy of the extract, remove all non-essential words from sentences.

⑤ Discussion time

Read the task with the class. Elicit a response with 'hands up'. Remind students that celebrations are about celebrating something that is important and worth celebrating. Ask students to research two or three traditional festivals they feel support their view. They should then use their findings to support their argument. Students present their research and evidence to the class as a short talk.

⑥ Extension

Students design and make a poster advertising the festivals they researched for Discussion time.

④ Student Book teaching notes and comprehension answers

A

Remind students that before selecting an answer they need to find the reference in the extract to support their choice.

Answers:

1 b **2** a **3** b **4** c **5** a

B

Ask students how many subheadings are used and what they are. (How people enjoy Trung Thu, Trung Thu masks, Moon cakes.) This should ensure they understand the feature and how it is used. Explain that questions 2 and 3 are asking for their own opinion. Point out that in order to provide a reasoned and rational point of view they will need to support this with evidence from the extract.

Answers:

1 **a**: To tell the reader what each paragraph is about.
2 There are many facts students can choose from. ***Examples:*** 'Van is twelve years old and lives in Vietnam.' / 'This mid-autumn festival celebrates the beauty of the moon' / 'Moon cakes are a traditional part of the Trung Thu festivities'.

Learning objective

① Use connectives to structure an argument or a discussion.

Students learn about a range of different connectives and how they can be used to connect and link ideas for the reader.

 Remember to display the child-friendly learning objective to the class along with the child-friendly checklist that students can use to assess how well they achieve it.

We know that we have achieved this because:

▶ We know that the right type of connective must be used to join sentences.

▶ We can use the right type of connective to join sentences in our own writing.

② Student Book teaching notes and grammar exercise answers

A

Read through the explanation of connectives. Explain that they are words or phrases that link one sentence to the next for the reader, so helping them follow ideas and make sense of things.

Answers:

a <u>Although</u> he was a good sportsman, John was not good at basketball.

b <u>When</u> he has had a new teacher, he quickly improved.

c <u>During</u> her time at junior school, she played in many tennis matches.

d <u>Since</u> leaving Hong Kong, Anya had not celebrated Chinese New Year.

B

Students complete the task on their own. They should read it through to check it makes sense and then swap with a partner for correction. Elicit feedback on incorrect answers to clarify for the whole class.

Answers:

<u>Firstly</u>, I would like to make the point that celebrations make people happier. <u>If</u> there were no celebrations, the world would be a very dull place. <u>On the other hand</u>, if there were too many celebrations, no work would get done! <u>Similarly</u>, if celebrations last too long, they can get in the way of daily life. <u>However</u>, I would like to make a plea that we do not lose our celebrations across the world. They are very important!

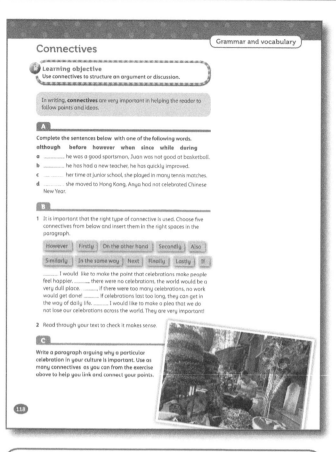

Connectives

Learning objective
Use connectives to structure an argument or discussion.

In writing, **connectives** are very important in helping the reader to follow points and ideas.

A

Complete the sentences below with one of the following words.

although　before　however　when　since　while　during

a _____ he was a good sportsman, Juan was not good at basketball.

b _____ he has had a new teacher, he has quickly improved.

c _____ her time at junior school, she played in many tennis matches.

d _____ she moved to Hong Kong, Anya had not celebrated Chinese New Year.

B

1 It is important that the right type of connective is used. Choose five connectives from below and insert them in the right spaces in the paragraph.

| However | Firstly | On the other hand | Secondly | Also |
| Similarly | In the same way | Next | Finally | Lastly | If |

_____ I would like to make the point that celebrations make people feel happier. _____ there were no celebrations, the world would be a very dull place. _____ if there were too many celebrations, no work would get done! _____ If celebrations last too long, they can get in the way of daily life. _____ I would like to make a plea that we do not lose our celebrations across the world. They are very important!

2 Read through your text to check it makes sense.

C

Write a paragraph arguing why a particular celebration in your culture is important. Use as many connectives as you can from the exercise above to help you link and connect your points.

118

C

Students write the paragraph using a variety of connectives. Ask for volunteers to read their paragraphs to the class. Correct any errors and clarify with the whole class.

③ Extension

Ask students to keep a tally of the number of connectives they use in their writing over the period of a day or a week. Individual targets can be set for students based upon frequency and range.

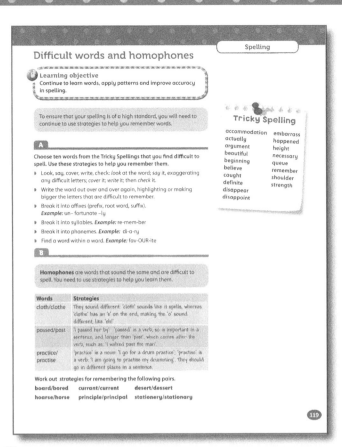

Spelling

Difficult words and homophones

Learning objective
Continue to learn words, apply patterns and improve accuracy in spelling.

To ensure that your spelling is of a high standard, you will need to continue to use strategies to help you remember words.

A

Choose ten words from the Tricky Spellings that you find difficult to spell. Use these strategies to help you remember them.

▶ Look, say, cover, write, check: *look* at the word; *say* it, exaggerating any difficult letters; *cover* it; *write* it; then *check* it.
▶ Write the word out over and over again, highlighting or making bigger the letters that are difficult to remember.
▶ Break it into affixes (prefix, root word, suffix). *Example:* un– fortunate –ly
▶ Break it into syllables. *Example:* re-mem-ber
▶ Break it into phonemes. *Example:* di-a-ry
▶ Find a word within a word. *Example:* fav-OUR-ite

B

Homophones are words that sound the same and are difficult to spell. You need to use strategies to help you learn them.

Words	Strategies
cloth/clothe	They sound different. 'cloth' sounds like it spells, whereas 'clothe' has an 'e' on the end, making the 'o' sound different, like 'oh!'
passed/past	'I passed her by': 'passed' is a verb, so is important in a sentence, and longer than 'past', which comes after the verb, such as: 'I walked past the man'.
practice/ practise	'practice' is a noun: 'I go for a drum practice'; 'practise' is a verb: 'I am going to practise my drumming'. They should go in different places in a sentence.

Work out strategies for remembering the following pairs.

board/bored   currant/current   desert/dessert
hoarse/horse   principle/principal   stationery/stationary

119

Tricky Spelling

accommodation   embarrass
actually   happened
argument   height
beautiful   necessary
beginning   queue
believe   remember
caught   shoulder
definite   strength
disappear
disappoint

Learning objective

④ **Continue to learn words, apply patterns and improve accuracy in spelling.**

Students learn new strategies to remember spelling rules for difficult vocabulary.

Remember to display the child-friendly learning objective to the class along with the child-friendly checklist that students can use to assess how well they achieve it.

We know that we have achieved this because:

▶ We can use strategies to remember the spelling of difficult words.
▶ We can spell words correctly.

⑤ **Student Book teaching notes and spelling exercise answers**

Books closed. Tell students they are going to do a spelling test. Choose a selection of words (up to ten) from the tricky spellings list. Check answers as a class, and keep a tally of the words most often spelt incorrectly. Use these as additional examples when you present strategies for remembering spelling rules. Explain that to remember spellings, students will need to help their brain remember — and that is what they are going to learn in this lesson.

⇨

A

Demonstrate each of the strategies for students, and allow them to ask any questions concerning these. Explain that remembering spellings is to do with visual memory. The brain likes patterns, so finds it difficult to remember individual letter; therefore, it is important to use patterns and groups such as: a spelling rule based on a letter group or a letter string such as 'lastic' in 'plastic elastic'; finding a word within a word; breaking a word into syllables or phonemes. Point out that when using the 'look, say, cover, write, check' system it needs to be premised on some system of visual recall.

B

Read through the explanation text with the class. Ask the class if they can think of any other examples of homophones. Elicit examples such as: allowed/aloud, sea/see, board/bored, etc.

Read through the exercise for students, pointing out that everyone will have different ways of remembering these words. However, the notes should give students some clues to how words with the same sound can be remembered.

Students should write down the strategies they have devised and share these with the class.

⑥ **Extension**

Ask students to keep a spelling notebook. They should write a difficult spelling on each page. They should also write down the strategies they want to use for remembering these. These should include a spelling rule (if applicable) or similar letter string. In both these cases, the student should write out words with the same pattern/letter string.

① Learning objective

Comment on the writer's use of language, demonstrating awareness of its impact on the reader.

Students to identify features of language in the poem and its impact on the reader.

 Remember to display the child-friendly learning objective to the class along with the child-friendly checklist that students can use to assess how well they achieve it.

We know that we have achieved this because:

▶ We understand how language has been used to create a particular impact.

▶ We can explain why particular words have been used.

② Teaching notes on the poem

Direct students attention to the photograph of the Boab tree, its strange shape, upturned branches and explain that there is a huge hole (cavern) in its trunk. Explain that it was used in the 1890s as a jail for prisoners on their way to the nearby court for sentencing. It was also used to store water to keep it cool. It has been estimated that 120,000 litres of water can be stored in the trunk and branches of the tree itself. It is now a tourist attraction and a week-long 'Tree Festival' is held there when its flower, called the wattle, blooms. This includes events such as mud football and watermelon seed spitting!

Explain that Aboriginal people are indigenous to Australia, and lived there long before the British arrived in the 18th century. Point out that one reason for the festival is that the Boab tree is next to an Aboriginal site where meetings, ceremonies, dances and songs were performed. This is a kind of religious theatre space, called the Corroboree.

Before the poem is read explain the glossary words. Explain that the Dreamtime is the time when the religious beliefs of the Aboriginal Australians are celebrated and explored. Many of these ceremonies are sacred.

Refer to the CD-ROM or read the poem while students follow in their books. In pairs or small groups, they read it again and write down a one sentence summary of what they think the poem is about, and which words and phrases they do not understand. Ask students to report these either orally or in writing. This will inform the subsequent teaching of the poem.

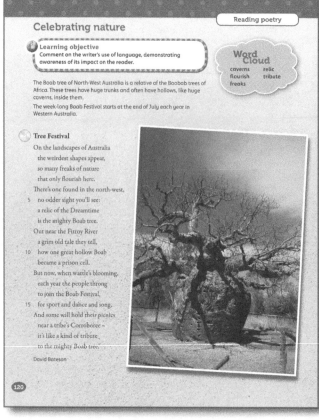

Celebrating nature

Learning objective
Comment on the writer's use of language, demonstrating awareness of its impact on the reader.

Word Cloud
caverns   relic
flourish   tribute
freaks

The Boab tree of North-West Australia is a relative of the Boobab trees of Africa. These trees have huge trunks and often have hollows, like huge caverns, inside them.
The week-long Boab Festival starts at the end of July each year in Western Australia.

Tree Festival

On the landscapes of Australia
  the weirdest shapes appear,
  so many freaks of nature
  that only flourish here.
5 There's one found in the north-west,
  no odder sight you'll see:
  a relic of the Dreamtime
  is the mighty Boab tree.
  Out near the Fitzroy River
  a grim old tale they tell,
10 how one great hollow Boab
  became a prison cell.
  But now, when wattle's blooming,
  each year the people throng
  to join the Boab Festival,
15 for sport and dance and song.
  And some will hold their picnics
  near a tribe's Corroboree –
  it's like a kind of tribute
  to the mighty Boab tree.

David Bateson

120

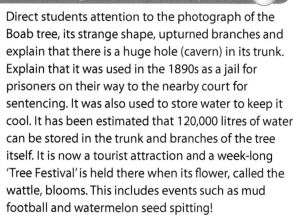

③ Word Cloud definitions

Direct students attention to the Word Cloud and refer to the CD-ROM. **Ask:** *Which word means a large, dark space?* (Cavern.) *What does cavernous mean?* (Like a cavern in size, shape, or atmosphere.) **Ask:** *Which word means unusual physical irregularity?* (Freak.) Can students explain the term 'freaks of nature'? Elicit responses around the fact that the Boab tree is unusual, weird and strange.

caverns large, dark places or spaces in a cave or chamber

flourish grow or develop in a healthy or vigorous way

freaks people, animals, or plants with an unusual physical irregularity

relic an object that has survived from an earlier time, especially one of historical interest

tribute an act or gift that is intended to show gratitude, respect, or admiration

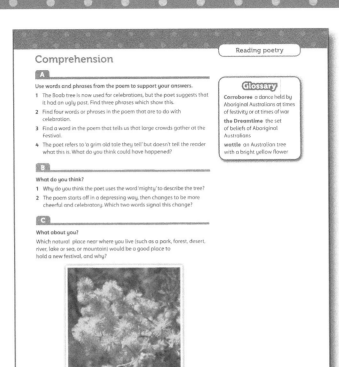

Comprehension

A

Use words and phrases from the poem to support your answers.

1 The Boab tree is now used for celebrations, but the poet suggests that it had an ugly past. Find three phrases which show this.

2 Find four words or phrases in the poem that are to do with celebration.

3 Find a word in the poem that tells us that large crowds gather at the Festival.

4 The poet refers to 'a grim old tale they tell' but doesn't tell the reader what this is. What do you think could have happened?

Glossary

Corroboree a dance held by Aboriginal Australians at times of festivity or at times of war

the Dreamtime the set of beliefs of Aboriginal Australians

wattle an Australian tree with a bright yellow flower

B

What do you think?

1 Why do you think the poet uses the word 'mighty' to describe the tree?

2 The poem starts off in a depressing way, then changes to be more cheerful and celebratory. Which two words signal this change?

C

What about you?

Which natural place near where you live (such as a park, forest, desert, river, lake or sea, or mountain) would be a good place to hold a new festival, and why?

The golden wattle is the national flower of Australia.

121

(4) Student Book teaching notes and comprehension answers

Explain that the poem, *Tree Festival* refers to the Boab Tree Festival which is held every year in Australia. The tree is next to the site of the place where the Aboriginal people would perform dances and other activities in 'the Dreamtime' — the Corroboree. This makes the tree especially significant — not only in how to looks, but its past and its situation near an Aboriginal performance ground.

The poem tells us that people who go to the festival are very mindful of this, 'It's like a mighty tribute, to the mighty Boab tree.' Tell students they are going to investigate the language used by the poet to create the unsettling effect on the reader, and affirming the presence of the 'mighty Boab tree.'

A

Students need to reference extracts from the poem as evidence for their answers.

Answers:

1 'many freaks of nature / that only flourish here'; 'no odder sight you'll see; 'a relic of the Dreamtime'; 'a grim old tale they tell'; 'became a prison cell.'

2 Sport, dance, song, picnics.

3 Throng

4 Students' suggestions will be varied. They could pick up on the prison or water aspect and relate these to the Corroboree or the Dreamtime.

Example: Someone died in the prison there inside the tree and the body was only discovered much later; someone died in the Boab tree during a fight, and whose body was never found. Perhaps a ghost haunts the tree and the nearby Corroboree; the spirits of the dead prisoner are said to join in a dance of the Aboriginal people, etc.

B

Explain that the term 'mighty' is almost personifying the tree – saying it is strong and forceful. The tree has had an effect on the environment and the people around it, and continues to do so. So much so, people want to hold a festival here. **Ask:** *Why is the reference to the 'mighty Boab tree' the last line of the poem?* (To leave the reader with the impression of its dominance, strength, and the respect with which it is held.)

1 'Mighty' means possessing great and impressive power or strength.

2 'But now . . .'

C

Brainstorm with students all the nearby natural places in the local environment, and then decide on what features are required of a festival site:

▷ Good roads, and accessible transport links.

▷ Large enough space to accommodate lots of people.

▷ Seems beautiful, special in some way.
Example: lots of unusual trees, good views, etc.

Learning objective

①

Adapt the conventions of the text type for a particular purpose

Students find out about the features of instruction texts and adopt these in their own writing.

Remember to display the child-friendly learning objective to the class along with the child-friendly checklist that students can use to assess how well they achieve it.

We know that we have achieved this because:

▶ We know what features are required to write an instruction text.

▶ We can adopt these features in the writing of our own instructions.

② Writing workshop teaching notes

Read the description of instructions and explanations. Point out that instructions give you the step by step journey of how to do something. Explanations generally give you the reasons of how, or why, something works. Give some examples of instructions — recipes, how to install a new computer game, etc. Tell students that instructions will often include short snippets of explanation — that is, giving the reason why something has to be done. ***Example:*** in a pastry recipe requiring that cold butter is needed as part of a recipe. An explanation would then tell you why it has to be cold: to ensure the pastry will be flaky and light. This will make the reader more inclined to make sure the butter is cold!

Model writing

Take students through the features of instructions:

▶ Purpose stated as a headline. ***Example:*** 'How to make a lantern.'

▶ Materials needed are listed at the outset. **Ask:** *Why?* (So that they can be assembled beforehand.)

▶ Instructions are numbered and in chronological order, with the imperative (command) verb starting each instruction. **Ask:** *Why?* (So it is immediately clear what action has to be done. If instructions were not clearly numbered, someone may think that the order is not important.)

▶ Adverbs are used when actions have to be performed in a particular way. ***Example:*** carefully, quickly, etc.

▶ The conclusion is how to serve the product, or a use for it.

⇨

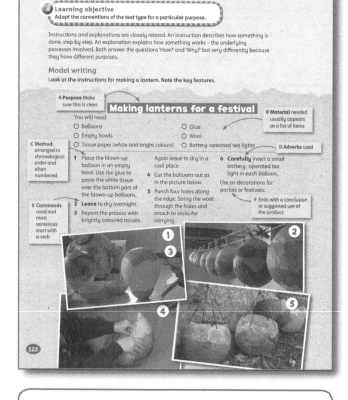

▶ The role photographs and diagrams can play in making points clear to the reader.

▶ Sentences are not very long, so there is not too much information to process at any one time.

▶ Explanation is sometimes used to give a reason for an instruction. These sentences will often begin, 'This is to . . . ' 'The reason for this is . . .'

Students should copy the features for writing instructions into their notebooks.

③ Extension

Students collect examples of instructions, and annotate their features for display on the classroom wall. In addition, students could write out instructions for a game such as 'Snakes and Ladders' and ask a partner to follow it through. They can then confer on which instructions need to be changed to make them more effective.

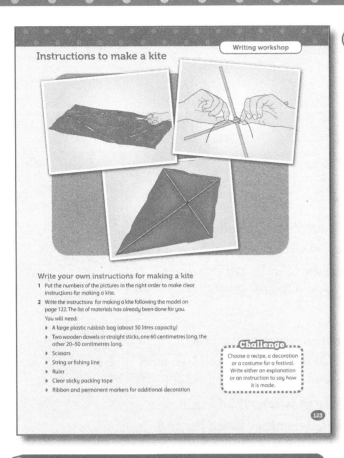

6 Extension

1 Using their own instructions students attempt to make a kite at home. They can write a short summary of how the instructions worked and write amendments to their original instructions to clarify them or correct them where required.

2 Students who chose to write explanations for the Challenge can now write instructions for the same chosen topic.

4 Writing workshop teaching notes

Write your own instructions for making a kite

1 Students number the images to show the order in which you make a kite. They should notice that the bottom illustration is the completed kite.

2 Model the writing of the first two or three steps of the instructions, ticking features off as they are used. Deliberately get some features wrong. ***Example:*** overlong sentences, not inserting an adverb when it is needed, not having an imperative verb at the beginning of a sentence, etc. Ask students to correct the errors in your features.

Instruct students to tick the features as they use them. After students have completed their own instructions they should swap with another student. **Ask:** *Are they clear? Would they be able to make a kite based on these instructions?* Instructions could also be tried out by someone at home, and feedback given.

5 Challenge

Ask students to choose an example from the list provided. Students writing explanations could be asked to read them in class and answer questions on their chosen topic. Those students who choose to write instructions could illustrate them and then swap with a partner for testing.

End of Unit Test

Question Paper

Reading: fiction

Read the extract and answer the questions.

> ### The puppet master
>
> She watched until the show came to an end. The audience applauded. The red-haired girl picked up a brightly painted box and went to collect the coins from the crowd. Clara fumbled in her purse until she found a half crown. She wished it was a sovereign. The red-haired girl accepted it with a little curtsy.
> 5   She met Clara's eyes and smiled.
>
> It was an extraordinarily friendly smile. Clara was struck to the heart. Improbable as it might seem, this girl liked her. Of the seventeen children who were coming to her birthday party, there was not one, Clara felt, who really liked her. They were the children of her parents' friends, who lived in Chester
> 10   Square. Clara thought them dull, and she suspected that they pitied her and thought her queer. But the red-haired girl liked her. Of that Clara was sure.
>
> She had scarcely time to tell the girl how much she had enjoyed the show before the puppet master sidled over. He bowed before Clara, a florid showman's bow: knees bent, wrists cocked, toe flexed. A dirty handbill
> 15   materialized between his fingertips. He stayed frozen in his jester's position until Clara ventured forward and took the handbill. There was something unnerving about the fixed grin on his face...
>
> That night, she gave the handbill to her father and begged to have the puppets at her birthday party.
>
> From *Fire Spell* by Laura Amy Schiltz
>
> ---
>
> **Glossary**
> **curtsy** a woman's or girl's formal greeting made by bending the knees with one foot in front of the other
> **florid** elaborate
> **handbill** a small printed notice, advertisement or leaflet, usually for distribution by hand

Comprehension

A

Give evidence from the extract to support your answers.

1 How much money did Clara give the red-haired girl at the end of the puppet show?

_____ [1]

2 How many children have been invited to Clara's birthday party?

_____ [1]

3 Who gave Clara the handbill about the puppet show?

_____ [1]

B

Give evidence from the extract to support your answers.

1 How does Clara know that the red-haired girl liked her?

_____ [2]

2 Why does Clara want to have the puppet show at her birthday party? Tick two correct boxes.

a The other children will like it. ☐

b She was impressed by the puppet master. ☐

c She likes puppets. ☐

d The red-haired girl will come. ☐ [2]

3 Find evidence from the extract which shows that the birthday party might not be a happy one for Clara?

_____

_____ [3]

C

Give evidence from the extract to support your answers.

1 Give two features about the puppet master that Clara might find frightening.

_____ [3]

2 Put these phrases from the extract (a–e) in the correct order (1–5).

a He stayed frozen in his jester's position.

b She met Clara's eyes and smiled.

c The audience applauded.

d Clara thought them dull.

e That night she gave the handbill to her father.

_____ [2]

Reading: non-fiction

Read the extract and answer the questions.

Happy Birthday!

While we typically celebrate birthdays today with cake, treats, family and fun, the history of birthday parties was not always such a jovial occasion.

Originally, a person feared their upcoming birthday. It was seen as a fearful experience because people believed bad spirits could harm you on
5　this day. Birthday parties were devised as a way to keep those spirits away by surrounding yourself with friends and loved ones who often brought small tokens and food to share. People would use noisemakers to scare off any evil spirits that may be lurking around the house.

It was in the Middle Ages that birthday parties began to take on a more
10　celebratory state, but they were not yet commonplace among people who had little money. In fact, most birthday parties were only celebrated by royalty or the very wealthy, which possibly explains the custom of wearing birthday 'crowns' as time went on. It wasn't until the 16th century that the birthday party became a more common occurrence in England. People then
15　began to make cakes and treats for the birthday person and would often tuck small fortune tokens into the cake for guests.

The Germans are given credit in birthday history for starting celebrations of children's birthdays. The word 'kinderfeste' is derived from two German words 'kinder' meaning children and 'feste' meaning festival or party.

20　The song 'Good Morning to You' was composed in 1893, but nobody really paid much attention to it until the words were changed to 'Happy Birthday to You'.

Adapted from www.lovingyourchild.com

Glossary
jovial cheerful and friendly

Comprehension

A

Give evidence from the extract to support your answers.

1 Why were people once afraid of their birthday?

_____

_____ [3]

2 When did birthday parties become common, and why?

_____

_____ [3]

B

Give evidence from the extract to support your answers.

1 How did the custom of 'birthday crowns' originate?

_____

_____ [3]

2 Why was very little attention first given to the song, 'Good Morning to You?'

_____

_____ [3]

C

1 How is the extract structured? Tick the correct box.

a From present then back through the past. ☐

b From the past then through to the present. ☐

c From the present then through to the future. ☐   [3]

Writing: fiction

Write the next three paragraphs of the fiction extract. The story could be about the day of Clara's birthday party. Please use a separate sheet of paper.

Use these plot points to develop your story:

The puppet master is accompanied by the red-haired girl.

The puppet show is enjoyed by all the guests – and Clara becomes popular.

Clara and the red-haired girl become friends.

[30]

Writing: non-fiction

Write about a celebration you have been involved in recently. It could be a birthday, a festival, a wedding or a party. Please use a separate sheet of paper.

Remember!

The first paragraph should describe the lead up to the celebration.

The second paragraph should describe what happens during the celebration.

The third paragraph should describe the end of the celebration.

[20]

Media mayhem

① Warm up objective

Explore definitions and use new words in context.

Students find out new words and their definitions, which they then explain to someone else, using language that is clear and concise.

 Remember to display the child-friendly learning objective to the class along with the child-friendly checklist that students can use to assess how well they achieve it.

We know that we have achieved this because:

▶ We are able to understand new words and their meanings.

▶ We are able to explain new words and their meanings.

Speaking and listening

9 Media mayhem

"The things most people want to know about are usually none of their business."
George Bernard Shaw

124

Let's Talk
1 Where do you get news and information? Use the photos on this page for some ideas.
2 Do you think we get too much news? Why?

② Unit warm up

Explain that the term 'media' means mass communication such as television, films, radio, magazines, and newspapers — and 'mayhem' means mess, confusion, and disorder. **Ask:** *How could our daily media create chaos and disorder?* (Because there is so much communication that it has all become too much.) Everything and anything can be communicated by anyone at any time, and because it is able to be processed quickly, can often result in being about nothing — apart from gossip!

Sometimes there are not quite enough facts to fill the newspapers and television channels, so often material is exaggerated – just for the sake of giving people constant 'news.' This is particularly the case with 24-hour rolling news, which means information is reported throughout the day and night. Explain that the unit will give students the opportunity to explore some of the issues surrounding the media in our lives today. **Ask:** *Is there too much? Do we always need to be receiving and sending information? Has the media got too strong a hold on us?*

Books open. Explain that George Bernard Shaw (who was a playwright) died in 1950. At this time there would have only been newspapers, films, and radio and just the beginnings of television. Even then, he thought that what the media was doing was just reporting information people did not really need to know about. **Ask:** *Do you believe his opinion is still valid today? Why?*

③ Let's Talk

1 Focus students' attention on the photos. **Ask:** *Which media do you use the most?* Elicit a hands-up response to the most popular type of media. **Ask:** *What media would you like to use more?*

2 Elicit a 'hands up' response from students who read or hear the news: daily/sometimes/never. Ask those responding in each group if they would like more or less news coverage. **Ask:** *What do they find interesting about the news? Is there a news story recently that has been of particular interest? Do they think it's a good thing for children to listen to or read the news? Do they ever feel there is too much news?* Write key phrases from students' answers on the board, divided into positive and negative opinions.

The Student Book page shown reads:

Information overload

Speaking and listening

Learning objective
Structure talk to aid a listener's understanding and engagement.

A

1 How many different ways do you or your family get news or information?

2 How do you think you'll get news in the future? Can you think of a new way?

B

Read the notes below and prepare to give a short talk to the class about information overload.

1 Today we live in a multi-media world. The term, media, used to mean TV, radio, newspapers and magazines. But now we can get our news, information and entertainment in all sorts of ways, such as through smart phones with apps.

2 People can also keep in touch through social media websites.

3 Television news is updated as it happens, twenty-four hours a day, seven days a week. We can read newspapers on paper, on the Internet, or on phones or tablet computers.

4 We learn about world events as they happen because people send images from their phones.

5 Famous people are pursued by paparazzi – photographers – who sell pictures and information to the media.

6 Although it is exciting, there is a danger that we can suffer from information overload.

7 We cannot always be sure that what we see or hear is true. It may be the opinion of the person who is writing or taking the photograph.

C

1 Many children now communicate through mobile phones. What are the advantages and disadvantages of these?

2 Outside school, where do you get most of your information from – family, friends, television, newspapers or magazines?

Word Cloud
blog
communication
media
overload
privacy

Glossary
apps software applications which can be downloaded onto multi-media devices
multi-media the use of sound, text and film as well as the printed word
paparazzi an Italian word for photographers who chase after celebrities
social media a collective term for communication by text, instant messaging, blogs and email

Paparazzi

125

Learning objective

(4)

Structure talk to aid a listener's understanding and engagement.

Students to gather vocabulary related to the media and use some of this in a structured talk.

Remember to display the child-friendly learning objective to the class along with the child-friendly checklist that students can use to assess how well they achieve it.

We know that we have achieved this because:

▸ We are able to use appropriate vocabulary in a talk focused on information overload.

▸ We can structure a talk so that it builds up towards a suitable conclusion.

▸ We can present a talk on information overload.

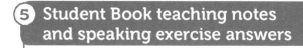

(5) Student Book teaching notes and speaking exercise answers

A

1 Explain that the definition of information is 'facts provided or learned about something or someone.' Point out that often the media is

---

presenting opinion rather than facts. Through 'hands up', find out the different sources of information that students and their families use: newspapers, radio, magazines, smart phones, etc.

2 In pairs or small groups, students brainstorm their ideas on how they think we will get news in the future. ***Example:*** no print media, but constant news streamed into 'screen walls' in homes.

B

Read through the notes for the talk, asking students if there are any words or concepts they do not understand. Explain that point 1 gives an overview of the talk, summarizing the ways we can get the news. Points 2–5, provide details on how news is brought to us, and points 6–7 are the downsides of receiving too much news and information. Encourage students to add factual examples to the numbered notes, so as to give their talk substance and validity.

Students work in groups to write and present the talk, splitting the points between them. Suggest students bring in photographs and examples of media to incorporate into their talk. Ask students to incorporate at least 10 media-specific words.

C

1 Ask one half of the class to list the advantages of mobile phones and devices (easy and instant communication with family and friends; good in an emergency; and music, etc.). Ask the other half to list the disadvantages (they might be bad for your health; addictive; they encourage bullying through text messaging; expensive, etc.)

2 Take responses from students and write them on the board. **Ask:** *What is the most popular source of information?* Show students how this could be represented in a simple graph or chart.

(6) Word Cloud definitions

Focus students' attention on the Word Cloud, then ask them if they know any other media related words. Write responses on the board. Students research, and present the definitions for the additional words.

blog a website on which an individual, or a group, regularly records their opinion

communication the exchange of information

media the main means of mass communication

overload an excessive amount of something

privacy being free from public attention

① Learning objective

Look for implicit meanings and make plausible inferences based on more than one point in the text.

Through answering comprehension questions, students infer how a range of meanings are created across a text.

 Remember to display the child-friendly learning objective to the class along with the child-friendly checklist that students can use to assess how well they achieve it.

We know that we have achieved this because:

▶ We can infer meaning from what characters think, from what they say and how they say it.

▶ We understand that meaning is not always explicit: some meaning needs to be inferred, with the reader picking up on clues on how the writer presents characters.

② Reading fiction notes

Tell students that the extract entitled 'Adam Explains' focuses on children who are so good at figure-skating they attend a special training school. Explain that figure-skating is a sport where competitors skate on ice and are marked for technical and artistic excellence in performing a series of patterns on the ice.

The extract opens at the moment the head teacher at the Skate School (Madame) informs the students that they are going to be filmed over a period of time for a weekly reality show which will be seen by everyone in the country. **Ask:** *What changes might this mean for them?* (Students will no longer be private individuals, but known publically, and all their good and bad points exposed for everyone to see. It could change their lives forever. If they are made into mega — huge – stars their lives will certainly never be the same again.) Point out how students put forward their anxieties and objections in the conversation with the producer about:

▶ Being filmed in their personal space: 'They won't be allowed into the bedrooms will they?' (Line 11)

▶ Filming of them falling over or making mistakes: 'And what if I fall over on the ice . . . I don't want to look like an idiot on national television.' (Lines 18–19)

▶ Being distracted from training: 'Isn't it going to be distracting having video cameras following our very move? What if our training suffers?' (Lines 26–28)

⇨

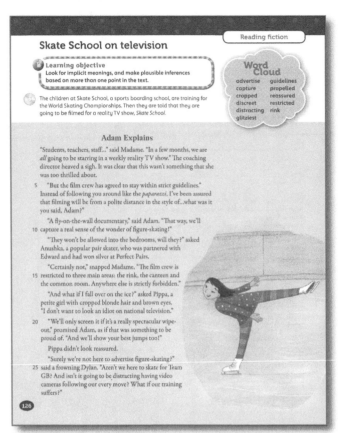

Refer to the CD-ROM or read the text while students follow in their books. Point out how at each objection Madame or Adam has an answer. **Ask:** *Why do some of Adam's answers not sound very convincing?* **Example:** "We'll only screen it if it's a really spectacular wipe out." (Line 20) Students could also be asked to find evidence that the students are not convinced by the arguments. **Example:** 'Pippa didn't look reassured.' (Line 23)

③ Word Cloud definitions

Ask students to work through what the Word Cloud words mean, and to then compare their answers with a partner. You can also refer to the CD-ROM.

advertise draw attention to a product, service, or event in order to promote sales or attendance

capture record accurately in words or pictures

cropped hairstyle in which the hair is cut very short

discreet careful in one's speech or actions, especially in order to keep something confidential or to avoid embarrassment

distracting thing that prevents someone from concentrating on something else

glitziest glamorous and showy

guidelines general rules, principles, or pieces of advice

propelled driven or pushed forwards

reassured told somebody that something is definitely true or is definitely going to happen

restricted kept under control and limited

rink an enclosed area of ice for skating

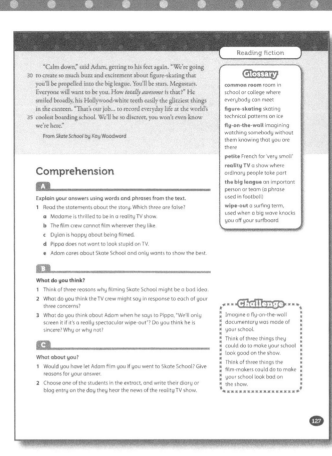

"Calm down," said Adam, getting to his feet again. "We're going
30 to create so much buzz and excitement about figure-skating that
you'll be propelled into the big league. You'll be stars. Megastars.
Everyone will want to be you. How *totally awesome* is that?" He
smiled broadly, his Hollywood-white teeth easily the glitziest things
in the canteen. "That's our job... to record everyday life at the world's
35 coolest boarding school. We'll be so discreet, you won't even know
we're here."

From *Skate School* by Kay Woodward

Comprehension

A

Explain your answers using words and phrases from the text.
1 Read the statements about the story. Which three are false?
   a Madame is thrilled to be in a reality TV show.
   b The film crew cannot film wherever they like.
   c Dylan is happy about being filmed.
   d Pippa does not want to look stupid on TV.
   e Adam cares about Skate School and only wants to show the best.

B

What do you think?
1 Think of three reasons why filming Skate School might be a bad idea.
2 What do you think the TV crew might say in response to each of your three concerns?
3 What do you think about Adam when he says to Pippa, "We'll only screen it if it's a really spectacular wipe-out"? Do you think he is sincere? Why or why not?

C

What about you?
1 Would you have let Adam film you if you went to Skate School? Give reasons for your answer.
2 Choose one of the students in the extract, and write their diary or blog entry on the day they hear the news of the reality TV show.

Glossary

common room room in school or college where everybody can meet
figure-skating skating technical patterns on ice
fly-on-the-wall imagining watching somebody without them knowing that you are there
petite French for 'very small'
reality TV a show where ordinary people take part
the big league an important person or team (a phrase used in football)
wipe-out a surfing term, used when a big wave knocks you off your surfboard

Challenge

Imagine a fly-on-the-wall documentary was made of your school.
Think of three things they could do to make your school look good on the show.
Think of three things the film-makers could do to make your school look bad on the show.

127

④ Student Book teaching notes and comprehension answers

A

Ask: *If Madame does not want the reality show TV show, why is she letting it happen?* Elicit positive aspects of reality television such as publicity and money for the school, promotion of figure-skating as a sport, etc.

Answers:
a False. Madame is not thrilled to be in a reality TV show.
b True. It is restricted to three areas.
c False. Dylan is not happy about being filmed.
d False. Adam doesn't care about Skate School and only wants to show the best TV.

B

1 The text gives many clues as to why the filming might turn out to be a bad idea. ***Examples:***
▶ Students will be followed while they are training, eating and socializing. The only personal space they will have is the bedroom. This is bound to cause tension and arguments.
▶ Any significant falls or mistakes on the ice will be used. This makes for good television, but could be detrimental to students' self-esteem.
▶ The film crew will show students' best jumps – so encouraging them to show off, and could cause falls and injuries.

▶ The film crew isn't concerned with the training, but with creating stars out of the students.

2 Students work in pairs. One student states a reason for concern, and the other has to respond as a member of the film crew. ***Example:***

Concern: Students will be followed while they are training, eating and socializing. The only personal space they will have is the bedroom. This is bound to cause tension.

Response: *We promise that we will focus on the training. We will not interfere in your private life.*

Concern: Why will falls on the ice be used. Is it just because that makes for good television?

Response: *Believe us; we will only use falls or accidents that the viewer might be interested in. The occasional slips and falls you make won't be used. We have to show how difficult it is for you.*

Concern: You aren't concerned with the training, but with creating stars out of the students.

Response: *Surely, that's not a bad thing? If skaters become stars they will get more opportunities, and more money. They will thank us in the end.*

Concern: You say you would be discreet – but how can a whole camera crew there every day not be noticed?

Response: *You will get used to the cameras and hardly notice we are there . . .*

3 Adam only wants to see falls that are funny or dramatic in some way. He is not sincere, because he is just after shots of students falling and slipping which will be of interest to viewers. He is not concerned about the impact of injury.

C

1 Students respond to the question with a reasoned argument for their decision. Remind students they can look back at the previous questions for guidance on possible concerns and intentions of the TV producer.
2 Students choose to write as Pippa or Dylan and write a diary, or blog extract, about how they feel when they hear the news of the show. Remind students that they need to consider how the characters infer their concerns, as well as their spoken reaction.

⑤ Challenge

Students work in groups and make lists of the positive and negative aspects of such a documentary. Ask each group to present their ideas to the class. What are the most common issues?

Learning objective

Explore word origins and derivations and the use of words from other languages.

Students learn about the origins and derivations of some words.

Remember to display the child-friendly learning objective to the class along with the child-friendly checklist that students can use to assess how well they achieve it.

We know that we have achieved this because:

▶ **We are able to recognize the origin and derivations of some words.**

▶ **We are also able to use an etymological dictionary.**

2 Student Book teaching notes and vocabulary exercise answers

A

Read the explanation of how the seemingly modern word 'advertisement' used in the extract is actually based on a 15th century French word. This is the case for much of the English language. What seem like modern, contemporary words actually come from very old words with origins in countries across the world. **Ask:** *Why would the paparazzi be likened to a mosquito?* (Buzzing, fast moving, irritating, etc.)

The explanations should be sufficient to enable students to work out the origin, without having to refer to an etymological dictionary.

Answers:

petite - From the French *petit* (little)

idiot - From the Greek *idiwtes*

spectacular - From the Latin *spectaculum* (a show, spectacle) and *spectare* (to view, watch)

filming - From the Old English, *filmen* (a thin skin)

paparazzi - From the Italian *pappataci* (a small mosquito)

B

Provide students with links to an etymological dictionary online.

Answers:

average: England (Middle English)

iceberg: Holland

bangle: India

bamboo: Malaysia

luck: Holland

hamster: Germany

guitar: Spain

ketchup: China

orchestra: Greece

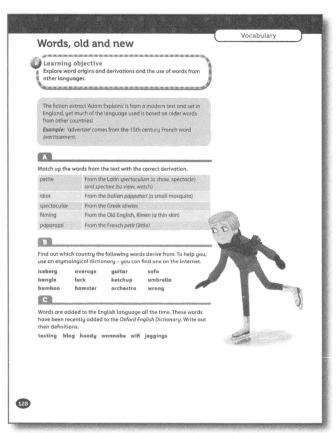

Words, old and new

Learning objective
Explore word origins and derivations and the use of words from other languages.

The fiction extract 'Adam Explains' is from a modern text and set in England, yet much of the language used is based on older words from other countries!
Example: 'advertise' comes from the 15th century French word *avertissement*.

A

Match up the words from the text with the correct derivation.

petite	From the Latin *spectaculum* (a show, spectacle) and *spectare* (to view, watch)
idiot	From the Italian *pappataci* (a small mosquito)
spectacular	From the Greek *idiwtes*
filming	From the Old English, *filmen* (a thin skin)
paparazzi	From the French *petit* (little)

B

Find out which country the following words derive from. To help you, use an etymological dictionary – you can find one on the Internet.

iceberg   average   guitar   sofa
bangle   luck   ketchup   umbrella
bamboo   hamster   orchestra   wrong

C

Words are added to the English language all the time. These words have been recently added to the *Oxford English Dictionary*. Write out their definitions.

texting   blog   hoody   wannabe   wifi   jeggings

128

sofa: Iran

umbrella: Italy

wrong: Denmark

C

Working in pairs, students attempt their own definitions of these new words, and then compare them with a dictionary definition.

Answers:

blog a website on which an individual, or group, regularly records opinions, links to other sites, etc.

jeggings tight-fitting stretch trousers for women, styled to resemble a pair of denim jeans.

hoody hooded sweatshirt, jacket, or other top.

texting sending a text message.

wannabe a person who tries to be like someone else or to fit in with a particular group of people.

wifi facility allowing computers, smartphones, or other devices to connect to the Internet.

3 Extension

Ask students to research what the following words once meant: pen, naughty, and treacle.

Answers:

pen – feather; naughty – worth nothing; treacle – a wild animal.

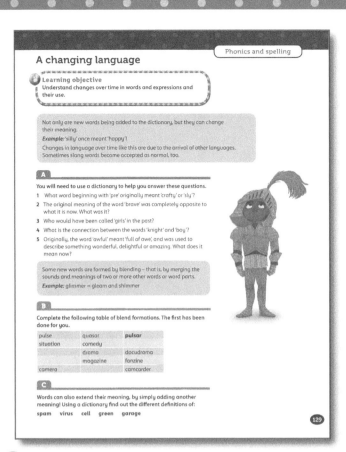

Phonics and spelling

A changing language

Learning objective
Understand changes over time in words and expressions and their use.

Not only are new words being added to the dictionary, but they can change their meaning.
Example: 'silly' once meant 'happy'!
Changes in language over time like this are due to the arrival of other languages. Sometimes slang words become accepted as normal, too.

A

You will need to use a dictionary to help you answer these questions.
1 What word beginning with 'pre' originally meant 'crafty' or 'sly'?
2 The original meaning of the word 'brave' was completely opposite to what it is now. What was it?
3 Who would have been called 'girls' in the past?
4 What is the connection between the words 'knight' and 'boy'?
5 Originally, the word 'awful' meant 'full of awe', and was used to describe something wonderful, delightful or amazing. What does it mean now?

Some new words are formed by blending – that is, by merging the sounds and meanings of two or more other words or word parts.
Example: glimmer = gleam and shimmer

B

Complete the following table of blend formations. The first has been done for you.

pulse	quasar	**pulsar**
situation	comedy	
	drama	docudrama
	magazine	fanzine
camera		camcorder

C

Words can also extend their meaning, by simply adding another meaning! Using a dictionary find out the different definitions of:
spam   virus   cell   green   garage

(129)

---

4   In earlier times a slightly older boy would have been called a knight.
5   terrible, dreadful

B

Answers:

sitcom, documentary, fan, recorder

C

Encourage students to write down the meaning of all the words.

spam irrelevant or unwanted messages sent randomly over the Internet, typically to large numbers of users, for the purposes of advertising, etc.; a tinned meat product made mainly from ham.

virus infective agent that is too small to be seen by a microscope, and able to multiply within the living cells of a human being or animal causing infection and disease; piece of code which is capable of copying itself and can destroy data on computers.

cell small room in which a prisoner is locked up or in which a monk or nun sleeps; the smallest unit of a living organism; the local area covered by a transmitter in a telephone system – hence a cell phone.

green colour; fresh green vegetables; make an area more fertile by planting trees or other vegetation; a piece of public grassy land, especially in the centre of a village; not harmful to the environment; inexperienced or naïve.

garage building for housing a motor vehicle; an establishment which sells fuel or which repairs and sells motor vehicles; a style of rough, energetic rock music.

Learning objective

Understand changes over time in words and expressions and their use.

Students learn how words change in meaning due to the: arrival of other languages; acceptance of informal vocabulary as formal; blending words together.

Remember to display the child-friendly learning objective to the class along with the child-friendly checklist that students can use to assess how well they achieve it.

We know that we have achieved this because:

▶ We understand that many words have changed in meaning over time, and know some of the reasons for this.

▶ We can recognize specific words that have changed meaning over time.

6 Extension

Instruct students to write 6–8 sentences using the following words with the meanings they **used** to have: sly, awful, pretty, girl, knight, pen, awful.

5 Student Book teaching notes and phonics exercise answers

A

Answers:

1   pretty
2   cowardice – from the word 'bravado'
3   boys and girls

Learning objective

Recognize key characteristics of a range of non-fiction text types.

Students to analyse non-fiction texts for persuasive features and then use this to devise their own persuasive text.

Remember to display the child-friendly learning objective to the class along with the child-friendly checklist that students can use to assess how well they achieve it.

We know that we have achieved this because:

▸ **We are able to distinguish persuasive features of layout and content in relation to audience.**

Investigate adverts

Learning objective
Recognise key characteristics of a range of non-fiction text types.

Word Cloud
advertisements product
buyers puzzles
festival teen
persuasion

On Sale Now!

Advertisements in magazines, on television, through the post or on hoardings use the language of persuasion and bright colourful images to attract attention from buyers.

5 **Fabulous fashion**
Nearly everyone wants to be fashionable and pages like this, in teen magazines, are aimed at getting young girls to buy all the 'latest fashions'. Well-known celebrities and models
10 show off the clothes. This article uses captions such as 'so cool' and 'rocks the festival look' to show that they are up-to-the-minute and you can be, too.

These adverts have been written to
15 appeal to girls, while the adverts for boys are more likely to be for the latest console or computer game.

FASHION ● FASHION ● FASHION
ST★R STYLE
Cool shades give you star style
Complete the look with sparkle earrings
Red is hot right now
Stand out from the crowd with cute animal prints.
Must have heels this season

130

② Reading non-fiction notes

Ask the class if they read teen magazines that look like the page of the one in the Student Book? **Ask:** *What does the page suggest the reader wants to know and read about?* (Fashion, looking cool, dressing like a pop star called Jesy.) Point out that all the items and products — sunglasses, leggings, shoes, etc. — featured on the page are the same as Jesy's. Explain this is called 'celebrity endorsement', that is, 'because a celebrity wears these clothes they must be good'. Explain that, however, some girls would not want to wear these clothes. They may go against the accepted code of dress for their culture or they want to follow their own style. So, the article is representing girls in a way that might not be true!

Ask: *Why are articles like these not found in boy's magazines?* (Boys are more often represented as being more interested in activities such as sport and computer games than fashion and what they look like.) Ask students to focus on the Little Big Planet game. Draw their attention to all the words that are linked to doing things and having fun. **Example:** fun, exciting, places to explore, items to collect and puzzles to solve. They are not represented as being shown how they dress. **Ask:** *Do you think this is right or fair?*

Refer to the CD-ROM or read the text while students follow in their books. Working in pairs or small groups, ask students to list two pieces of information they found surprising.

Point to the glossary and read out the definitions. Ask students to locate these terms in the text. **Ask:** *Which other words do they think are important?*

③ Word Cloud definitions

Focus students' attention on the Word Cloud and refer to the CD-ROM for help with pronunciation.

advertisements notices, pictures or films telling people about a product, job or service

buyer a person who makes a purchase

festival an organized series of concerts, plays, or films, typically held annually in the same place

persuasion the action or process of persuading someone or of being persuaded to do or believe something

product something that is manufactured for sale

puzzles games, toys, or problems designed to test cleverness or knowledge

teen relating to teenagers

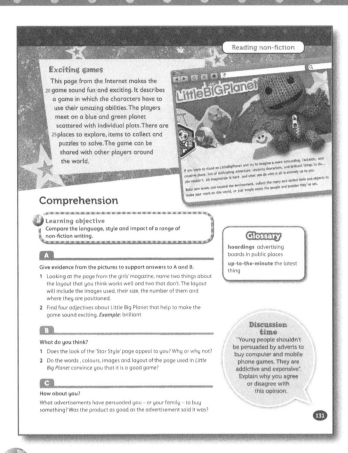

Answers:

Positive: All the images are a good size so can be seen clearly; there are lots of images; the colours are bright and attractive; the captions for each item give helpful advice; large letters (font size) are used for titles, so things are clear.

Negative: There are a lot of images on the page, so it looks messy and confusing; the sizing of some images makes it difficult to see things; captions do not give the price or where they can be bought; the colours are too bright, takes a time to distinguish some items against the blue background.

2 **Ask:** *Why have so many of this type of adjective been used across a small amount of text?*
(Advertisers really want to enforce the idea to the reader that the game is exciting.)

Answers:

amazing, enthralling, fantastic, uncanny, brilliant

1 Using their responses to A, students decide if the magazine layout is appealing or not. As well as thinking about how it looks encourage students to consider if it is targeted at them or others.
Ask: *What types of magazines do you read?*

2 Ask students to consider if they would be more interested in the game if they had not seen the image and just heard the description? Which adjectives used to describe Little Big Planet did students find most convincing?

C

Ask students to share the details of their purchase with the class. They should explain which details of the advertisement, persuaded them to buy it.
Ask: *What did they think was effective about the advertisement? Are they glad they made the purchase?*

4 **Learning objective**

Compare the language, style and impact of a range of non-fiction writing.

Students analyse the language and style in non-fiction writing.

Remember to display the child-friendly learning objective to the class along with the child-friendly checklist that students can use to assess how well they achieve it.

We know that we have achieved this because:

▶ We are able to compare the language and style of a range of non-fiction texts.

▶ We understand why certain language is used in non-fiction texts.

6 Discussion time

Ask: *Who plays Internet games?* Elicit reasons from those that play them why they play them and when. Explain that addictive means something that could cause a dependence on it. Ask students to each provide a reason to support their opinion and write these on the board. **Ask:** *What are the most popular opinions?*

5 Student Book teaching notes and comprehension answers

A

1 Explain that the layout means the organization of information on the page, and how it is presented. This will include the images used, their size, the number of them and where they are positioned. Point out that students should also consider how colour and fonts are used.

① Learning objective

Revise language conventions and grammatical features of different types of texts.

Students learn which language and grammatical features are used in persuasive texts.

 Remember to display the child-friendly learning objective to the class along with the child-friendly checklist that students can use to assess how well they achieve it.

We know that we have achieved this because:

▶ We can identify key language and grammatical features.

▶ We can incorporate these techniques in our own persuasive text.

② Student Book teaching notes and grammar exercise answers

A

1 Books open. Read the language and grammar techniques that are used for persuasive purposes.

Answers:

Personal pronouns: your, you, us, we

Short sentences: use of 'but' and 'and' at the beginning of a sentence; 'And if you don't have time today . . .'

Apostrophes for omission: can't, you're, It's, don't

Adverbs: simply, just, still

Adjectives: best, top, fantsastic

Rhetorical questions: Want to cut broadband bills? . . . you're too busy? What difference can we make?

Connectives: Of course . . .

Alliteration: broadband bills, we will

Modal verbs: can, will

2 Answers:
Other techniques: makes process of buying seem easy; makes the company seem as if they care about the buyer.

B

Show students examples of advertisements in magazines. Point out the use of colour, font choice and font size. Explain that the majority of advertisements will use images. Students should consider these factors when making their own advertisement more persuasive.

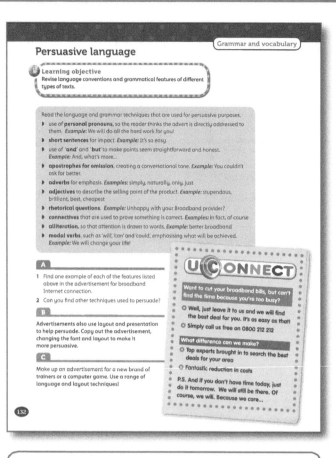

C

Advise students to design and write the advert in pencil first, and then to insert the persuasive techniques. Check this first draft, before students work on their final version. Encourage students to use ICT in their final work. The final assessment could be based on the use of a set language and grammar criteria.

③ Extension

Ask students to annotate their advertisements for language and grammar features.

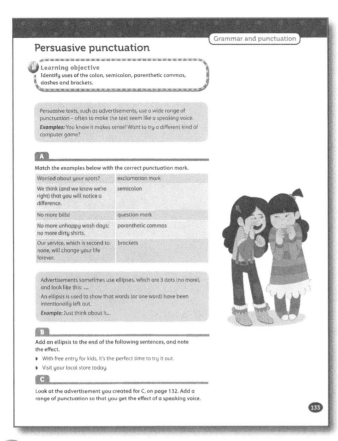

again without. This will show the difference the correct punctuation can make to a text.

Answers:

Worried about your spots?	question mark
We think (and we know we're right) that you will notice a difference.	brackets
No more bills!	exclamation mark
No more unhappy wash days; no more dirty shirts.	semicolon
Our service, which is second to none, will change your life forever	parenthetic commas

Read the information on ellipses in the grammar and punctuation box with students.

Encourage students to read out their examples, pronouncing the ellipses as 'dot-dot-dot'. Ask students to comment on the effect. The effect is to make the words more studied as the talker is thinking about what and how to say what he or she wants to say.

C

Tell students they should use up to four features of punctuation. Explain that if too much punctuation is used, it will seem overdone and distract attention from words. Ask selected volunteers to read their advertisements out without — and then with — the punctuation added. **Ask:** *What is the difference?*

⑥ Extension

Ask students to cut out examples of punctuation used effectively in magazines or newspapers. Use the examples to create a class poster and display on the wall.

Learning objective

④

Identify uses of the colon, semicolon, parenthetic commas, dashes and brackets.

Students learn how punctuation is used in persuasive texts.

Remember to display the child-friendly learning objective to the class along with the child-friendly checklist that students can use to assess how well they achieve it.

We know that we have achieved this because:

▸ **We can identify key punctuation.**

▸ **We can correctly use punctuation in our own persuasive text.**

⑤ Student Book teaching notes and grammar exercise answers

A

Read the information in the grammar box with students. Explain that using punctuation in writing can make it seem that a voice is 'speaking' with pauses and intonation conveying emotion and inference. These punctuation marks can be as simple as an exclamation mark or a question mark. Read the example with the class with the punctuation, then ⇨

① ## Learning objective

Read and interpret poems in which meanings are implied or multi-layered.

Students identify how different layers of meaning in the poem are conveyed to the reader.

 Remember to display the child-friendly learning objective to the class along with the child-friendly checklist that students can use to assess how well they achieve it.

We know that we have achieved this because:

▶ We understand that the poem has a literal and metaphorical meaning.

▶ We can see that the poem is written in free verse.

② ## Student Book teaching notes and comprehension answers

Explain that in this lesson and the next, students are going to focus on two poems which are to do with celebrities and the media.

Ask: *What does the title of the poem, 'The Price of the Fame' mean?* (Fame has been achieved through hard work and setbacks: fame has not come easy.) Point out that as students read the poem they might not find it as straightforward as this. Who the hero is, and who would like to be the hero, become quite confused!

Refer to the CD-ROM or read *The Price of Fame* to the class. Explain that the poem starts off stating that actually being famous is not easy, so the reader knows what the poem is going to be about. However, this is made more complex by the fact that someone with the same name as the poet was a hero by scoring a goal with a 'glancing header.' (Line 5) Then events go from illusion to reality, when the poet misses the chance of an easy goal, and is sent off for a professional foul. The writer is not a good football player, but wishes he was as good as his namesake, 'Everyone's blaming me, and calling me names.' (Line 14) The final two lines — 'If it goes on like this, I'm going to ask Sir for a transfer' — show humour in that, unlike a professional football player, there is no possibility of being transferred to another team; he just wants to get away from the failure and the pressure, and another chance to start again.

A

Remind students that they need to provide evidence, and line references from the text to support their answers.

1   Point out the extreme shift from hero to villain and how this often happens to celebrities.

Ups and downs

Learning objective
Read and interpret poems in which meanings are implied or multi-layered.

John Foster started to make up poems for his children to stop them from getting bored on long car journeys.

 The Price of Fame

It's not easy being famous.

Last week I was a hero.
In injury time
5   my namesake scored the winner
with a glancing header.

Everyone ran round the playground
chanting my name.

Today I'm a villain.
10 Last night I missed an open goal.
Then, just after half time,
I was sent off for a professional foul.
We lost two-nil.

Everyone's blaming me and calling me names.

If it goes on like this,
I'm going to ask Sir for a transfer.

John Foster

Word Cloud

chanting   transfer
half time   villain
playground
scored

Comprehension

A

Give evidence from the text to support your answers.

1   Which line tells us how the player was treated as a hero? Which as a villain?

2   Which line within the poem tells us what this poem is really about?

3   The title of the poem is 'The Price of Fame'. What alternative title would also give the reader an idea of what the poem is about?

134

Glossary

foul when you have played unfairly during football
injury time extra time at the end of a football match
namesake somebody with the same name as you
nil means no score
Sir formal way of greeting a teacher or sports coach

Answers:

'Last week I was a hero.' (Line 2); 'Today I'm a villain.' (Line 9)

2   The reality is that he is not a very good football player, but wishes he was.

Answer:

'It's not easy being famous.' (Line 1)

3   Students suggest alternative titles. *Example:* At what cost?

③ ## Word Cloud definitions

Ask if anyone in the class plays or watches football. They could be asked to explain the football related Word Cloud words. Refer to the CD-ROM.

chanting repeated rhythmic phrase, typically one shouted or sung in unison by a crowd
half time a rest period in the middle of a game
playground an outdoor area provided for children to play in, especially at a school or public park
scored gained (a point, goal, run, etc.) in a competitive game
transfer move to another team
villain the person responsible for problems

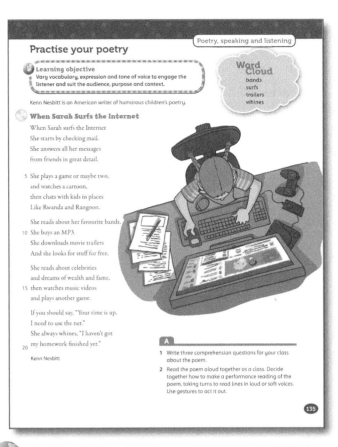

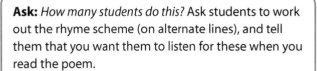

Ask: *How many students do this?* Ask students to work out the rhyme scheme (on alternate lines), and tell them that you want them to listen for these when you read the poem.

Refer to the CD-ROM or read the poem to the class. After the poem has been read, ask students to confer in pairs and answer two questions. **Ask:** *How would they sum up Sarah in one sentence?* (She spends all her time on the computer.) **Ask:** *What is the purpose of the last two lines?* (Sarah spends too much time on the computer when she should be doing homework. She wants to literally live through the Internet.)

Explain that the word 'whines' means a complaining and sulky tone of voice. It also suggests that Sarah is just thinking about herself, and possibly a little bit addicted to the Internet. **Ask:** *Do you behave as Sarah does?* Discuss some of the possible issues of using the Internet too much, such as neglecting friends, ignoring family, not finishing chores or homework, etc.

Students could walk round the room saying the poem over and over again, possibly getting louder or softer as directed. Freeze. Select students to say the last two lines, students should make it sound suitably sulky and complaining.

A

1   Students work alone to develop three questions about the text. Ask students to consider not only the subject but also the language and rhythm. When students have finished they can swap questions with a partner and complete an individual comprehension exercise.
2   Arrange students in a block triangle and give each a random line number, so that line number 1 might be spoken by someone at the back. Give some lines to four people to say at once. All of the class should read the direct speech, 'Your time is up, I need to use the net', and 'I haven't got my homework finished yet'. One half as Sarah, the other as the person she is talking to.

Learning objective

(4)

Vary vocabulary, expression and tone of voice to engage the listener and suit the audience, purpose and context.

Students identify how sound and tone can affect a spoken poem.

Remember to display the child-friendly learning objective to the class along with the child-friendly checklist that students can use to assess how well they achieve it.

We know that we have achieved this because:

▶ **We understand tone and expression can enhance the meaning of a poem.**
▶ **We can read poetry with expression.**

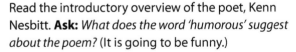

(5) Student Book teaching notes and exercise answers

Read the introductory overview of the poet, Kenn Nesbitt. **Ask:** *What does the word 'humorous' suggest about the poem?* (It is going to be funny.)

Before reading *When Sarah Surfs the Internet,* explain that 'surfing' the Internet means moving from site to site on the Internet. Explain that often people start looking at one thing, and then they see a link to something else, then they press that, going on and on, moving further away from the thing they started on. ⇨

(6) Extension

Students present their performance of the poem to another class at school assembly, or in class time.

1 Learning objective

Use the styles and conventions of journalism to write reports.

Students find out about the features of interviews and how questions should be constructed.

Remember to display the child-friendly learning objective to the class along with the child-friendly checklist that students can use to assess how well they achieve it.

We know that we have achieved this because:

▶ We know the features of interview texts.

▶ We can recognize closed and open questions.

▶ We can devise our own interview using these features.

2 Student Book teaching notes and writing workshop exercise answers

Ask: *What is an interview?* (A session in which someone questions someone else to find out more about them.) *Have they ever read or seen an interview?* Elicit responses on where they have seen or read these, and who was being interviewed. Explain that in the lesson which follows students will find out about some of the techniques that interviewers used. It may sound quite easy to ask someone questions — but it isn't!

Read through the explanatory boxes on interviewing techniques.

Examples

Answers:

a One initiates a much longer, more informed response than another.

b The second question is not premised on receiving a 'yes or no' answer, but an answer where the interviewee has to give their opinions. Questions need to be designed to make the interviewees talk.

c Questions which only generate a 'yes or no' answer or short responses would make for a very short interview! There would be very little to write about. While you would have responses you wouldn't generate reasons for opinions or examples of anecdotes. These are the features that make interviews interesting and generate publicity.

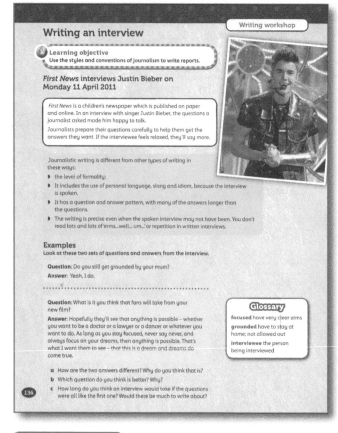

Writing an interview

Learning objective
Use the styles and conventions of journalism to write reports.

First News interviews Justin Bieber on Monday 11 April 2011

First News is a children's newspaper which is published on paper and online. In an interview with singer Justin Bieber, the questions a journalist asked made him happy to talk.

Journalists prepare their questions carefully to help them get the answers they want. If the interviewee feels relaxed, they'll say more.

Journalistic writing is different from other types of writing in these ways:

▶ the level of formality;

▶ It includes the use of personal language, slang and idiom, because the interview is spoken.

▶ It has a question and answer pattern, with many of the answers longer than the questions.

▶ The writing is precise even when the spoken interview may not have been. You don't read lots and lots of 'erms...well... um...' or repetition in written interviews.

Examples

Look at these two sets of questions and answers from the interview.

Question: Do you still get grounded by your mum?

Answer: Yeah, I do.

Question: What is it you think that fans will take from your new film?

Answer: Hopefully they'll see that anything is possible – whether you want to be a doctor or a lawyer or a dancer or whatever you want to do. As long as you stay focused, never say never, and always focus on your dreams, then anything is possible. That's what I want them to see – that this is a dream and dreams do come true.

a How are the two answers different? Why do you think that is?

b Which question do you think is better? Why?

c How long do you think an interview would take if the questions were all like the first one? Would there be much to write about?

> **Glossary**
> **focused** have very clear aims
> **grounded** have to stay at home; not allowed out
> **interviewee** the person being interviewed

136

3 Extension

Ask students to find examples of interviews in magazines or newspapers to bring to class. Ask them to annotate the interviews to show how the interviewer has structured their questions to generate interesting responses.

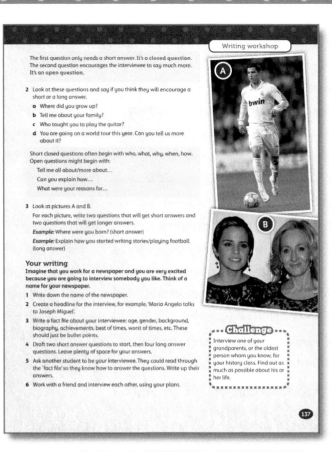

The first question only needs a short answer. It's a closed question. The second question encourages the interviewee to say much more. It's an open question.

2 Look at these questions and say if you think they will encourage a short or a long answer.

a Where did you grow up?

b Tell me about your family?

c Who taught you to play the guitar?

d You are going on a world tour this year. Can you tell us more about it?

Short closed questions often begin with who, what, why, when, how. Open questions might begin with:

Tell me all about/more about…

Can you explain how…

What were your reasons for…

3 Look at pictures A and B.

For each picture, write two questions that will get short answers and two questions that will get longer answers.

Example: Where were you born? (short answer)

Example: Explain how you started writing stories/playing football. (long answer)

Your writing

Imagine that you work for a newspaper and you are very excited because you are going to interview somebody you like. Think of a name for your newspaper.

1 Write down the name of the newspaper.

2 Create a headline for the interview, for example, 'Maria Angelo talks to Joseph Miguel'.

3 Write a fact file about your interviewee: age, gender, background, biography, achievements, best of times, worst of times, etc. These should just be bullet points.

4 Draft two short answer questions to start, then four long answer questions. Leave plenty of space for your answers.

5 Ask another student to be your interviewee. They could read through the 'fact file' so they know how to answer the questions. Write up their answers.

6 Work with a friend and interview each other, using your plans.

Challenge

Interview one of your grandparents, or the oldest person whom you know, for your history class. Find out as much as possible about his or her life.

137

Direct students to look at the images of Cristiano Ronaldo (footballer) and Emma Watson and JK Rowling (actress and author). Confirm with the class that they know who they are and what they do. Elicit suggestions from the class as to the topics they could discuss in the interview. *Example:* Current performance on the pitch (Ronaldo); forthcoming film or book (Watson/ Rowling). Now students write their short and long answer questions. In pairs, students adopt the role of the interviewer and the celebrity, and role-play the interview. **Ask:** *Did the interviewees respond as expected?*

Your writing

Students decide who they are going to interview and make a plan covering themes and topics. Next they decide which newspaper or magazine they are writing for. Following their practice in the previous exercise students should now have a clear understanding on how to structure questions to elicit factual and opinion based responses. Using their plans students conduct the interviews with a partner. Select volunteers to carry out their interviews in front of the class.

4 **Student Book teaching notes and writing workshop exercise answers**

2 Read the explanation of open and closed questions.

Answers:

a short answer

b long answer

c short answer

d long answer

3 Read through example interviews with the class; this will help them source questions for their own interviews, and to decide what information they want to structure the theme of the interview. Point out some tips for structuring their interviews.

▶ There are only six key questions. Who? What? Where? When? How? Why?

▶ Ask the most important question first.

▶ Try to ask a maximum of four questions. You want to generate interesting feedback, and encourage the interviewee to talk — this is your content.

▶ Shorter questions are better than longer ones — you don't to confuse your interviewee.

▶ Never ask more than one question at a time, linking questions can add confusion and reduce responses to all questions.

▶ Do your research! You should know some basic facts about your interviewee, how old they are, what they do, where they are from, etc.

5 **Challenge**

Students structure the interview using the same planning model they created for the exercises. Stress that students will need to consider where they do the interview. They need to make sure it is quiet and free from distractions. A successful interview will be one in which a great story is unravelled or a fascinating personality is discovered.

End of Unit Test

Question Paper

Reading: fiction

Read the extract and answer the questions.

> ### Jake and the Commercial
>
> Jake had been selected to star in a commercial for Olympic Edge, a new performance-aiding sports drink manufactured by the camp's main sponsor: LGE. He didn't even want to be in the stupid commercial. All he wanted to do was to play world-class football. He didn't like all the politics and marketing,
> 5   but he'd learned from his dad that it was all part of the game.
>
> 'Hey, you,' said the director, a skinny guy whose accent was pure Brooklyn. 'Thanks for joining us. Stand over there by the blonde, will ya?'
>
> Jake smiled, taking his position beside the tanned American girl. He certainly wouldn't be forgetting Veronika Richardson's name. She'd won last year's junior
> 10   Wimbledon, and was tipped to be in the top twenty by the end of her first pro season.
>
> 'Right, I want all of you together in a group. Act like you're having fun!'
>
> The Olympic Advantage hopefuls came together, as instructed. A team of young women with make-up brushes at the ready descended on the group.
> 15   Jake tried to protest, but everyone was getting the same make-over treatment. They didn't lay a brush on Veronika.
>
> The director finally called, 'action' while they all pretended to be enjoying themselves. After the director yelled, 'Cut!', they were each given a bottle of Olympic Edge, ready for close-ups. Jake held the 'Riptide' flavour, which
> 20   was sickly blue.
>
> From *The Edge* by Nick Hale
>
> ---
>
> **Glossary**
> **commercial** live advertisement

Comprehension

A

Give evidence from the extract to support your answers.

1   What product is the commercial selling?

_____ [1]

2   Who is the sponsor for the product?

_____ [1]

3 What sport does Jake play?

_____ [1]

4 Find a quotation which shows Jake did not want to be involved in the commercial.

_____ [2]

B

Give evidence from the extract to support your answers.

1 Why had Jake decided to take part in the commercial?

_____

_____ [2]

2 Why do the sponsors want Jake and Veronika to be involved in the commercial?

_____ [2]

3 Why does the director ask the group to 'act like you're having fun'?

_____ [2]

C

Give evidence from the extract to support your answers.

1 'The Olympic Advantage hopefuls came together.' Who might these be?

_____ [2]

2 What indication is there in the last sentence that Jake does not like the product he is advertising?

_____ [2]

Reading: non-fiction

Read the extract and answer the questions.

The problems with watching television

Television has changed the way families interact. Before television, families sat round the dinner table at night to discuss and share the events of the day, whereas, now, many families eat in front of the television, and any sharing of thoughts and ideas are reduced to almost nil.

5   This means that children are not learning the social skills of eating together and the cultural importance of traditions. Some children are spending up to six hours a day in front of the television. A recent university study found that spending too much time watching television results in more time eating snacks and so leads to overeating. Young people are
10 becoming more and more unfit and overweight, and are 15 to 20 per cent less fit than their parents at the same age. Obesity among adolescents has trebled over the past 15 years.

    Alternatively, families who watch less television tend to do more activities together. They play more sport and become involved in cultural and social
15 activities. The parents know what their children are doing and what they are interested in.

From *Step Ahead Book 4/5* by Robyn Mann

Glossary
obesity the state of being grossly fat or overweight

Comprehension

A

Give evidence from the extract to support your answers.

1 Give two reasons why the writer thinks that watching television is not good for families.

_____ [2]

2 Read the statements. Tick the correct box.

  a Children spend six hours a day watching television. ☐

  b Children have a 15% higher rate of obesity. ☐

  c Children are 25% less fit than 15 years ago. ☐ [1]

3 Give one reason why watching television can be bad for families.

_____ [2]

B

Give evidence from the extract to support your answers.

1 According to the writer, how does eating in front of the television impact on social development? Give two reasons.

_____ [2]

2 Write definitions for *'enriching'* and *'interacting'.*

_____

_____ [3]

C

Give evidence from the extract to support your answers.

1 Give one fact and one opinion from the extract. Explain your examples.

_____

_____ [3]

2 Which word is used to indicate a change in the writer's argument?

_____ [2]

Writing: fiction

Write the next two paragraphs of the fiction extract. Please use a separate sheet of paper.

Consider the following questions:

What will the director ask the group to do next?

Will Veronika have a star part? Will Jake be happy?

[30]

Writing: non-fiction

Write a letter to the writer of the non-fiction extract, giving your own views on television. Please use a separate sheet of paper.

Organize your description in four paragraphs. Include:

A short introduction summing up your views.

The advantages of watching television.

The disadvantages of watching television.

A conclusion.

[20]

10 Learning for life

① Warm up objective

Develop opinions based on information and experience.

Students ask and answer questions, and develop their own opinions in order to partake in informed discussions.

Remember to display the child-friendly learning objective to the class along with the child-friendly checklist that students can use to assess how well they achieve it.

We know that we have achieved this because:

▶ We can ask questions to develop our understanding of something.

▶ We can answer questions to help others understand something.

▶ We can use our own opinions and experience to aid discussion.

Speaking and listening

10 Learning for life

Let's Talk

The Tree of Knowledge is an old metaphor.

1 Why do you think knowledge is shown as a tree?

2 Which picture do you like best? Why?

3 Which picture puzzles you most? What do you think it means?

"Aim for success, not perfection. Never give up your right to be wrong, because then you will lose the ability to learn new things and move forward with your life."
David M. Burns

138

② Unit warm up

Books closed. Write title, 'Learning for life' on the board. With students, brainstorm on one quarter of the board what students have learned in life so far. **Example:** learning to ride a bike, operate a computer, etc. On another quarter of the board, list reasons why it is important to learn. **Example:** knowledge enables you to do more things; it helps make sense of the world, etc. On a third quarter, list reasons why learning is sometimes difficult. **Example:** not being able to understand something straight away, making mistakes, etc. Steer students towards an appreciation of how learning can be complex and difficult — and that failure should be viewed positively; you learn from your mistakes. The final quarter of the board should be about what makes for effective learning. **Example:** asking questions, trying something new, etc. Ask for volunteers to share a particular experience of a learning experience which went well.

Books still closed. Ask students in pairs to come up with a quote bubble which sums up why learning is important. **Example:** 'Keep on learning and love life'; 'To be alive is to learn'; 'If you know things, you will know life,' etc. Ask selected pairs to read out their examples.

Books open. Read the quote. **Ask:** *How does this compare with their own quotes? What two key messages does it convey?* (Aim to be an effective learner, not a perfect learner; no one can know everything. It is the

process of learning that is important, not the 'knowing'.) The second message of the quote bubble is that making mistakes is a really important way of learning, and of developing as a person.

③ Let's Talk

Explain that a metaphor means likening one thing to another without using the words 'like' and 'as'. So, the 'tree of knowledge' is the same as knowledge — it grows and develops.

1 To confirm the metaphor, ask students to copy the tree and draw in human characteristics. **Example:** eyes and mouth on the trunk, and to select five or six key learning words or phrases from the board to position in particular places on the branches.

Answer:

Our knowledge keeps growing and developing like the trunk, but it also branches out into lots of different areas — growing outwards as well as upwards. A tree will keep on growing — the same as learning.

2 Elicit responses from the class through 'hands up'. Ask students to give reasons and opinions for why they like a particular picture.

3 Ask students to give reasons and opinions for why they find particular images puzzling.

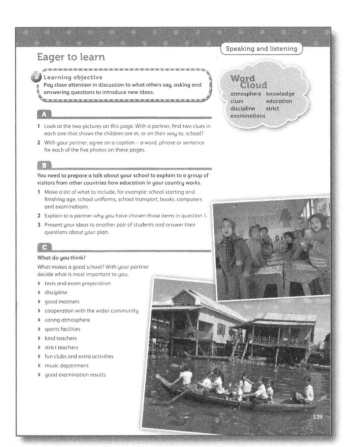

2 Students confer with a partner to write a caption for each photograph. Remind students to consider the setting, the people in it and the action it details.

B

1 Working in pairs, students add facts of their own that they think students from another country might be interested in. This could be school transport, school food, dinners, holidays, length of school day, behaviour, discipline, and facilities.

2 Encourage students to make suitable, precise notes which will subsequently give them something to talk about. *Example:* School subjects: 'In primary schools English, mathematics, science, humanities are each taught for one hour a day.'

3 Allocate each pair a two minute slot for their talk. For each talk, select some students to ask questions written on cards. *Example:* Could you tell me more about . . .? What happens if . . .? Why do students . . .?

C

Read the features that make for a good school. Clarify any words that students may not understand. *Example:*

cooperation the action or process of working together.

community area or place where inhabitants live.

Working in pairs, students write out the features in order of priority, and then share and compare their answers with another pair.

Write each item on the board and elicit whole class feedback. Use this information to collate the most important features of a good school.

Learning objective

④

Pay close attention in discussion to what others say, asking and answering questions to introduce new ideas.

Listen carefully to what students say and ask questions which make them elaborate upon their ideas.

Remember to display the child-friendly learning objective to the class along with the child-friendly checklist that students can use to assess how well they achieve it.

We know that we have achieved this because:

▶ **We are able to listen carefully to what others say.**

▶ **We are able to use a range of questions that make them elaborate upon their ideas and extend them.**

⑥ Word Cloud definitions

Books closed. Explain that there is one word in the Word Cloud that sums up the process of teaching and learning experienced by children all over the world. **Ask:** *What word is this?* (Education.) If students don't know, prompt with clues such as it begins with 'ed' and ends in 'n', or write an anagram of 'education' on the board.

atmosphere the air in any particular place

clues facts that serve to reveal something

discipline the practice of training people to obey rules

education a process of teaching and learning, to improve knowledge and develop skills

examinations detailed inspections or tests

knowledge facts, information, and skills acquired through experience or education

strict following rules or beliefs exactly

⑤ Student Book teaching notes and speaking exercise answers

A

1 Elicit ideas from students on items to do with school. *Example:* uniforms, transport, book bags, etc.

Learning objective

1

Understand aspects of narrative structure such as the handling of time.

Students consider how narrative is used to suggest the future and past.

 Remember to display the child-friendly learning objective to the class along with the child-friendly checklist that students can use to assess how well they achieve it.

We know that we have achieved this because:

▶ We can understand how narrative time is created.

▶ We can identify how the past and future are created.

2 Reading fiction notes

Books closed. Explain that science fiction texts are set in the future, often focusing on imaginary scientific and technological developments. **Ask:** *What do you imagine schools will be like in the future?* Encourage students to be imaginative with their responses and base them on current reality.

Tell students that they are going to read an extract from a book called 'Earth is Room Enough' by the famous writer of science fiction stories, Isaac Asimov. It is set in 2155. **Ask:** *How many years from now is the story set?* (about 142 years.) Read the brief overview. **Ask:** *Why would it be unusual, or strange that a character has found an old book?* (We are already moving away from printed books, so it is likely that in the future electronic books will replace printed books.)

Explain that the extract presents school as it could be in the future, and the problems and difficulties Margie (one of the two main characters) has with this.

Refer to the CD-ROM or read the text while students follow in their books. **Ask:** *What facts do we find out about future schools as imagined by the author?* ***Example:*** Teachers are now robots called mechanical teachers; students feed their answers through a punch code (a special code password) into a mechanical teacher, and are given feedback straight away; mechanical teachers obtain their information from bigger computers known as 'sectors'; if these malfunction, the mechanical teacher cannot operate. Through 'hands up', ask who would like an education like this.

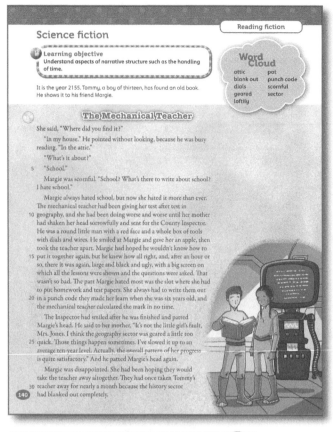

Science fiction

Reading fiction

Learning objective
Understand aspects of narrative structure such as the handling of time.

It is the year 2155. Tommy, a boy of thirteen, has found an old book. He shows it to his friend Margie.

Word Cloud
attic   pat
blank out   punch code
dials   scornful
geared   sector
loftily

The Mechanical Teacher

She said, "Where did you find it?"

"In my house." He pointed without looking, because he was busy reading. "In the attic."

"What's it about?"

5   "School."

Margie was scornful. "School? What's there to write about school? I hate school."

Margie always hated school, but now she hated it more than ever. The mechanical teacher had been giving her test after test in
10 geography, and she had been doing worse and worse until her mother had shaken her head sorrowfully and sent for the County Inspector. He was a round little man with a red face and a whole box of tools with dials and wires. He smiled at Margie and gave her an apple, then took the teacher apart. Margie had hoped he wouldn't know how to
15 put it together again, but he knew how all right, and, after an hour or so, there it was again, large and black and ugly, with a big screen on which all the lessons were shown and the questions were asked. That wasn't so bad. The part Margie hated most was the slot where she had to put homework and test papers. She always had to write them out
20 in a punch code they made her learn when she was six years old, and the mechanical teacher calculated the mark in no time.

The Inspector had smiled after he was finished and patted Margie's head. He said to her mother, "It's not the little girl's fault, Mrs. Jones. I think the geography sector was geared a little too
25 quick. Those things happen sometimes. I've slowed it up to an average ten-year level. Actually, the overall pattern of her progress is quite satisfactory." And he patted Margie's head again.

Margie was disappointed. She had been hoping they would take the teacher away altogether. They had once taken Tommy's
30 teacher away for nearly a month because the history sector had blanked out completely.

140

3 Word Cloud definitions

Refer to the CD-ROM. Ask students to identify the words which are associated with technology or mechanics. (Dial, punch code, sector.) **Ask:** *What are the adverb and adjective used to sum up Tommy's character?* (Loftily, superior.) Emphasize that the emotions and differing characteristics of Tommy and Margie make them seem very real. Explain that if everything was too futuristic, it would be too confusing for the reader. Science fiction books have to combine both the future and a present that readers can relate to.

attic a space or room inside the roof of a building

blank out forget; unable to remember

dials plates or discs turned to select a setting on a piece of equipment

geared the gears in a machine that give it a specific speed or power output

loftily conceited and self-important

pat touch quickly and gently with the flat of the hand

punch code a code on a card that is recognized by a computer

scornful a feeling and expression of strong dislike for someone or something

sector an area that is different from others

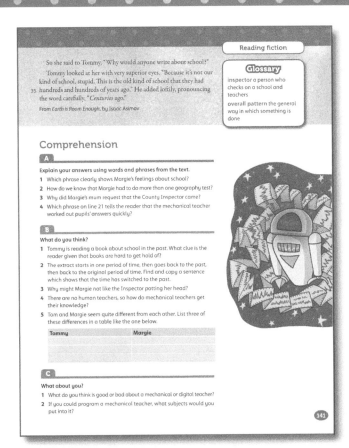

So she said to Tommy, "Why would anyone write about school?"
Tommy looked at her with very superior eyes. "Because it's not our kind of school, stupid. This is the old kind of school that they had 35 hundreds and hundreds of years ago." He added loftily, pronouncing the word carefully, "*Centuries* ago."

From Earth is Room Enough, by Isaac Asimov

Glossary

inspector a person who checks on a school and teachers

overall pattern the general way in which something is done

Comprehension

A

Explain your answers using words and phrases from the text.

1 Which phrase clearly shows Margie's feelings about school?
2 How do we know that Margie had to do more than one geography test?
3 Why did Margie's mum request that the County Inspector came?
4 Which phrase on line 21 tells the reader that the mechanical teacher worked out pupils' answers quickly?

B

What do you think?

1 Tommy is reading a book about school in the past. What clue is the reader given that books are hard to get hold of?
2 The extract starts in one period of time, then goes back to the past, then back to the original period of time. Find and copy a sentence which shows that the time has switched to the past.
3 Why might Margie not like the Inspector patting her head?
4 There are no human teachers, so how do mechanical teachers get their knowledge?
5 Tom and Margie seem quite different from each other. List three of these differences in a table like the one below.

Tommy	Margie

C

What about you?

1 What do you think is good or bad about a mechanical or digital teacher?
2 If you could program a mechanical teacher, what subjects would you put into it?

141

---

④ Student Book teaching notes and comprehension answers

Tell students that in this lesson they will analyse and discuss the characters and their respective feelings, and how time is handled in the extract. Explain that time in fiction is called narrative time. It is not real time. It is a technique used by the writer to get the reader to imagine what they are reading is set in the future, present or past. Writers can also make readers imagine that time has passed slowly or quickly.

A

Remind students to support their answers with references from the text.

Answers:

1 'Margie was scornful.' (Line 6) 'Margie always hated school.' (Line 8)
2 'The mechanical teacher had been giving her test after test in Geography.' (Lines 9–10)
3 She had not been making progress in her school work. 'She had been doing worse and worse.' (Lines 10–11)
4 '. . . the mechanical teacher calculated the mark in no time.' (Line 21)

B

1 Margie asks, 'Where did you find it?' This suggests that books are not openly available. In addition, Tommy finds it in the attic, a room in the house

---

where old, unused items are usually hidden and stored away.

2 **Example:** '. . . and she had been doing worse and worse until her mother her mother had shaken her head sorrowfully and sent for the County Inspector.'; 'She always had to write them out in a punch code which they made her learn when she was six years old.'; 'They once had taken Tommy's teacher away for nearly a month.'

3 Point out to students that it is noticeable that Margie doesn't say anything to the Inspector and let's herself be treated like this. She might be frightened of him.

Answer:

Patting her head is quite a patronizing action, and an invasion of her personal space.

4 They seem to get it from subject sectors: computer areas that focus on particular types of knowledge such as history or geography. All the information from the sector is fed into the mechanical teachers.

5 Tommy: thinks he knows a lot; acts superior; positive about school; interested in school

Margie: not performing well at school, negative, not interested in school

C

1 Students list the advantages and disadvantages of having a mechanical teacher. Collate responses from the class.

Disadvantages: no sense of humour, human qualities; does not look very attractive — just a large computer; all teachers would be the same; would be able to detect instantly if you weren't doing well or not doing homework; could break down; could be set at the wrong level

Advantages: wouldn't have to worry if a teacher was strict or not; work could be marked quickly so you would know straight away how you were doing; if the teacher broke down there might be an opportunity for a rest; doesn't need lunch breaks

2 Discuss with the class and elicit suggestions. Tell students this can be any subject they like! But point out how a mechanical teacher might be more useful for some subjects than others (ICT/Art).

⑤ Extension

Students research Isaac Asimov, and write up a short profile about him or an imaginary interview they have carried out with him.

Learning objective

Use apostrophes accurately for omission and possession.

Students learn that apostrophes are used for both omission and possession.

 Remember to display the child-friendly learning objective to the class along with the child-friendly checklist that students can use to assess how well they achieve it.

We know that we have achieved this because:

▶ We are able to recognize apostrophes of omission and possession.

▶ We are also able to use them correctly in sentences.

② Student Book teaching notes and punctuation exercise answers

Read the definition of apostrophes for omission and possession. Provide a short test for students at the onset of the lesson so as to assess their knowledge and understanding. This may well indicate that additional time and/or focus is needed on this area, with some initial exercises.

A

1 Ask students to write their examples out in full and write a short explanation of why the apostrophe has been used. *Example:* We use an apostrophe in 'What's' for omission. The full term is 'what is'.

Answers:

What's/wouldn't/wasn't/it's/I've

2 Ask students to provide a full reference to the text.

Answers:

Margie's head; little girl's

B

Extend the task by asking students to provide an explanation on why the use of the apostrophe is correct or incorrect.

1 Correct
2 Correct
3 Incorrect (there should be no apostrophe in *it's*)
4 Incorrect (there should be an apostrophe in *tree's*)
5 Incorrect (there should be apostrophes in *Tommy's teacher's*)
6 Incorrect (there should be an apostrophe in *boy's*)
7 Incorrect (the apostrophe should be here: *week's*)
8 Incorrect (the apostrophe is missing from *That's*)
9 Correct

Apostrophes

 **Learning objective**

Use apostrophes accurately for omission and possession.

Apostrophes are used in two ways.
▶ To show that letters have been missed out of a word (apostrophes for omission)
Example: it's = it is
▶ To show that something belongs to something else (apostrophes for possession)
Example: The pen belonging to the man = the man's pen

A

1 From the extract on pages 140–1, find five examples of the apostrophe used to show letters have been missed out. (apostrophe for omission)

2 From the extract, find two examples of the apostrophe being used to show that something belongs to something else. (apostrophe for possession)

Top Tip
If there is more than one owner and an -s is added, the apostrophe comes after the -s. *Example:* the shoes belonging to several boys = the boys' shoes.

B

Decide if apostrophes in these sentences are used correctly, and if not write them correctly.

1 Rodriguez's mother's Australian.
2 It's not the little girl's fault.
3 The mechanical teacher has lost it's data.
4 The trees leaves have fallen to the ground.
5 Tommys teachers pen was on the table.
6 The boys' father is looking for him.
7 Next weeks' school council meeting has been cancelled.
8 Thats not mine. That's Tommy's.
9 Margie said that everything has to go in its place.

C

Insert the missing apostrophes in the sentences below.

The boys rucksacks were found by the dogs bed. Marias mother also discovered all the ladies handbags by the dogs bed. Why? Whats going on? Whos to blame? Its a mystery. Theres no doubt about it.

142

C

Students complete this task individually. Confirm answers with the whole class.

Answers:

The **boys'** rucksacks were found by the **dog's** bed. **Maria's** mother also discovered all the ladies handbags by the **dog's** bed. Why? **What's** going on, everyone asked? **Who's** to blame? **It's** a mystery, everyone agreed. **There's** no doubt about it.

③ Extension

Students write a short paragraph describing what is in their bedroom. Set a target for them to use four apostrophes for omission and four apostrophes for possession in their text.

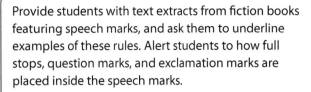

Direct speech

Punctuation

Learning objective
Punctuate speech accurately.

A

Use the sentences of dialogue below as a model. Explain the rules for how speech and dialogue should be punctuated and set out. There should be four rules.

She said, "Where did you find it?"

"In my house." He pointed without looking, because he was busy reading. "In the attic."

"What's it about?"   *A new line is used to show a new speaker*

"School."

Margie was scornful. "School? What's there to write about school? I hate school."

B

Below is another extract from *Earth is Room Enough*, by Isaac Asimov. Write out the lines and add in missing punctuation and some reporting clauses, such as 'he said' and 'she shouted'.

She read the book over his shoulder for a while, then said, "Anyway, they had a teacher

"Sure they had a teacher, but it wasn't a *regular* teacher. It was a man

A man? How could a man be a teacher"

"Well, he just told the boys and girls things and gave them homework and asked them questions"

"A man isn't smart enough"

"Sure he is My father knows as much as my teacher."

"He cant A man can't know as much as a teacher.

C

In comics, the words in the speech bubble are the words actually spoken. Make up two speech frames for a comic strip about *The Mechanical Teacher*.

143

Learning objective

(4) Punctuate speech accurately.

Students learn the rules for the punctuation and layout of direct speech.

Remember to display the child-friendly learning objective to the class along with the child-friendly checklist that students can use to assess how well they achieve it.

We know that we have achieved this because:
- We understand that direct speech has to be punctuated and laid out in accordance with particular rules.
- We can insert missing punctuation in direct speech, and lay it out correctly.

5 Student Book teaching notes and punctuation exercise answers

Brainstorm with students the rules for punctuating direct speech, listing these on the board with examples.

- Words actually spoken are enclosed in speech marks.
- If there is a comment or reporting clause, the speech marks should be stopped then started again.
- When someone new speaks a new line should be taken.

Provide students with text extracts from fiction books featuring speech marks, and ask them to underline examples of these rules. Alert students to how full stops, question marks, and exclamation marks are placed inside the speech marks.

A

Encourage students to copy out the sentences so that they are in the middle of the page, with enough space left around the sides for annotation.

Answers:

- "Where did you find it?" Question mark placed inside speech marks.
- "In my house." He pointed without looking… "In the attic." There is a reporting clause, so the speech marks are stopped, and then started again.
- "What's it about?" Someone new is speaking so a new line is taken.

B

Answers:

She read the book over his shoulder for a while, and then said, "Anyway, they had a teacher."

"Sure they had a teacher, but it wasn't a regular teacher. It was a man."

"A man? How could a man be a teacher?"

"Well, he just told the boys and girls things, and gave them homework and asked them questions."

"A man isn't smart enough."

"Sure he is. My father knows as much as my teacher."

"He can't. A man can't know as much as a teacher."

C

Students draw up two speech frames depicting *The Mechanical Teacher* as a comic book. Remind students that they can use the illustration to convey the tone and context of the story.

6 Extension

Ask students to write a conversation between two young students on their very first day at school. One is enjoying school, the other one is not. Remind students to use speech marks correctly, and to take a new line when there is a new speaker.

① Learning objective

Explore autobiography and first person narration.

Students explore the features of first person narration and use these in their own narration.

 Remember to display the child-friendly learning objective to the class along with the child-friendly checklist that students can use to assess how well they achieve it.

We know that we have achieved this because:

▶ We are able to identify features of autobiographical and first person narration.

▶ We are able to incorporate these features in our own writing.

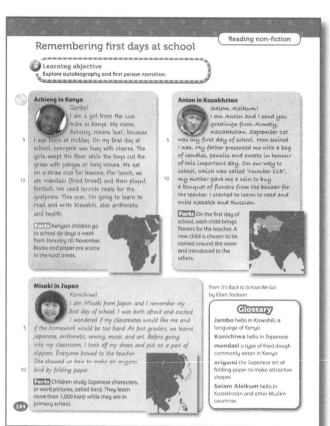

② Reading non-fiction notes

Books closed. Explain that children all over the world go to school in order to learn and receive an education, but that some of these schools will be very different from the ones students currently attend. Ask students to identify where Kenya, Kazakhstan and Japan are on the map. Books open. Point out the respective maps with the respective countries identified. Were the students correct?

Take students through the glossary words. To confirm understanding, ask students to memorize the greetings used in Japan, Kazakhstan, and Kenya. Books closed. Can students repeat the greetings? Tell students they are now going to find out about children's experience in these countries on their first day at school.

Refer to the CD-ROM or read the text while students follow in their books. Ask students to scan the text and identify words which they find difficult. Explain and contextualize any queries before reading further. Ask students to consider which features of the schools and the school day they have read about that are similar and different to their own school life.

arithmetic the branch of mathematics dealing with numbers

bouquet an arranged bunch of flowers, presented as a gift or carried at a ceremony

chores routine tasks, especially household ones

panga bladed African tool like a large knife

scarce small numbers or quantities; rare

slippers a comfortable, soft slip-on shoe that is worn indoors

termite small, pale insect that lives in large colonies within a small stack of cemented earth

③ Word Cloud definitions

Focus students' attention on the Word Cloud and refer to the CD-ROM. Tell them to find one word that refers to flowers (bouquet); one word relating to insects (termite); and a word which means jobs (chores)

Ask: *If you are wearing slippers, what are you wearing?* (Soft, indoor shoes.)

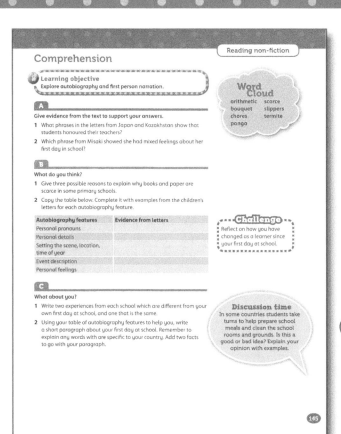

Event description: 'I took off my shoes...' (Misaki)
Personal feelings: 'How excited I was' (Anton)

C

1 Students consider their own first day at school experiences then compare them with those in the Student Book.
2 Ask students to tick the features in the autobiographical table each time they use them in their writing. Emphasize that the two facts added must be of interest to children in other countries. Discuss with the class any features of the students' own education system which might be unusual or distinctive.

5 Challenge

In pairs, students share memories of their first day at school and how they felt. **Ask:** *How would they compare their first day experience with how they are now?* (Older, less anxious, can read and write, etc.)

6 Discussion time

Ask students to put their hand up according to whether they think it is a good or bad idea. Elicit reasons why. ***Example:*** gives students responsibility; makes them care more about their school; students go to school to learn, not do chores; it could interfere with school work; etc.

4 Student Book teaching notes and comprehension answers

A

1 Remind students to give evidence from the text to support their answers.

Answers:

Kazakhstan: 'My mother gave me a coin to buy a bouquet of flowers from the bazaar for the teacher.'

Japan: 'Before going into my classroom, I took off my shoes and out on a pair of slippers. Everyone bowed to the teacher.'

2 Mixed feelings: 'I was both afraid and excited. I wondered if my classmates would like me and if the homework would be too hard.'

B

1 Many schools around the world cannot afford pencils or paper, let alone computers and tablets. Discuss the costs of educational resources, the geographical location of some schools, and how education is not as rigidly enforced in some countries.

2 **Example answers:**

Personal pronouns: I, we, me, our, my
Personal details: Achieng born midday
Setting the scene, location, time of year: 'first day at school' (Anton)

1 Learning objective

Revise different word classes.

Students learn about dynamic, action, statue, and non-finite verbs.

 Remember to display the child-friendly learning objective to the class along with the child-friendly checklist that students can use to assess how well they achieve it.

We know that we have achieved this because:

▶ We know what active, stative, and non-finite verbs are.

▶ We can successfully identify each of these types of verbs.

2 Student Book teaching notes and grammar exercise answers

Read the explanation, highlighting verbs' importance as an essential word class. Check that students can identify straightforward verbs within a sentence, before embarking on the subsequent exercise.

A

Confirm that these kinds of verbs can be seen, as they describe something happening within a limited period of time, and have a definite beginning and end. (See Top Tips) Ask for volunteers to mime each of the sentences so that the actions and verbs can be clearly 'seen.'

Answers:

1 brings
2 swept, cut
3 took, put, bowed

B

Use the explanation in Top Tips and the summary explanation provided, and confirm that stative verbs cannot be mimed or shown easily because they describe states or conditions which continue over a period of time.

Answers:

1 Your classmate <u>seems</u> very nice.
2 We <u>were</u> all there on time.
3 The loss of the school rucksack <u>was</u> my fault.
4 Anton <u>became</u> quite excited about the first day at school.

There are numerous stative verbs in the three extracts. A useful exercise would be for students – working in pairs – to underline all the verbs in the paragraphs and to then decide which are active and which are stative.

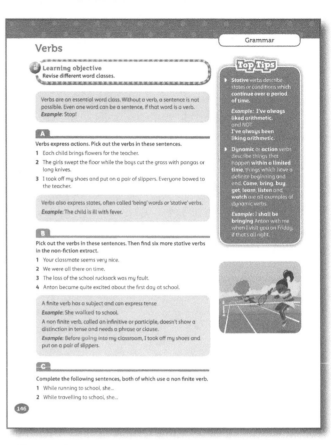

C

Read the explanation of finite and non-finite verbs. Encourage students to use additional non-finite verbs at the beginning of a sentence such as walking, waking, dancing, and laughing. Check that students have wrapped these in a phrase or a clause, and a comma added. ***Example:*** Walking slowly and carefully, she. . .

3 Top Tip

Read through the tip with the class and ask students to write three sentences using dynamic verbs.

4 Extension

Set students a target to use a particular number of active, stative and non-finite verbs in their own writing over a period of time.

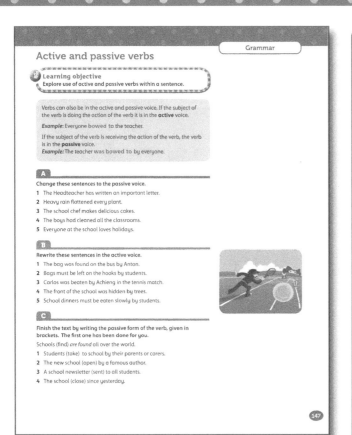

Student Book page reproduced:

Active and passive verbs

Grammar

Learning objective
Explore use of active and passive verbs within a sentence.

Verbs can also be in the active and passive voice. If the subject of the verb is doing the action of the verb it is in the **active** voice.
Example: Everyone bowed to the teacher.

If the subject of the verb is receiving the action of the verb, the verb is in the **passive** voice.
Example: The teacher was bowed to by everyone.

A
Change these sentences to the passive voice.
1 The Headteacher has written an important letter.
2 Heavy rain flattened every plant.
3 The school chef makes delicious cakes.
4 The boys had cleaned all the classrooms.
5 Everyone at the school loves holidays.

B
Rewrite these sentences in the active voice.
1 The bag was found on the bus by Anton.
2 Bags must be left on the hooks by students.
3 Carlos was beaten by Achieng in the tennis match.
4 The front of the school was hidden by trees.
5 School dinners must be eaten slowly by students.

C
Finish the text by writing the passive form of the verb, given in brackets. The first one has been done for you.
Schools (find) *are found* all over the world.
1 Students (take) to school by their parents or carers.
2 The new school (open) by a famous author.
3 A school newsletter (sent) to all students.
4 The school (close) since yesterday.

147

 A

Explain that in changing verbs in the active voice to the passive voice, a good tip is to take the object of the sentence, and shift it to the front of the sentence as the subject. This reduces the importance of the previous subject; they now simply receive the action.

Answers:
1 An important letter was written by the Headteacher.
2 Every plant was flattened by heavy rain.
3 Delicious cakes have been made by the school chef.
4 All the classrooms have been cleaned by the boys.
5 Holidays are loved by everyone at the school.

 B

Answers:
1 Anton found the bag on the bus.
2 Students must leave their bags on the hooks.
3 Achieng beat Carlos in the tennis match.
4 Trees hid the front of the school.
5 Students must eat their school dinners slowly.

C

Students should note that the passive voice is formed using the 'help' of the verb 'to be.'

Answers:
1 Students are taken to school by their parents or carers.
2 The new school was opened by a famous author.
3 A school newsletter was sent to all students.
4 The school has been closed since yesterday.

Learning objective

(5) **Explore use of active and passive verbs within a sentence.**

Students learn how active and passive verbs are used.

Remember to display the child-friendly learning objective to the class along with the child-friendly checklist that students can use to assess how well they achieve it.

We know that we have achieved this because:
▸ We know what active and passive verbs are.
▸ We can successfully identify each of these types of verbs.

(7) **Extension**

Students create a poster for a younger class explaining the difference between the active and passive voice.

(6) **Student Book teaching notes and grammar exercise answers**

Tell students they are going to learn about the use of active and passive verbs within a sentence. Read the grammar rule with students before embarking on the exercises.

⇨

1 ## Learning objective

Articulate personal responses to reading, with close reference to the text.

Students will investigate the poem closely and, based on this, respond personally.

Remember to display the child-friendly learning objective to the class along with the child-friendly checklist that students can use to assess how well they achieve it.

We know that we have achieved this because:

▶ Through close investigation, we understand how a range of meaning is created within the poem.

▶ We can make close reference to the poem, and from this, articulate personal responses.

2 ## Student Book teaching notes and comprehension answers

Tell students that some poems, such as *Let No-One Steal Your Dreams*, are written to inspire the reader, urging them to believe in themselves.

Tell students to scan the poem, and to find particular lines they find inspiring. **Ask:** *Why has the poet, Paul Cookson, written the poem especially for 11-year-olds about to leave primary school and go on to secondary schools?* (The message of the poem is to keep on climbing up the ladder of opportunity and personal development, to aim high and be the best they can be.) Emphasize that this is a message that could apply to anyone at any time in their lives. Everyone needs to have faith in themselves, not to be put off by their own fears or the negative words of anyone else.

Focus on the title. **Ask:** *What does this mean?* (Don't let anyone take away your ambition.)

Refer to the CD-ROM and read the poem through, asking students to consider the number of times the poet uses the personal pronoun 'you' or 'your'. Explain that this is because the poem is directly talking to the reader.

A

Ask for volunteers to share their answers with the class. Clarify any misconceptions or queries.

Answers:

1 Working individually, student summarize the meaning of the first verse in their own words.

2 If you set your sights on something, it becomes the target of your ambition or the object of your attention.

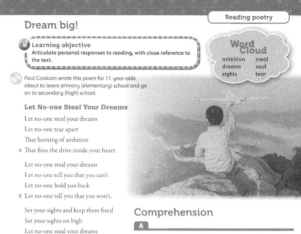

Reading poetry

Dream big!

Learning objective
Articulate personal responses to reading, with close reference to the text.

Word Cloud
ambition   steal
dreams   soul
sights   tear

Paul Cookson wrote this poem for 11-year-olds about to leave primary (elementary) school and go on to secondary (high) school.

Let No-one Steal Your Dreams

Let no-one steal your dreams
Let no-one tear apart
That burning of ambition
4 That fires the drive inside your heart.

Let no-one steal your dreams
Let no-one tell you that you can't
Let no-one hold you back
8 Let no-one tell you that you won't.

Set your sights and keep them fixed
Set your sights on high
Let no-one steal your dreams
12 Your only limit is the sky.

Let no-one steal your dreams
Follow your heart
Follow your soul
For only when you follow them
17 Will you feel truly whole.

Set your sights and keep them fixed
Set your sights on high
Let no-one steal your dreams
21 Your only limit is the sky.

Paul Cookson

Comprehension

A

Use words and phrases from the poem to explain your answers.

1 Rewrite the meaning of the first verse into four sentences of your own words.

2 What does 'set your sights on' mean?

3 Which five things in the poem must you not let people do to you?

B

Poet's use of language

1 Which two words does the poet use in verse 1 to describe heat?

2 Which two phrases does the poet use in verse 3 to indicate 'there's no upper limit'?

C

What about you?

How did the poem make you feel? Give phrases from the poem as part of your explanation.

148

---

3 Steal your dreams; tear apart the burning of ambition; tell you that you can't; hold you back; tell you that you won't (achieve your dream).

B

1 'burning', 'fires'

2 'Set your sights on high'; 'Your only limit is the sky'

C

You can extend the exercise by asking students to work in pairs and share their ambitions with each other. They should consider what they are going to do to achieve them: work hard, pass examinations, etc.

Example answers:

Inspiring, encouraging, determined, positive, etc.

3 ## Word Cloud definitions

Focus students' attention on the Word Cloud and refer to the CD-ROM. **Ask:** *Which is another word for 'rip'?* (Tear.)

ambition a strong desire to achieve something

dreams special aspirations, ambitions, or ideals.

sights future ambitions

steal take another person's property without permission and without intending to return it

soul person's emotional nature or sense of identity

tear pull (something) apart with force

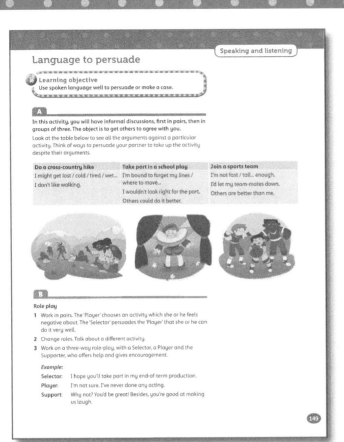

Language to persuade

Speaking and listening

Learning objective
Use spoken language well to persuade or make a case.

A

In this activity, you will have informal discussions, first in pairs, then in groups of three. The object is to get others to agree with you.

Look at the table below to see all the arguments against a particular activity. Think of ways to persuade your partner to take up the activity despite their arguments.

Do a cross-country hike	Take part in a school play	Join a sports team
I might get lost / cold / tired / wet...	I'm bound to forget my lines / where to move...	I'm not fast / tall... enough.
I don't like walking.	I wouldn't look right for the part.	I'd let my team-mates down.
	Others could do it better.	Others are better than me.

B

Role play

1 Work in pairs. The 'Player' chooses an activity which she or he feels negative about. The 'Selector' persuades the 'Player' that she or he can do it very well.
2 Change roles. Talk about a different activity.
3 Work on a three-way role-play, with a Selector, a Player and the Supporter, who offers help and gives encouragement.

Example:
Selector: I hope you'll take part in my end-of-term production.
Player: I'm not sure. I've never done any acting.
Support: Why not? You'd be great! Besides, you're good at making us laugh.

149

A

Students should work on this activity in pairs, with the requirement to add four or five further objections to each column. Point out how these negative thoughts have grown and grown into a worst case scenario. They would be very powerful in making someone not want to take part in any of the activities – and deny themself valuable opportunities. Explain that students will not develop their potential if they are not taking part in things.

B

Students work in pairs. Using the activities listed in A they try to persuade each other to take part, and be positive about the personal attributes they could bring to an activity or event.

Explain to students that it isn't just the words that are important when writing persuasive text. They also need to consider punctuation and expression, so that when the text is spoken it is engaging and effective.

Learning objective

(4)

Use spoken language well to persuade or make a case.

Students persuade each other to participate and be positive.

Remember to display the child-friendly learning objective to the class along with the child-friendly checklist that students can use to assess how well they achieve it.

We know that we have achieved this because:

▶ We understand how to make a persuasive case or argument.
▶ We can use language to persuade others.

6 Extension

Students anonymously write down an activity or event that they are not keen to participate in. Put these in a box and mix them up. Each student draws out an example. Their job is to really convince one of their classmates to try something! Can they do it? Once they have the topic, students should identify both sides of the argument — for and against. They need to be objective and rational, and should list any relevant facts and anticipate any objections. Finally they should make a list of statements to support their position. Ask for volunteers to present their work to the class — has it worked?

5 Student Book teaching notes and exercise answers

Explain that sometimes students do not achieve or fulfil their ambitions because they foreground their fears and worries and what they can't do, rather than what they can do. Emphasize that it is important to stay positive, and adopt a 'can do' attitude. Explain that the following activities will help students deal with negative thoughts of 'worse case scenarios.'

① Learning objective

Select appropriate non-fiction style and form to suit specific purposes.

Students write an information non-fiction text – a school handbook for new students – and adopt an appropriate range of text and language features.

Remember to display the child-friendly learning objective to the class along with the child-friendly checklist that students can use to assess how well they achieve it.

We know that we have achieved this because:

▶ We can structure an appropriate handbook with topic sentences and paragraphs.

▶ We can link and develop ideas using suitable connectives.

▶ We can use features which help personalize the text such as personal pronouns and opinions.

Writing a handbook

Writing workshop

Learning objective
Select appropriate non-fiction style and form to suit specific purposes.

Guided writing
You have been asked by your Headteacher to write part of a student handbook which is given to new students coming to the school. You need to write key facts about the school, but also some helpful advice, such as how to make friends or what school rules are especially important.

Copy the paragraph boxes below and their subheadings, then make notes inside each. Some ideas have been given to help you.

Paragraph 1 Some key facts about the school
- name of school
- name of Headteacher
- subjects studied
- some information about the actual school building e.g. two floors, gymnasium, science laboratories
- number of pupils
- teachers' names and year groups
- facilities like sport, creative arts
- school uniform
- some key achievements/awards
- you could include a map drawing of inside the school.

Paragraph 2 The school day
- what time the school starts
- morning assembly -or whole school meeting
- how pupils are registered
- break and lunch times - with tips on how to get there on time/ get a place in the queue.
- what snacks or meals you recommend
- lesson finishing time
- times for after school clubs

Paragraph 3 Lessons and Learning
- a learning experience you have had which you will never forget or a favourite teacher or subject you enjoyed.
- extracurricular activities available and annual competitions
- advice on homework and preparing for tests.
- advice on how to be organized and reflective about your own learning to do their best.

Paragraph 4 Final advice and suggestions
- behaviour rules new pupils must follow
- what to do if you feel lost, lonely, sick or have a problem
- how to encourage parents / carers to be involved with your school

150

---

② Writing workshop teaching notes

Show students examples from their own school handbook, or other schools in your area. This will provide additional guidance for students on what it should include. Explain to students that their 'audience' is likely to be similar to their own age, so it will be really useful to include students' own positive experiences about the school in the leaflet.

Ask students to consider the following questions:

▶ What is the best thing about your school?

▶ What advice would you give to someone who was going to come to our school?

Guided writing

Students write notes to accompany each feature listed in the paragraphs. Students may not know all the answers to some of these questions. Suggest that before they move on to 'Your writing' they write a list of any information they might need, such as the number of students in the school, extra-curricular activities available, etc.

③ Extension

1 Ask students to write a short description of themselves at school. This should consist of a few sentences outlining who they are and what they like to do at school. They shouldn't write their name in these descriptions. Display these in the class and ask other students to guess the student by the sentences.

2 Students can then develop their descriptions into short profiles which could be used in the handbook to welcome new students.

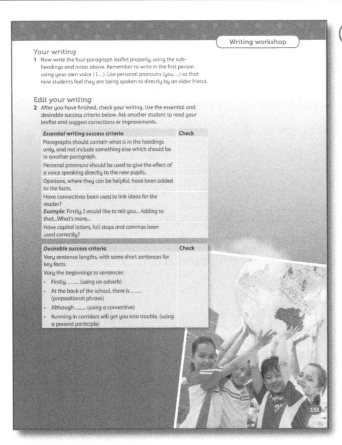

Writing workshop

Your writing

1 Now write the four-paragraph leaflet properly, using the sub-headings and notes above. Remember to write in the first person, using your own voice (I...). Use personal pronouns (you...) so that new students feel they are being spoken to directly by an older friend.

Edit your writing

2 After you have finished, check your writing. Use the essential and desirable success criteria below. Ask another student to read your leaflet and suggest corrections or improvements.

Essential writing success criteria	Check
Paragraphs should contain what is in the headings only, and not include something else which should be in another paragraph.	
Personal pronouns should be used to give the effect of a voice speaking directly to the new pupils.	
Opinions, where they can be helpful, have been added to the facts.	
Have connectives been used to link ideas for the reader? *Example:* Firstly, I would like to tell you... Adding to that...What's more...	
Have capital letters, full stops and commas been used correctly?	

Desirable success criteria	Check
Vary sentence lengths, with some short sentences for key facts.	
Vary the beginnings to sentences:	
• Firstly, ____ (using an adverb)	
• At the back of the school, there is ____ (prepositional phrase)	
• Although ____ (using a connective)	
• Running in corridors will get you into trouble. (using a present participle)	

151

⑤ Extension

Students should consider what images they think would be useful in the handbook — pictures of the school, pupils, teachers, etc. Students then create an artwork list with captions for images that they would ideally like to use. If there is photographic equipment available students can take their own pictures to use.

④ Writing workshop teaching notes

Take students through the success criteria. Explain that these are the features students will be assessed upon, so they will need to show evidence of them in their writing. If possible, provide model writing on the board which shows evidence of some of the success criteria for students to refer to.

Your writing

Encourage students to write up the notes in the paragraphs in the order they are written, possibly putting each bullet point into one or two sentences. Remind students to write as 'I', and to talk directly to the students they are addressing as 'you.' Emphasize that if 'we', 'us' and 'our' are used this can also help reinforce the sense of a school community, and make the new students feel more welcome.

After students have checked their work against the success criteria, they should swap work with another student. Students should then provide suggestions for improvement or correction.

End of Unit Test

Question Paper

Reading: fiction

Read the extract and answer the questions.

A New School

On the first day of high school, I stood in the sun and watched, but pretended not to watch, the others. They stood in groups and talked and knew each other, all except one — a girl though — in a faded blue dress, carrying a sack lunch and standing near the corner looking everywhere but at the crowd.

5   I might talk to her, I thought...

    That first day was easier when the classes started. Some of the teachers were kind; some were frightening. Some of the students didn't care, but I listened and waited; and at the end of the day I was relieved, less conspicuous from then on.

    But that day was not really over. I hurried to carry my new paper route.
10 At the last house, just as I cut across a lot and threw to the last customer, I saw the girl in the blue dress coming along the street, heading on out of town, carrying books. And she saw me.

    "Hello."

    "Hello."

15   And because we stopped we were friends. I didn't know how I could stop, but I didn't hurry on. There was nothing to do but to act as if I were walking on out too. I had three papers left in the bag, and I frantically began to fold them — for throwing. We had begun to walk and talk.

    "Have you gone to school here before?" I asked.

20   "Yes, I went here last year."

    A long pause. I kicked through the dust of the road.

    I began to look ahead. Where could we be possibly walking to? Fortunately, there was only one more house, a gray house by a sagging barn, set two hundred yards from the road.

25   "I thought I'd see if I could get a customer here," I said, waving towards the house.

    "That's where I live..."

From *The Osage Orange Tree* by William Stafford

Glossary

conspicuous something conspicuous stands out and is easy to see or notice

sack lunch a packed lunch

sagging sinking, subsiding, or bulging downwards under weight or pressure or through lack of strength

Comprehension

A

Give evidence from the extract to support your answers.

1 What line in the extract tells the reader that the weather is pleasant?

_____ [1]

2 Where does the girl in the blue dress live?

_____ [2]

3 The writer experiences a range of feelings in the extract. Tick two correct boxes.

   a He feels upset. ☐

   b He feels awkward. ☐

   c He feels confident. ☐

   d He feels angry. ☐ [2]

B

Give evidence from the extract to support your answers.

1 Find a quotation in the extract suggesting the writer does not know anyone at the school.

_____ [2]

2 What similarity is there between the writer and the girl? Tick the correct box.

   a This is their first day at a new school. ☐

   b They are both outsiders. ☐

   c They both live on the north edge of town. ☐

   d They both deliver newspapers. ☐ [1]

3 Is the writer a boy or girl? Explain your answer.

_____ [2]

C

Give evidence from the extract to support your answers.

1 What evidence is there that the girl in the story might be poor?

_____ [2]

2 When the writer first starts walking with the girl, he tries not to show his feelings. Find the adverb which shows his real feelings.

_____ [1]

3 Suggest an alternative title for the extract.

_____ [2]

Reading: non-fiction

Read the extract and answer the questions.

Learning for Life

Education is an important part of British life. There are hundreds of schools, colleges and universities, including some of the most famous in the world. It is free for all children between the ages of 5–16. Current government proposals say that children must continue to receive some form of education
5 or training to 18. Education is compulsory, but school is not, as children are not required to attend school. They can be educated at home.

Children's education in England is normally divided into two separate stages. They begin with primary education at the age of five and this usually lasts until they are eleven. Then they move to secondary school, there they
10 stay until they reach sixteen, seventeen or eighteen years of age.

The school year runs from September to July and is 39 weeks long. Compulsory testing takes place at the ages of eleven in England. Most young people take GCSE (General Certificate of Secondary Education) examinations at 16, and many take vocational qualifications, A/S and
15 A Levels (Advanced Levels), at 17 and 18. These exams determine whether a student is eligible for university.

Teachers in primary schools (5–11-year-olds) are always addressed by their surname by parents and pupils alike, always Mr, Mrs or Miss Smith. In secondary schools (11–16 years), teachers are usually addressed as Miss or Sir.

Adapted from www.woodlands-junior.kent.sch.uk

Glossary
compulsory required by law or a rule; obligatory

Comprehension

A

Give evidence from the extract to support your answers.

1 Read the statements below. Tick two correct boxes.

  a Some children are educated at home. ☐

  b School is compulsory for all children. ☐

  c Children attend both primary and secondary schools. ☐

  d All children go to university. ☐   [2]

2 What three examinations can children take at the age of seventeen?

_____ [3]

B

Give evidence from the extract to support your answers.

1 It is acceptable to call a teacher by their first name. True or false? Explain your answer.

_____

_____ [2]

2 All young people take GCSE examinations. True or false? Explain your answer.

_____

_____ [2]

C

Give evidence from the extract to support your answers.

1 Which two paragraphs could have the subheadings: _Assessment_ and _Education in Britain_?
Explain your answer.

_____ [3]

2 Give another word or phrase which could be used instead of the word _'eligible'._

_____ [3]

Writing: fiction

Write a short fictional story. In the story you make a new friend and include answers to the questions listed below. Please use a separate sheet of paper.

Consider the following:

Where did you meet them? How old were you both?

What was your first impression of them? What did you like about them?

How did you start a conversation and how did it develop?

[30]

Writing: non-fiction

Write a blog entry describing what happened during your school day. Please use a separate sheet of paper.

Consider the following:

What did you do? What did you learn?

How do you feel about school?

Write in the first person.

Consider your audience and write in the correct tone and style.

[20]

Revise and Check ❶

Vocabulary

1 Read these sentences. Write words or phrases that mean the same as the emboldened words.

  a Unless urgent action is taken, these amazing creatures could become **extinct**.

  b In 2000, the drowned cities were discovered as well as the **ancient** harbour.

  c We were travelling now on a **lagoon** when the trail began to tremble.

2 Write a sentence for each phrase.

  a good cause

  b lend a hand

  c a ripple of applause

3 Write down four words that mean the same as:

  a observe

  b replica

  c journal

  d voyage

Punctuation

1 Add a colon, semicolons, and a full stop to this sentence.

This is the shopping list two large fresh tomatoes one packet of noodles 500 grams of cheese one kilo of oranges a small bag of rice

2 Add two adjectives before each of the two nouns. Also add punctuation.

  a A _____ _____ car
  b A _____ _____ baby

3 Punctuate this sentence.

My brother is tall but my father and mother are not.

Grammar

1 Choose the correct subordinating connectives to complete these sentences.

which   what   since   where   that   why   who   when

a The house _____ my friend lives has a blue door _____ will be painted tomorrow.

b I haven't seen her _____ last week _____ she fell off the wall after school.

2 Make up three sentences placing the clause "when I am hungry" in a different place in each sentence.

3 Write out the sentences below. Then write simple, compound or complex after the right one.

a She ate her meal and then she did her homework.

b John Ramsay says she's aboard for the Gentlemen and officers, so they might have fresh cream when they please.

c He walked to school.

4 Choose two modals from the list below to add to this complex sentence.

should   will   can   must

You _____ do your homework, so that you _____ watch your favourite programme later.

5 Make these adverbs into adjectives.

carefully   dangerously   quickly   heavily

Spelling

1 Complete these words with the correct 'shun' ending.

–cian   –sion   –ssion   –tion
–otion   –ution   –ition   –ation

musi _____   discu _____   direc _____
explor _____   instit _____   emo _____
pos _____   sta _____

Revise and Check ②

1 Write the correct word for the following definitions.

   a a ruler in ancient Egypt

   b a small picture that represents a word in Egyptian writing

   c information obtained by a spy

   d to demand money as payment for not telling a secret

   e a person who writes for people who can't write

   f a tiny robot

   g an instrument used to look at very small things

2 Write the root and meaning of these words.

   valuable   solution   disappearance

3 Complete the sentences with the correct idiom.

   to show his hand   to keep an eye on her

   a When he was talking to the suspected spy he did not want _____

   b She looked very suspicious so he decided _____

4 Choose the correct word.

   typhoons lava tsunami volcano hurricanes floods earthquake tornadoes twisters

   When the ground shakes it is an **(a)** and if it happens in the sea it makes a big wave called a **(b)** which **(c)** the land. An erupting mountain is a **(d)** and hot **(e)** pours down the mountain. Tropical rainstorms with very strong winds are called **(f)** or **(g)**. Tall spirals of wind that suck everything up are called **(h)** or **(i)**.

1 Put in the correct punctuation in the dialogue below.

   I feel sick said Jenna. It's your own fault cried her brother. You ate twelve chocolate brownies, you greedy girl. But you ate ten yourself said Jenna. I saw you.

2 Write out the sentence below twice, once using dashes, once using brackets.

   James Bond the fictional spy is the hero in many books and films.

Grammar

1 Change these sentences from passive to active.

  a The dinner was cooked by my grandmother.

  b The visitors were frightened by the howling wolves.

  c My mother was terrified by the storm.

2 Make two sentences from each word, once as a noun and once as a verb.

  permit   spell

3 Make adjectives from these verbs.

  sleep   explode   please   talk

Spelling

1 Give two examples for each prefix.

  dis–   im–   il–   un–   re–

2 Write a word for each ending.

  –able   –ible   –or   –er   –ck   –k   –less   –ness

3 Add prefixes to the words in brackets to change the meaning.

  Our neighbour is very (kind). He keeps our ball when it goes into his garden. It is (possible) to get it back. He is very (helpful) and (patient).

4 Spell these words correctly.

  imprefect   dissappointed   unnhapy

Revise and Check ③

Questions

Vocabulary

1 Write down the names of three kinds of circus acts.

2 Which part of speech – 'noun', 'verb', or 'past participle' – is each of the following?

   celebrate   preparation   decoration   greeting   introduce   presented

3 Write out the sentences below adding the correct idiom from the list.

   to cut a long story short   from scratch   speaking my mind   tip of my tongue

   a I made the cake _____
   b _____ I broke my leg falling on the ice.
   c Sometimes I get into trouble for _____ without thinking.
   d I can't remember her name but it's on the _____

Punctuation

1 Write out the sentences inserting the missing apostrophes.

   a Its not my fault!
   b The childrens party was last week.
   c Next weeks skating lesson is on Tuesday.
   d Thats not mine. Its Sorayas.

2 Punctuate the dialogue below. Start each speech on a new line.

   Hello Achieng. Hello Jacob. Did you have a good holiday? Great thanks, we went to Mombasa to see my auntie. Did you stay there for the whole holiday? No I had to help my mother in our shop in Nairobi for four weeks.

3 Write out these sentences using the correct punctuation from the list.

   commas   brackets   colon

   a The Vietnamese festival Trung Thu is celebrated in autumn.
   b Here is an example path sounds like bath.
   c The petite very small skater whirled around the rink.

Grammar

1 Add the correct connectives to the sentences.

while   as soon as   before   after

a _____ going to bed, she had a glass of water.

b _____ dinner Kim played computer games.

c _____ driving to school, we saw my friend Bo.

d _____ we get home, I'll feed the dog.

2 Write out the passive form of these sentences.

a The students (take) to the party by their parents.

b The new gym (opened) by a famous footballer.

3 Write two sentences for each of these present participles. In one sentence put it in the middle, in the other put it at the beginning.

a running

b crying

c shouting

Spelling

1 Write a sentence for each pair of homophones.

a their   there

b meat   meet

c knows   nose

d flower   flour

2 Write the meaning of each prefix below, then write one word which uses it.

micro–   auto–   trans–   sub–   im–   dis–   super–   tele–

3 Write down four words which end in a 'k' sound.

Pulling together

Synopsis
This legend from the Arctic tells of how an Inuit boy harnesses wolves to his sledge to help in his search for his sister.

Background information
Many cultures tell stories about dogs — a testament to the longstanding relationship between man and canine. Many stories celebrate or explain the dogs' loyalty and usefulness, while others show them as ferocious. This will often depend on a culture's relationship with the animal and whether the dogs are tame or still wild

Group or guided reading

Introducing the story
▸ Ask the students to share their thoughts on the literal and metaphorical meanings of the title *Pulling together*.

▸ Look at the pictures and ask them to find clues about who or what will pull together.

▸ In which country or region is the story set? Do they think it is a good place for the author to set a story on this theme? Why?

Strategy check
Remind the children to use a combination of sound blending, words-within-words and sentence and story context to make sense of unfamiliar words. Encourage them to use sound blending to read the names 'Anuat', 'Oki' and 'Puja'.

Check the children's ability to decode and understand these words: 'kayak' on line 4, 'trudged' on line 23, 'Baffled' on line 34, 'folly' on line 68, 'harness' on line 85 and 'descendants' on line 153.

During reading
Ask the children to read page 154 of *Pulling together* and to think about the style in which it is written.

▸ **Ask:** *What genre of story is it?* (Story from another culture) *How do you know?* (**Example**: the landscape, characters' clothes and lifestyle.)

▸ Ask the students to describe how the daily life of the characters in the story differs from their own. Can they find examples in the text to support their answer? (**Example**: 'She liked running out along the shore, hunting small birds and taking them home to eat.')

▸ Ask them to explain what happens at the end of the page — how Oki discovers that Anuat is missing. **Ask:** *How do you think Oki feels? Why do you think the author has deliberately not told the reader what has happened to Anuat?* **Learning objective**: Consider how the author manipulates the reaction of the reader. (**Example**: how characters are presented.)

▸ As they read independently, encourage the students to look for one good example of language that the author uses to create an impact on the reader or to build suspense, (**Example**: Lines 29–30: 'All around, the snow had been churned up, as if there had been a struggle'.)

Independent reading
Ask the students to read the rest of the story independently. As they read, listen to each of them in turn, noting the decoding strategies they use and prompting them if necessary.

Returning and responding to the text

Once the students have finished reading the story, ask them in pairs to discuss the story. **Ask:** *Can you describe to each other what happened? Was there anything you didn't understand that your partner can clarify for you?*

As a group, explore the story.

Ask:

- *On lines 42 and 43, Oki says, "If Anuat is still alive, she must be far away". What makes him so sure about that?*
- *What gave Oki the idea to train the bear and the wolves to carry his sledge?*
- *Why did Oki wait until winter before setting out to find his sister Anuat?*
- Ask the students to find evidence in the story to show that his parents weren't happy about him doing this. (Lines 101–102: "We've lost one of our children," they said. "How could we bear to lose another?")
- Ask the students to comment on any language they felt would have an impact on the reader or create suspense. Discuss how the author could have expressed the sentence in a more mundane way. Why has the author's choice of words had a stronger impact on the reader? **Learning objective:** Analyse the success of writing in evoking particular moods. (*Example*: suspense.) **Learning objective:** Comment on writer's use of language, demonstrating awareness of impact on reader.
- *The idea of the story is to present a reason why people first used wolves to pull their sledges across the Arctic landscape. Do you think this story is true? Why or why not?*

Further reading activities

- Ask the students in pairs to find further examples of language that created suspense in the story. Can they think of other words and phrases that the author could have used to express the same event or situation? Compile good examples of language on a chart for students to refer to when doing their own writing

Speaking and listening activities

- Debate the topic 'Animals should be used to work for man'. Allow students time to prepare their arguments, based on whether they agree or disagree with this statement. **Learning objective:** Use spoken language to persuade or make a case.

E-books

The e-books have various tools which you can use in your lessons. Some of the functions are explained below but please go to the 'User Guide' tab on the CD-ROM for further information.

The e-books can be displayed on an interactive whiteboard and are a fun way of reading through the fiction, non-fiction texts and poetry. They have a variety of tools which can be used effectively in your lessons:

1 The **Spotlight** tool can be used to focus on one image or character on the page. Everything else is hidden so the students remain focussed on what they can see. You can use this tool to introduce the students to the story. Using the example pictures below we could ask: *who do you think this is?* (one of the main characters), *what is he doing?* (he is going on a journey), *what do you think this story is about?* (the Arctic), etc.

2 You can use the **Highlighting Pen** tool to highlight words in different colours. You might want to highlight difficult words in green which you would like to explain, verbs in red, nouns in blue etc.

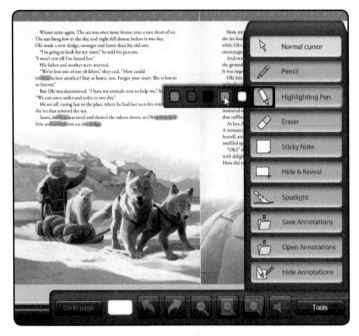

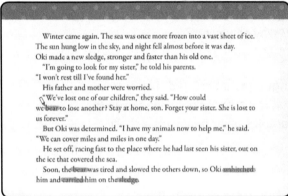

3 The **Sticky Note** tool can be used to add any teacher notes or reminders to any e-book page. These can be hidden if necessary.

4 If you make a mistake then simply select the **Eraser** tool and then click on the text which you would like to delete.

5 Finally, click on the 'Play' button to hear the audio. This will help students with their pronunciation.

Glossary

adjective An *adjective* is a word that describes somebody or something.

1 *Adjectives* are usually found in front of a noun.
Example: Green emeralds and glittering diamonds

2 *Adjectives* can also come after a verb.
Example: It was big. They looked hungry.

3 Sometimes you can use two *adjectives* together.
Example: tall and handsome
This is called an adjectival phrase.

4 *Adjectives* can be used to describe degrees of intensity. To make a comparative adjective you usually add –er (or use more).
Example: quicker; more beautiful

5 To make a *superlative* you add –est (or use most).
Example: quickest; most beautiful

adverb An *adverb* adds further meaning to a verb. Many are formed by adding –ly to an *adjective*.
Example: slow/slowly
They often come next to the verb in a sentence. *Adverbs* can tell the reader:

How: quickly, stupidly, amazingly
Where: there, here, everywhere
When: yesterday, today, now
How often: occasionally, often

agreement An *agreement* is the link between the subject of a sentence and the verb.

Example: I am/I was; you are/you were
The storm was becoming worse
The storms were becoming worse

alliteration *Alliteration* occurs when two or more nearby words start with the same sound.
Example: A slow, sad, sorrowful song

antonym An *antonym* is a word or phrase that means the opposite of another word or phrase in the same language.
Example: *shut* is an antonym of *open*.

apostrophe An *apostrophe* (') is a punctuation mark that is used in two ways.

1 To show where letters are missing
Example: don't, can't, I'm

2 To show possession
Example: My dog's collar. This explains that the collar belongs to my dog. In the plural the apostrophe follows the *s*. *Example:* the boys' cards. This explains that the cards belong to the boys.

bold Letters or words can be written in *bold* print, which is darker than normal. It can help to highlight words for the reader.
Example: Promise me, you will **never** do that again.

brackets These can be used to add an extra comment, fact or aside into a sentence.
Example: I am as thirsty (who wouldn't be?) as a camel.

capital letter A *capital letter* starts the first word of a new sentence. It is a letter written in the upper case.
Example: **J**oin now.

The names of persons and places, the days of the week, and the months of the year also begin with a capital letter.

caption A *caption* is a short sentence or phrase used with a picture.

clause A *clause* is a group of words that contains a subject and a verb.
Example: I ran. In this clause, I is the subject and ran is the verb.

colon/semicolon A *colon* is a punctuation mark (:) often used either:

1 To introduce a list in instructions
Example: You will need: a notebook, a pencil, etc.

2 To add further information to a sentence
Example: I am quick at running: as fast as a cheetah.

A *semi-colon* is a punctuation mark (;) that separates two main clauses.
Example: I like cheese; it is delicious.

comma A *comma* is a punctuation mark (,) used to separate parts in a sentence. When reading you have to pause when there is a comma. Commas can be used:

1 To separate items in a list
Example: a sunny day, a stretch of sand, a pile of good books, several rock pools and an ice-cream van

2 To separate pieces of information
Example: That's true, yes, that's true.

3 When addressing someone by name
Example: I know, Wayne.

4 After a subordinate clause which starts a sentence
Example: Although it is cold, I am warm.

5 After many connecting conjunctions used to start a sentence
Example: However, penguins can get cold…

comparative See *adjective*

conjunction A *conjunction* is a word used to link clauses within a sentence.
Example: and, but, so, until, when, as.
Example: He had a book in his hand when he stood up.

connective A *connective* is a word or a phrase that links clauses or sentences. *Connectives* can be conjunctions.
Example: but, when, because. *Connectives* can also be connecting adverbs.
Example: then, therefore, finally.

context The *context* is the part of a spoken or written text that immediately precedes and follows a word or passage and clarifies its meaning.

definition A *definition* is an explanation of the meaning of a word.
Example: **purse** a small bag for holding money.

dialogue A *dialogue* is an oral or written conversation.

discussion This type of text sets out both sides of an argument and draws a conclusion, supported by reasoning and evidence. Discussion texts set out to provide a balanced argument.

exclamation mark An *exclamation mark* is a punctuation mark (!) used to end an exclamation of joy, anger, surprise.
Example: Oh dear!

explanation This type of text explains a process: how or why things happen.
Example: How a kite flies.
Explanations based on a description of 'cause' and 'effect'.

full stop A *full stop* (.) is a punctuation mark used at the end of a sentence.

heading A *heading* is a title that shows the reader what a paragraph or section of text is about.

hyphen A *hyphen* is a short dash used to join words together.
Example: snake-pit.

idiom An *idiom* is a colourful expression which has become fixed in the language.
Example: It's raining cats and dogs.

instruction This type of text helps readers to make something or to carry out a sequential operation.

metaphor A *metaphor* is a figure of speech in which one thing is actually said to be the other.
Example: This man is a lion in battle.

noun A *noun* is a word that names something or somebody.
Example: fox, chicken, brother, rock.

Nouns can be singular (dog) or plural (dogs).
A collective noun refers to a group.
Example: a flock of birds.
A proper noun begins with a capital letter and names something specifically.
Example: Mrs Brown, London.

onomatopoeia Words that imitate sounds, sensations or textures.
Example: bang, crash, prickly, squishy.

person (1st, 2nd or 3rd person) The *1st person* is used to talk about oneself – I/we. The *2nd person* is used to address the person who is listening or reading – you. The 3rd person is used to refer to someone else – he, she, it, they.

Example: I feel like I've been here for days.
Look what you get, when you join the club.
He says it takes real courage.

persuasive writing This type of text intends to persuade the reader to a certain standpoint. Powerful language may be used with supporting arguments and evidence.

playscript A *playscript* is the written down version of a play and is used by actors.

plural See *singular*.

poem A *poem* is a text which creates or recreates experience in a compressed and intense way, using rhythm, or rhyme and language effects to create images and sound effects.

point of view In fiction, the narrator's position in relation to the story being told.

prefix A *prefix* is an element placed at the beginning of a word to modify its meaning.

preposition A *preposition* is a word that indicates place (on, in), direction (over, beyond) or time (during, on) among others.

pronoun A *pronoun* is a word that can replace a noun.
Example: I, me, mine, myself.

punctuation Is the term given to those marks used to help a reader.
Example: full stop (.), question mark (?), comma (,), exclamation mark (!), speech mark ("), colon (:) and semicolon (;)

question mark A *question mark* (?) is a punctuation mark that is used to end a question sentence.
Example: What part will you play?

recount This type of text tells the reader about what has happened.
Example: news, a diary.

report This type of text provides information about a given subject.

sentence A *sentence* is a group of words that expresses a complete thought. All sentences begin with a capital letter and end with a full stop, question mark or exclamation mark. There are four types of sentences:

1 Statements – that declare something and end in a full stop (.).
Example: The class yelled in triumph.

2 Questions – that ask something and end in a question mark (?).

3 Exclamations – that exclaim and end in an exclamation mark (!).

4 Imperatives – that command or instruct.

Simple *sentences* are made up of one clause.
Example: I am hungry.

Compound *sentences* are made up of two or more main clauses, usually joined by a conjunction.
Example: I am hungry and I am thirsty.

Complex *sentences* are made up of one main clause and one, or more, subordinate clauses. A subordinate clause cannot stand on its own and relies on the main clause.
Example: When I joined the drama club, I did not know that it was going to be so much fun.

simile A *simile* is a figure of speech in which two things are compared using the linking words 'like' or 'as'.
Example: In battle, he was as brave as a lion.

singular/plural *Singular* refers to one thing. *Plural* refers to more than one thing.
Example:

dog (singular)	dogs (plural)
sky (singular)	skies (plural)
wolf (singular)	wolves (plural)

speech marks *Speech marks* ('and') are punctuation marks that enclose speech, including the relevant sentence punctuation.
Example: 'What is it?' she gasped.

In direct speech you write down what is said.
Example: 'Hello children,' said Tom.

In indirect speech you report on what was said.
Example: Tom said hello to the children.

speech verbs *Speech verbs* are the verbs used before or after speech to show how the words have been spoken. The most common is said. Others include – roared, whispered, chanted, muttered.

standard English *Standard English* is the form of English used in most writing and by educated speakers. It can be spoken with any accent. There are many slight differences between standard English and local ways of speaking.
Example: 'We were robbed' is standard English but in speech some people say, 'We was robbed.'

story A *story* is a text type that recounts an invented tale. It is usually used to entertain. Stories normally have a setting, characters and are structured by a plot.

subheading A *subheading* comes below a heading and indicates to the reader the contents of smaller units of text.

suffix A *suffix* is an element placed at the end of a word to modify its meaning.

superlative See *adjective*.

synonym A *synonym* is a word or phrase that means exactly or nearly the same as another word or phrase in the same language.
Example: shut is a synonym of close.

tense A *tense* is a verb form that shows whether events happen in the past, present or the future.
Example:

The Pyramids are on the west bank of the River Nile. (present tense)

They were built as enormous tombs. (past tense)

They will stand for centuries to come. (future tense)

Most verbs change their spelling by adding –ed to form the past tense.
Example: walk/walked.

Some have irregular spellings.
Example: catch/caught.

thought map A *thought map* helps present information by dividing the key points of an oral or written presentation into main topics and subtopics branching off the main topics. Colour is used to highlight the different 'branches' in a thought map.

title A *title* is the overall heading given to a text.

verb A *verb* shows the action in a sentence and can express a process or state.

1   Verbs are often known as 'doing', 'being' or 'happening' words.
     Example: The boys run down the hill. In this sentence the word *run* is the *verb*.

2   Sometimes several words make up the verb.
     Example: The boys are running. In this case *running* is the main verb and *are* is an extra verb that adds to the meaning. It is called an auxiliary *verb*.

Notes